GIMME ALL YOUR LOVIN'

THE BLUES, BOOGIE,
AND BEARD OF
ZZ TOP'S
BILLY F. GIBBONS

CHRISTOPHER McKITTRICK

Backbeat Books

Essex, Connecticut

Backbeat
Books

An imprint of Globe Pequot, the trade division of
The Rowman & Littlefield Publishing Group, Inc.
4501 Forbes Blvd., Ste. 200
Lanham, MD 20706
www.rowman.com

Distributed by NATIONAL BOOK NETWORK

British Library Cataloguing in Publication Information available

Library of Congress Cataloging-in-Publication Data
Names: McKittrick, Christopher, author.
Title: Gimme all your lovin' : the blues, boogie, and beard of ZZ Top's Billy F. Gibbons /
    Christopher McKittrick.
Description: Essex, Connecticut : Backbeat, 2024. | Includes bibliographical references and
    index.
Identifiers: LCCN 2023057959 (print) | LCCN 2023057960 (ebook) | ISBN
    9781493074433 (paperback) | ISBN 9781493074440 (ebook)
Subjects: LCSH: Gibbons, Billy F., 1949- | ZZ Top (Musical group) | Rock musicians—
    United States—Biography. | Guitarists—United States—Biography.
Classification: LCC ML419.G49 M35 2024 (print) | LCC ML419.G49 (ebook) | DDC
    782.42166092 [B]—dc23/eng/20231226
LC record available at https://lccn.loc.gov/2023057959
LC ebook record available at https://lccn.loc.gov/2023057960

∞™ The paper used in this publication meets the minimum requirements of American
National Standard for Information Sciences—Permanence of Paper for Printed Library
Materials, ANSI/NISO Z39.48-1992

For Flynn

CONTENTS

PROLOGUE

THE TONE OF BILLY GIBBONS

It was not a tremendous shock in the music industry in September 2006 when ZZ Top, the then nearly four-decade-old "little ol' band from Texas," as the multigenre trio had become known since the early years of their career, announced the band was no longer under contract to RCA, one of the oldest and most prestigious record labels in the United States. The announcement came fourteen years and four albums into a five-album record deal reportedly worth more than $30 million. Even when RCA signed the band in 1992, there was skepticism that the band was worth the price tag. After all, at that time it had been nearly a decade since ZZ Top had released their top-selling album *Eliminator*, and the band's subsequent albums, 1985's *Afterburner* and 1990's *Recycler*, were released to diminishing, though still successful, sales.

It didn't help matters that in 1992 many in the industry viewed ZZ Top as a gimmicky band whose popularity had been bolstered by a series of ridiculous music videos in the wake of the release of *Eliminator*. Instead of focusing on the band members—guitarist and vocalist Billy Gibbons, bassist and vocalist Dusty Hill, and drummer Frank Beard—the videos instead featured leggy models, hot rods, and comedic bits, like a men's humor magazine come to life. Most of the conversation about ZZ Top centered on Gibbons's and Hill's most distinguishing feature—their chest-length beards—rather than on the band's music, even though the group charted seven Top 40 singles in the United States during the 1980s. Other critics pointed to the band's increasingly bombastic concert tours, which began to rival those of KISS in their reliance on special effects wizardry for both the visuals and the music.

A band that had once been a blues-based power trio in the tradition of the Jimi Hendrix Experience and Cream had evolved—or, in the estimation of critics and some fans, devolved—into a sideshow spectacle that heavily relied on promotional sponsorship and backing tracks. When ZZ Top signed the deal with RCA, it had been just over a year since the band's management had kicked then up-and-coming rock band the Black Crowes off the Recycler World Tour for rallying against corporate sponsorship while the tour was supported by a substantial marketing campaign—along with significant financial support—by Miller Lite beer. Following the dismissal, Chris and Rich Robinson, respectively the Crowes' singer and guitarist, made it no secret that they had grown disillusioned with ZZ Top's corporate sponsorship and use of prerecorded tracks to bolster their live sound, and the Crowes, at the time popular with the music press because of a highly regarded debut album and a propensity to ignore any semblance of tact in their interviews, were happy to share those views with anyone who would listen.

Still, at the time of the RCA signing, it was hard to deny ZZ Top's longevity. The Gibbons-Hill-Beard lineup had remained unchanged since Hill had joined the band in early 1970, and the band managed to become a top concert draw long before they had the record sales to support their success at the box office. The fact that the band had a massive hit record with *Eliminator* thirteen years into their career, followed by another enormous success two years later with *Afterburner*, was substantial proof that the group had staying power. The track record of success was there.

It's also fair to argue that RCA was also following the trend of massive record deals signed by bands like Aerosmith, Mötley Crüe, and the Rolling Stones around the same period as record companies had little idea of just how much digital distribution would disrupt the historical model of record sales a decade later.

But after ZZ Top's first RCA album, 1994's *Antenna*, barely managed to go platinum and failed to produce a hit on the pop charts, the band's next three albums—1996's *Rhythmeen*, 1999's *XXX*, and 2003's *Mescalero*—were released to diminishing returns, with RCA holding up the release of *Mescalero* for weeks as the label tried to determine if it could do anything to salvage the underwater deal. By 2006, the band had not even made a music video—the medium that had made Gibbons, Hill, and Beard superstars—for a decade after 1996's "She's Just Killing Me" video directed by fellow Texan and emerging filmmaker Robert Rodriguez.

As such, the announcement that ZZ Top and RCA were prematurely parting ways did not come as much of a surprise. The big shock was the second part of the announcement: the band was also parting ways with manager Bill Ham, who had encountered Gibbons in 1969 in the waning days of his involvement with locally famous Houston psychedelic rock band the Moving Sidewalks and steered ZZ Top from a group of blues-crazy musicians just barely out of their teens to international superstardom.

Ham, who had come to be known as the fourth member of ZZ Top, was a dozen years older than Gibbons, Hill, and Beard and, like the trio, was a native of Texas. Ham had unsuccessfully tried his hand at music in the late 1950s, releasing a doo-wop single under the name of Bill Ham and The Van Dels, produced by none other than 1950s chart topper Pat Boone, on Dot Records, a previously independent label that had recently been acquired by Paramount Pictures. While Ham wasn't destined to be a pop musician, he later turned his attention to attempting to create them instead—and in addition to ZZ Top, he helped shape the careers of dozens of artists as both band manager and music publisher.

Ham has been variously described as "brilliant," "shrewd," "intimidating," and "ruthless" by those who collaborated with him. "I will say that without Bill Ham there would have been no ZZ Top as we know it," notes Terry Manning, an acclaimed, industry-renowned recording engineer and producer who worked with ZZ Top for nearly twenty years. "Billy would have probably done something great and been a big star and success, and maybe the band would've gotten together with someone else, I don't know. But I know Bill Ham gave his heart, soul, and life to that group. He worked so hard to promote them."

Ham's guidance of ZZ Top's career has drawn more than a few comparisons to entrepreneurial promoters like Colonel Tom Parker, whose management of Elvis Presley's media career brought both unparalleled and unprecedented fame and financial ruin at different points in the career of the King of Rock and Roll. While comparisons to Parker are unfair in the scope of ZZ Top, his management of country superstar Clint Black ended after a lawsuit, in which Black accused Ham of pocketing too high a percentage of his publishing royalties, was filed the same year that ZZ Top signed their megadeal with RCA.

Ham managed ZZ Top with strict conditions to help ensure the success of the band. He was credited as the producer of all the band's albums from 1971's *ZZ Top's First Album* through 1990's *Recycler* and as coproducer of 1994's *Antenna* and 1996's *Rhythmeen*, even when at times his contributions to the technical musical direction of the material were minimal. He attempted to keep the band members away from bad influences when massive, expensive concert tours were at stake, and he promoted the band with gimmicks that would have made Texas showman Pappy O'Daniel proud. ZZ Top instead made their statement on stage, playing hundreds of concerts in the early 1970s while putting out well-reviewed—but not necessarily top-selling—albums, 1971's *ZZ Top's First Album* and 1972's *Rio Grande Mud*, before having a commercial breakthrough with 1973's *Tres Hombres* featuring a single that just missed the *Billboard* Top 40, "La Grange."

He also enforced an ironclad rule for the group: ZZ Top was a trio. They would only perform together and appear together. That meant no solo albums or one-off guest appearances on other artists' records, and interviews and photo sessions—which were both a rarity in the band's early years—would only be conducted in a group setting. By the time ZZ Top was making popular music videos on MTV and appearing as performers on television and award shows, it seemed like Gibbons, Hill, and Beard were an inseparable three-man team, as iconic a trio as the Three Musketeers, the Three Stooges, and the Good, the Bad, and the Ugly. During the peak of the band's popularity in the 1980s, nearly every ZZ Top public appearance was a group effort, with the trio typically conducting irreverent interviews, acting jovial yet cagey about revealing too much about themselves, often riffing on jokes about the band's curious name, their beards, or the state of Texas to dodge any questions of substance.

It was almost as if Gibbons had to sneak out of the country or go under an assumed name to accomplish any work outside ZZ Top—and that is not much of an exaggeration. Gibbons cowrote the song "One Step Back" with Dallas-born songwriter Jerry Lynn Williams, who had written songs for Eric Clapton, Bonnie Raitt, and B. B. King, as well as the song "Tick Tock" for Stevie Ray Vaughan and Jimmie Vaughan. Swedish singer Louise Hoffsten recorded "One Step Back" and released it on her *Message of Love* album in 1991. This songwriting arrangement was not undertaken without Ham's notice—Williams had at one point been signed to a copublisher agreement with Ham's publishing company Hamstein Music, though that arrangement would end acrimoniously, with several lawsuits between the parties, which carried on even after Williams died in 2005.

Gibbons also cowrote the song "Powder Keg" with German-born, Arizona-based bluesman Rainer Ptacek, known mononymously as Rainer, whose ability caught Gibbons's eye when he had seen Rainer perform at a club in Tucson in the early 1980s. The song appeared on Rainer's 1992 album *Worried Spirits*, with Gibbons credited under the pseudonym "Justis Walkert." Gibbons also was involved in a production role on Rainer's 1993 album *The Texas Tapes*, but he similarly could not be credited due to his contractual arrangement with Ham (a "Willie the Workingman" is credited as "dial fiend" in the liner notes, a possible alias for Gibbons). Similarly, the mysterious Justis Walkert also cowrote the song "Cruel Little Number" on the 1992 album *Feel This* by the Jeff Healey Band. But back in the early 1990s, ZZ Top fans would likely have no idea that these songs even existed—and Ham would have wanted to keep it that way.

In the final years of Ham's management of ZZ Top, the public solidarity of the group began to change. Though the band's music was credited equally to Gibbons, Hill, and Beard for most of their careers, it was no secret that Gibbons was the driving force behind ZZ Top. He was not only one of the founding members of the band in 1969, but as the guitarist and primary lead vocalist, he was the figure standing most prominently on the stage (though often just a few feet to the left of Hill). Though Ham made a substantial effort to promote the musical unity of ZZ Top, he never held back on extolling the guitar chops that Gibbons unleashed on the albums and on stage, frequently pushing in the band's press the story that Gibbons was once named as one of the nation's best young guitarists by none other than rock icon Jimi Hendrix, even if that wasn't quite the fact that Ham alleged. Ham was a firm believer that when it came to ZZ Top, the appeal and mystique earned by keeping the band at a distance from the public would leave the audience always wanting to learn more about them.

By the early 2000s, Gibbons began to emerge as the public face—or beard, if you will—of ZZ Top. He began by appearing as a guest musician on a handful of records by artists he admired and respected, like bluesman John Mayall and emerging country renegade Hank Williams III. Later in the decade, he began to step into the spotlight as the public face of the band, showing up solo on reality shows and award shows when he previously would only be seen along with and working with his two compadres.

It was a huge shift in approach to how ZZ Top normally conducted themselves in public. Over the last two decades, Gibbons has become positively verbose, spilling stories of a career that has stretched for more than half a century. When Gibbons finally started speaking regularly to the press, he revealed what had only been hinting at during his first three decades in pop culture in his rare interviews and lyrics—his infectious wit, a combination of the vocabulary of a bohemian, the sincerity of a street preacher, the perspective of a bluesman, and the humor of the guy at the end of a bar who will offer you a great joke if you buy him his next round. His offbeat humor is universally recognized—for example, Gibbons is known to hand out business cards that identify him as "Friend of Eric Clapton."

Pearls of wisdom frequently spill from the lips of the Pearly Gates axman, with colorful phrasing and observations. Take, for example, his description of Las Vegas in a 2017 interview with *Rolling Stone*: "Everything is square, nothing is round in Las Vegas. When you live this kind of uncertain life from being on the road, you don't like sitting in chairs with a round arm. You like sitting in a nice square chair because it has identifiable corners." It could safely be said with confidence that no other human being has ever thus described Sin City.[1]

In public, Gibbons never appears to lose his cool, except for an infamous 1990s Swedish interview in which, after being asked too many questions about the politics of ZZ Top's music, Gibbons walks out (the footage regularly pops up on music forums to the surprise of ZZ Top fans). And yet, many who have interviewed Gibbons have noted his continued knack for frequently changing the subject of a probing question with a whimsical anecdote or boilerplate ZZ Top lore. "When he doesn't want to answer a question, he'll offer up some mysterious non sequitur or Zen koan," wrote *Guitar World* back in 1994. "If you try to press your query, he'll just become more mysterious. When he does this, the underlying message is clear: 'Back off, hombre.'"[2]

Even more so, fans of ZZ Top have learned that Gibbons is often a cunning fabulist, content to add new layers to the ZZ Top mythology that don't necessarily fit with the established facts. Joe Hardy, an engineer and musical collaborator who worked extensively with Gibbons for nearly forty years, once said of Gibbons, "Here's one thing I can tell you that is absolutely true and that he will approve if I say this: He will lie about anything. Our saying is that he would rather climb a tree to tell a lie than stand on the ground and tell the truth."[3]

Gibbons's persistent promotion of ZZ Top by using his oft-repeated phrase "same three guys, same three chords" has also downplayed his musical leadership of the band. Though Hill and Beard have both contributed to ZZ Top's music as songwriters and have driven the band's incomparable rhythm, it is Gibbons who largely directed the artistic path that the band would follow, choosing to embrace synthesizers in the 1980s to expand the sonic parameters of what ZZ Top's music could be, as well as the various rhythmic experimentations—both satisfying and perplexing—during the band's ill-fated RCA period.

In addition, despite Gibbons's frequent "same three guys, same three chords" assertion, the truth is that the "little ol' band from Texas" has never been a three-man operation from the moment that Gibbons and Ham decided to go into business together. This is not a shot at the trio's musical abilities or their monumental accomplishments together—after all, most rock-and-roll bands are not simply the sum of their core membership. There are numerous candidates often dubbed the "Fifth Beatle" who helped the Fab Four conquer the world, and the Beach Boys' most-loved hits are the products of dozens of first-rate studio musicians backing up the famous voices. When Joan Jett and the Blackhearts were inducted into the Rock and Roll Hall of Fame in 2015, Jett's longtime manager and producer, Kenny Laguna, was among the inductees, and it's nearly impossible to write about the success of Bruce Springsteen without recounting his wildly successful partnership with manager Jon Landau. While it's no surprise that ZZ Top sought to preserve the iconic image of the "Tres Hombres" jamming together to develop their hits over more than five decades of partnership, there have been many more "hombres" involved to help the band succeed during that stretch.

Furthermore, it hasn't always been the "same three guys"—in the early months before Beard and Hill joined ZZ Top, Gibbons was originally joined by bassist/organist Lanier Greig and drummer Dan Mitchell (the lineup that recorded ZZ Top's first single), with Greig later replaced by bassist Billy Ethridge. However, Greig, Mitchell, and Ethridge's membership quickly became footnotes because the Gibbons-Beard-Hill lineup famously remained unchanged for over five decades until Hill died in 2021 at the age of seventy-two.

Another point that nearly all fans agree on is Gibbons's ability as a musician. While most people speaking about Gibbons first mention his beard, guitarists and guitar aficionados often look past the facial hair and talk about his tone—Gibbons's seemingly uncanny ability to make a guitar sound exactly how he wants it to in new and different ways, from a clean-sounding polished hum to a sludgy crunch. In the studio, Gibbons has been known to use whatever guitar he feels will give him the best sound and tone for the particular song he's working on. He has not always been forthcoming in identifying which guitars he has used on which tracks, which of course may be intentional in order for the magician to keep some of his tricks a secret. This extraordinary skill is widely admired by Gibbons's peers. "Billy Gibbons is one of the most creative people I have ever met," says Mark Erlewine, owner of the landmark Erlewine Guitars in Austin, Texas, who has built a variety of custom guitars for Gibbons, including a model called the Automatic. "He is an excellent guitar player. His tone is unique. I remember Mark Knopfler came in one time to have me build an Automatic for him because he had talked to Billy and asked him where he got his tone. To me, Billy is the tone master and he is really able to do pretty much anything. I feel like he is the creative force behind ZZ Top and he wrote most of their original music."

The same goes for his vocal tone. Though most would agree that Hill had the better voice of the two, Gibbons is the primary lead vocalist of the group and has used a variety of different voices throughout the band's career, from a gnarly, low growl (most famously in "La Grange") to funky phrasing ("Cheap Sunglasses") to a higher register howl ("Legs"). It was often a challenge to determine whether Gibbons, Hill, or some unknown entity was singing upon first listen, particularly because Gibbons has so many vocal stylings that shift from song to song to find the right groove for the tune.

Similarly, Gibbons is largely beloved by his musical peers, who revere him for his ability, persona, and—since the mid-2000s—willingness to collaborate. "He's just a beautiful man—a sweet, intelligent, and fucking funny-as-hell man," says Al Jourgensen, the musical force behind the industrial rock band Ministry and someone who has had several collaborations with Gibbons. "He's awesome, and there's nobody else I would rather hang out with on the planet than Mr. Billy fucking Gibbons. It's one of those things where

I've met a couple of my heroes where you are highly disappointed, but Billy is the opposite of that. You meet one of your heroes and he turns out to be even beyond your expectations as a human being and just as a really talented person. He exceeds your expectations, which is just amazing to me. I don't know anyone else like that."

And yet that's how Gibbons's history—both with ZZ Top and outside the group's history—has been woven and retold through interviews, profiles, documentaries, and other pieces documenting the life of the man affectionately called the Reverend Willy G by his friends, associates, and fans.

A few months after the end of the band's RCA contract and split with Ham, ZZ Top announced that they had acquired new management, Carl Stubner, a powerhouse manager who envisioned ways to broaden ZZ Top's appeal beyond the band's greatest hits and recording of new music that struggled to be noticed. The move was financially lucrative for the band—or, at that point, it would probably be far more accurate to say "brand." New music from ZZ Top was no longer the priority (the group has released just one album, 2012's *La Futura*, since the end of the RCA contract), and the edict was now to get the aging rockers as much publicity as possible to remind the world that ZZ Top are rock-and-roll legends. That required more visibility for a group that Ham had previously tried to hide behind the curtain. Gibbons, now acknowledged as the face and primary force behind the band, fully embraced his role as one of rock's elder statesmen. By the time ZZ Top made an appearance on the singing competition series *American Idol* in 2008 to perform "Sharp Dressed Man" with the winning contestant of that season of the reality show, it was clear that a new blueprint was in place—one that got the band face time on an episode of a television series watched by over thirty million viewers, including millions of younger viewers who may not have ever seen ZZ Top on TV before.

It would be impossible to fully capture Gibbons's sixty-plus years in music in one book, let alone to fully explore the career of ZZ Top. For one, many key figures have passed, including Bill Ham. There are also Gibbons's admitted tall tales about his own history.

But the constant remains that Gibbons has been one of the most mythologized, respected, and, in some cases, misunderstood figures in American rock music history, a place where he rightfully stands shoulder to shoulder with other guitar greats like Hendrix, Clapton, and Jeff Beck.

1
A GUITAR FOR CHRISTMAS

By the late 1970s, the fully bearded Billy Gibbons surely looked like he had stumbled into the spotlight out of a remote shotgun shack situated somewhere in the wild Texas badlands. In reality, Gibbons grew up in Houston, the son of Frederick "Freddie" Royal Gibbons, a musician and songwriter who had an impressive musical journey of his own.

Unlike his guitarist son, Freddie was not a native Texan. He was born on New Year's Eve 1907 in Gloversville, New York, an upstate town named for its once-prominent industry, glove making. Freddie, like his six siblings, was given piano lessons as a child, and as a teenager he formed a band that became a local sensation, just like his son would do decades later. Freddie became so proficient as a musician at a young age that he was recruited by a high school in Geneva, New York—150 miles west of Gloversville—not only to attend the school but to teach music classes to the other students. Though Freddie was apt at playing numerous instruments, by the time he graduated from high school his primary instrument had become the organ, and he earned additional money playing it as an accompanist for silent movies in theaters. It soon became Freddie's primary source of income and livelihood.

As the silent movie era began to sunset in the early 1930s, Freddie received a job offer to play the organ at the Texas Theatre in downtown Houston. Houston was a booming city—its population had more than doubled from 1920 to 1930—which led to the development of more leisure activities across the city. One of Freddie's roles at the theater was to perform "organ sing-alongs," many of which he would compose himself, which would fill time between features. The theater was owned by businessman Will Horowitz, whose daughter, Ruth Iris, would become Freddie's first wife.

The cinema industry trade paper *Box Office* reported in its July 20, 1940, edition that Freddie's Saturday Midnight stage shows in Houston at the "Texan" were a huge hit, noting that he was drawing crowds akin to a *Gone with the Wind*–size opening, an incredible benchmark for comparison, considering the immense popularity of the 1939 classic film, especially in the South. By the early 1940s, Freddie had found additional work playing music for radio broadcasts—the November 1947 edition of the *Radio Showmanship* trade magazine mentions Freddie as the organist of *Grand Prize Beer*, a show sponsored by Houston's Gulf Brewing Company and syndicated all over Texas. He would later perform with the Houston Symphony and conduct the Houston Philharmonic. Iris passed away due to an illness in 1946, and shortly afterward Freddie married his second wife, Lorraine Duffy. William "Billy" Frederick Gibbons, their second child, was born on December 16, 1949.

In the 1950s, Freddie was the regular Monday performer at the private Cork Club in the Shamrock Hilton Hotel, which merited several positive notices in the Hollywood bible *Variety*. Freddie's musical proficiency and connection to the entertainment industry led to occasional work in both Hollywood and Las Vegas. This included possibly working with his relative, Cedric Gibbons, an acclaimed Hollywood art director who became the supervising art director at Metro-Goldwyn-Mayer (MGM) when the studio was established in 1924. Cedric worked on iconic films like *Ben-Hur* (1925), *The Wizard of Oz* (1939), and *Singin' in the Rain* (1952), among hundreds of other movies, and married actresses Dolores del Río—a stunning Mexican-born starlet who appeared in films on both sides of the border—and Hazel Brooks, who was thirty-four years his junior. Cedric was one of the founding members of the Academy of Motion Picture Arts and Sciences and designed the iconic Academy Award statuette. He would go on to win eleven Oscars for Best Art Direction during his career. It is unclear if Billy ever had a relationship with Cedric, who died when he was ten years old—their relationship is often noted as a piece of trivia rather than a matter of serious exploration.

According to Billy Gibbons, his father found additional work as a music director for MGM and maintained his connections to Hollywood and Las Vegas while living in Houston, though records of what film or television projects Freddie may have performed on are difficult to locate (Billy has also claimed that his father performed with Frank Sinatra on several occasions). Still, he recalled as a youth going to the Tropicana in Vegas with his father for a birthday party for entertainer Dick Powell, where he encountered Humphrey Bogart poolside (it's no surprise that ZZ Top recorded "As Time Goes By," the Herman Hupfeld–penned standard made famous by *Casablanca*, as a hidden track on the band's 2003 album *Mescalero*). Also unsurprisingly, considering his pedigree, on several occasions Gibbons has identified himself as a film buff and a devotee of many things Hollywood.

Billy Gibbons grew up in the Tanglewood neighborhood of Houston, a then newly established insular upscale community, later home to many members of the Bush political family and other notable Texans. Gibbons's mother became acquainted with the Bush family during their years in Tanglewood ("They are a fine family," Gibbons would later say about the Bush clan before playing a concert in Washington, DC, to mark George W. Bush's inauguration).[1]

Gibbons has told several different stories about how he first became interested in music. Though his father's work was undoubtedly an influence, Gibbons credits Elvis Presley for inspiring his first interest in rock and roll. "When I was five, I saw Elvis and I knew I wanted to spank the plank," Gibbons shared with *Thrasher Magazine* in 2015. "It just looked like the coolest thing you could possibly do." Gibbons has said that his mother took him to a Presley concert in Houston when he was five years old (according to the website of Presley's guitarist Scotty Moore, Presley played over a dozen performances in Houston in 1955 and 1956, making it difficult to determine the exact show Gibbons might have seen). Gibbons would later say that he saw Presley around the time "Jailhouse Rock" became a hit, but the song was not released until September 1957, when Presley was playing far fewer live performances because of his recording and film commitments (none of Presley's 1957 performances were in Texas, and Presley began the military service that kept him off the road in March 1958). Gibbons would also later point to being inspired by Presley because of the singer's appearances on *The Ed Sullivan Show*, the first of which occurred on September 9, 1956—infamously, the crew only shot Presley from the waist up because of his controversial gyrations. Gibbons's future ZZ Top bandmate Dusty Hill saw Presley perform at the Cotton Bowl in Dallas on October 11, 1956, which could have very well been during Presley's swing through Texas when Gibbons saw him (Presley performed two shows in Houston on October 13, 1956).[2]

While music was the most influential subject on the mind of young Billy Gibbons, a close second was cars—he frequently quips that his first three words were "Ford," "Chevrolet," and "Cadillac." Cars would remain a tremendous influence on Gibbons, inspiring the lyrics of ZZ Top songs and becoming part of the band's music (the revving sound at the beginning of "Manic Mechanic" from *Degüello* is from Gibbons's father's 1964 Dodge Dart, which later became Gibbons's first car); in the MTV video era, they were an essential part of the group's image.

Gibbons would also say that he first crossed paths with the blues, the music that would define his career, about a year afterward, at around age seven, when his father took him to Audio Company of America (ACA) Studios, a prominent Houston recording studio, where B. B. King was recording at the time. The ACA Studios Master Books, which have been digitized and are part of the University of Houston's digital collections, list King's last session at the studio in September 1953, more than three months before what would be Gibbons's fourth birthday. However, King's booking agency at the time, Buffalo Booking Agency, was based in Houston, and the blues legend, with whom Gibbons would record decades later, may have dropped in on occasion at ACA Studios in later years.

Gibbons has also occasionally given an alternate explanation for his early love of the blues: he learned it from his family's Afro-Caribbean maid, "Big" Stella Matthews, and her daughter, "Little" Stella Matthews, recalling that they would sneak him blues records and that Little Stella would also bring him and his older sister to local shows at a club called the Mocombo in Fourth Ward Houston, much to the disapproval of his parents.

Gibbons's upbringing and introduction to the blues contrast starkly with the experience in Dallas of his future bandmates, Frank Beard and Dusty Hill, more working-class teenagers who performed in blues clubs—particularly Hill, who even began backing Texas blues great Freddie King on occasion starting when he was fifteen years old (decades later, ZZ Top would induct King into the Rock and Roll Hall of Fame posthumously in 2012).

Regardless of what hooked Gibbons on the blues, his parents attempted to foster their son's interest in music at a very young age. When he was about thirteen years old (Gibbons has cited the year 1963), he was sent to New York City to spend the summer studying percussion with mambo legend Tito Puente. "Tito was devoted to focusing into how things are structured rhythmically," Gibbons recalled to the *Providence Journal* in 2016. "That's certainly helpful when playing guitar since there's a very significant percussive element to that. I'm not entirely sure that 'El Rey del Mambo' was aware I even had a passing familiarity with any stringed instrument, but as noted, the lesson learned from him had an impact on just about everything that came thereafter."[3]

While Gibbons grew up surrounded by music, he did not often reveal his depth of musical knowledge and education in the early days of his fame. "I think what I learned about him later explained why I felt the way I did about him," shares Robin Hood Brians, who is credited as an engineer on ZZ Top's first four albums.

> *You know, he gives this image of "I'm just a poor ol' dude, I ain't got no money, I wandered in here with this ol' guitar that the dude down at the music store gave me 'cause it was broke and I kind of like to play the blues." Billy was raised in a home where music education was a big deal and I think he had a whole lot more musical knowledge than most people realized, and I think he's smart for never talking about it. You know, you're supposed to be cool, like it just seeps out of your soul. But it was seeping out of his education there and we didn't realize it at the time.*

The blues had a tremendous effect on Gibbons, but it was just one of the many genres of music that influenced him. His upbringing in Texas gave Gibbons—and his future bandmates—a bountiful musical crossroads to draw from. Because of its size and relative isolation from the media markets of the East and West Coasts, Texas' music scene was more insular in the 1960s and 1970s, though it was actually a net exporter of national talent. Some early rock-and-roll stars, like Buddy Holly and Roy Orbison, hailed from Texas. Rock singer Janis Joplin was born in the Lone Star State but left for San Francisco in 1963; aside from a brief return to Texas in 1965, she remained more identified with the counterculture scene of San Francisco until she died in Los Angeles in 1970. Outside Texas, the state's music output was largely recognized for its country music stars like Tex Ritter, Bob Wills, Buck Owens, and George Jones, among countless others, and later for its "outlaw" stars like Willie Nelson and Waylon Jennings. The constant stream of Texas-born country music talent continued to solidify Texas' identity with the spirit of the West even though the state was increasingly growing more diverse in population and culture.

For instance, Texas was also a hotbed of blues musicians—though this was far less nationally acknowledged than its country music scene—and gave Gibbons, Hill, and Beard ample opportunity to indulge in the music that inspired them. Blues pioneers like Blind Lemon Jefferson, Blind Willie Johnson, T-Bone Walker, Lightnin' Hopkins, Freddie King, and Albert Collins were all born in Texas, and many others born outside the state, like B. B. King and Clarence "Gatemouth" Brown, had professional success there. The Texas blues tradition would be kept alive not only by ZZ Top but by more traditional Texas-born blues musicians like Johnny Winter, Stevie Ray Vaughan, the Fabulous Thunderbirds, and even Rocky Hill, the older brother of ZZ Top's Dusty Hill.

Another tremendous musical influence on Gibbons, Hill, and Beard was later recounted by ZZ Top in the songs "Heard It on the X" and "Antenna Head": the proximity to Mexico and its high-powered AM radio stations known as "border blasters." Because the stations were situated outside the United States, they did not need to adhere to broadcast restrictions imposed by US law. The signals for these Mexican stations—which had call signs beginning with XE or XH, giving rise to the nickname "X stations"—could be as high as 250,000 watts, which was five times the US limit, and could be heard hundreds of miles away. The stations often featured all kinds of programming meant to attract American audiences, from country to blues to gospel to Chicano to mariachi, interspersed with advice from quacks selling fraudulent cure-alls. "Dr. B," who is mentioned in the lyrics of "Heard It on the X," refers to John R. Brinkley, an early-twentieth-century charlatan who presented himself as a doctor. Brinkley infamously promoted a male impotence cure involving goat glands (he would later tout the goat glands and other phony treatments as a cure for dozens of ailments). Despite his complete lack of legitimate medical knowledge, Brinkley amassed such wealth and popularity that he mounted campaigns for governor of Kansas in 1930 and 1932, drawing about 30 percent of the vote in each campaign.

After running afoul of the US Federal Radio Commission for providing fraudulent medical advice on the radio in Kansas, in 1932 Brinkley set up shop on Mexican radio's XER, a station the Mexican government launched to house his program. Brinkley packed the station with performances by country stars, including such notables as Gene Autry, Jimmie Rodgers, and the Carter Family, to help draw attention to his program. Though that station was initially a massive success—at one point it was so powerful it could even be heard in Canada—Mexico shut down XER after a short period. But XER proved to be a successful trial run for border blasters, and several other stations would broadcast from across the border until November 1972, when the United States and Mexico signed an agreement to limit the power levels of FM radio stations (however, AM border blasters continued to encroach on US airwaves). Most famously, American disc jockey Robert Weston Smith, better known as Wolfman Jack, became the voice of XERF-AM in 1963 and later XERB-AM in 1966, helping to make him an iconic radio figure across the United States.

Through X stations, the future members of ZZ Top were able to absorb all kinds of music as well as outlandish programming and advertising that would not have passed American regulations, likely helping to shape the irreverent, humorous lyrics of their later songs.

Perhaps influenced by what he was hearing on the X stations, Gibbons's interest soon turned from the drums to the guitar, and he begged his parents to buy him one. Though his parents were skeptical of rock and roll, for Christmas 1963 Gibbons received his first guitar, a sunburst 1962 Gibson Melody Maker, and a Fender Champ amp. Gibbons would later recall that the first songs he learned to play were Jimmy Reed's "Big Boss Man" and Ray

Charles's "What'd I Say" (the order of which he learned first changes depend-ing on the interview), and in early 1964 he formed his first band, the Saints, with other local kids. "Their first rehearsal hall was in our garage," Lorraine Gibbons remembered of Gibbons's early music pursuits in a 1986 interview. "At first they were in the den, but there was hardly room for a coffee pot in there with all the drums and guitars. Billy's father told the boys they could use the garage if they sound-proofed it, so they did."[4]

There is not a whole lot of information about Gibbons's earliest bands, but he clearly took to the guitar very quickly. Over the next two years, Gib-bons would form two other bands, Billy G. and the Ten Blue Flames, and the Coachmen. The latter group, which formed sometime in 1965, would bring Gibbons his first notable musical success and would at times include his future Moving Sidewalks bandmate (and very early ZZ Top member), drum-mer Dan Mitchell. Gibbons's Coachmen years revealed his savvy approach to marketing; decades later, business cards for the group—listing "Bill Gibbons" as one of the contacts—surfaced and were shared on the internet, much to the delight of "Bill Gibbons" himself.

Steve Ames, a figure in the Houston music scene who had gotten to know Gibbons during his very early years as a musician, would later become the manager of Gibbons's band the Moving Sidewalks. After his family moved from California to Houston in 1964, Ames was interested in becoming involved in the nascent music scene in the area. "I was trying to get into a band when I lived in California because I was new to music," remembers Ames. "That seemed like a fairly popular thing to do. In Houston, that wasn't even on most teenagers' minds. Billy was already playing at that point and I met him as a teenager that summer. He would've been in junior high, he was fourteen and I was sixteen, so that's how far back it goes."

While Ames points to Beatlemania as a major factor in the growth of the popularity of rock music in the United States, including Houston, he notes that it wasn't an overnight sea change. "Everybody didn't start forming garage bands," he recalls.

> *Bands at that point were more like R&B groups that would have brass and larger groups like that, which didn't appeal to people like me or Billy. I think what the Beatles did was make it okay to have a four or five-piece group, and I think that is what started the garage band idea. I met Billy and we just sort of talked and maybe rehearsed once because I was trying to put something together or get in a group, but our paths kept crossing. We lived in the same neighborhood, actually. Occasionally he would ask me to sit in with his band at that point, the Coachmen.*

Ames notes that even in those early years Gibbons stood out as a band-leader. "He had a charisma about him," he explains. "Nobody ever thought of it as being anybody else's but his band. It wasn't like he was a great singer; he just had something about him as well as being really good at guitar."

Ames, who played electric piano and organ, later joined the popular Houston group Neal Ford and the Fanatics, an established rock group that had already recorded and received airplay on local radio. However, he still kept in touch with Gibbons and made a pivotal introduction. "One night Billy asked me to sit in when the Coachmen were playing a pool party or something, but I was supposed to hang out with Dan Mitchell, who was one of the first people I started hanging out with and I had been in two bands with earlier," recalls Ames. "I said, 'I'll come play, but Dan's got to come with me,' or something. That was how Billy got introduced to Dan, and after that, he became his drummer in the Coachmen."

There is a lot of foggy history in Gibbons's life during this period, and it is challenging to fit all the events, encounters, and happenings that he's referenced in interviews in the known chronology of his life. At some point, the Coachmen—who in early 1966 consisted of Billy Gibbons (guitar), Bob

Bolton (guitar), Mike Frazier (bass), Dan Mitchell (drums), and Kelly Parker (keyboards)—became the Coachmen V. It is known that before the band name changed, in April 1966 the Coachmen stepped into Houston's Gold Star Studios to record the songs "99th Floor," which was written by Gibbons, and "Stay Away." Ames's older brother, Richard, who had made some money in the oil business, came on to manage Neal Ford and the Fanatics. Gibbons approached Richard to also manage the Coachmen, but Richard said he was too busy and suggested that the band work with his younger brother, Steve. "I'd been grumbling at that point to everyone in the band that I knew more than they did," Ames recalls, laughing. "This was several months before I quit the Fanatics, so [the Coachmen] came to me and I liked the idea of what they were doing. I had been interested for years in production. We made a demo, and it just came out terrible." These early Coachmen recordings—including demos of both songs—finally saw the light of day in 2012 as part of the two-disc set *Moving Sidewalks: The Complete Collection*.

Shortly afterward, the Coachmen V transitioned into a new band entirely when the group was whittled down to just Gibbons, Mitchell, and Parker. The new band originally approached Ames with the idea to name the group the Eleven Mile An Hour Moving Sidewalks. According to Gibbons, they came upon their personal transportation–themed name from the moving sidewalks that were installed at Dallas Love Field airport.

The band's original full name was an obvious tribute to the 13th Floor Elevators, an Austin-based rock band that originated the psychedelic sound and had become a regional sensation because of the antics of the band's guitarist and singer, Roky Erickson. Born Roger Kynard Erickson ("Roky" being a combination of his first and middle names) in Dallas, he was a gifted songwriter who had the foresight to see the "turn on, tune in, drop out" theme of the counterculture musically before almost anyone else, and the band is credited as the first to describe itself as "psychedelic rock."

The 13th Floor Elevators—which uniquely featured an "electric jug" player, Tommy Hall, who helped give the band a unique sound—had a song reach number fifty-five on the national *Billboard* charts with their debut single, "You're Gonna Miss Me," which was initially released in Houston in January 1966, just weeks after the band formed. The single featured Erickson's raspy, shrieking vocals, which made the song sound like Van Morrison's Them on mind-altering substances, giving the band national exposure. The success of the single pushed the 13th Floor Elevators' record label, International Artists, to lean heavily into the psychedelic sound, including signing the Red Crayola and Bubble Puppy, and quickly made the 13th Floor Elevators the band to emulate in the Texas rock scene, even more so after the band made an appearance on the popular music series *American Bandstand* in October 1966 shortly after the song peaked nationally.

The success of the 13th Floor Elevators (and the fad of psychedelic rock) was ultimately short-lived. Though they managed to release three studio albums and one "live" album (made up of alternate takes with overdubbed crowd noise) before the end of the 1960s, the 13th Floor Elevators never matched the success of "You're Gonna Miss Me," and Erickson's open advocacy of drug use soon ran afoul of Texas law. After being arrested for marijuana possession in 1969, Erickson avoided serving prison time by pleading not guilty because of insanity and was committed to an institution (he had previously been sent to a psychiatric hospital after an erratic performance during San Antonio's HemisFair '68). The band's final album, 1969's *Bull of the Woods*, was mostly cobbled together from previously recorded material and new songs written and recorded without Erickson.

At the beginning of the ascent of the 13th Floor Elevators, Gibbons and his bandmates were significantly influenced by the success of Erickson's group. Ames, however, thought the unwieldy Eleven Mile An Hour Moving

Sidewalks wouldn't have worked as a band name and suggested that they shorten it to just Moving Sidewalks.

Though Neal Ford and the Fanatics were having more commercial success, Ames would eventually quit the Fanatics before the summer of 1966 to go full-time into production. "I guess you could say it was a high-risk situation," Ames recalls. "My family thought there was something wrong with me!" He encouraged the Moving Sidewalks to rerecord "99th Floor" on October 4, 1966, at Andrus Studios in Houston, producing the session himself (Ames would later produce and engineer music with other bands, most notably rock band King's X, another trio with a longtime stable lineup).

While the few photos of the Coachmen demonstrate that they dressed much like the Ed Sullivan–era Beatles, the Moving Sidewalks—despite being largely the same band—had an aesthetic much more reflective of the late 1960s counterculture era. The stylistic differences between the two bands are highlighted in the two recordings of "99th Floor": The Coachmen's version is pure mid-1960s pop-rock, with a more surf-sounding guitar break and a longer harmonica solo; it is a pleasure of a pop tune in a succinct two minutes and twenty seconds but definitely the work of young musicians feeling their way into studio recording. The version by the Moving Sidewalks is just as much of a garage tune, but the more prominent organ, heavier distortion, and more far-out production of the vocals make it a more obvious product of its time and a tune ready for 1960s AM radio airplay—a more polished, more contemporary take than the original recording.

Later that month, New York–based Mainstream Records, a label that had released albums by blues artists like Charles Brown and Lightnin' Hopkins, as well as jazz records and movie soundtracks, signed the Moving Sidewalks to a recording contract. In 1967, the label would release the self-titled debut albums of Big Brother and the Holding Company (featuring Janis Joplin) and the Amboy Dukes (featuring Ted Nugent), so it was obvious that Mainstream

Records was on the lookout for dynamic new artists. "There was a process of a few months where we dealt with some record companies, which was a whole different ball game," recalls Ames, then the newly minted manager of the Moving Sidewalks and a few other, similar area groups, like the Magic Ring. "We had this one record deal and two of the band members, Billy and the keyboard player, were under sixteen, and the rest of them were all under twenty-one. I had to get them to sign contracts, and now I don't know how that works! Two of them had to go to their parents and say, 'Hey, we got a record deal and we think that we can really do well.' What's funny is that Billy's parents didn't flinch on that, but Kelly's parents wouldn't go along with that, so he had to leave the band." Keyboardist Kelly Parker left the Moving Sidewalks shortly after the single was recorded; he was replaced by Tom Moore, a former roadie for Neal Ford and the Fanatics, later that year (Ames notes that the band wanted him to join, but he passed to remain as manager). The classic Moving Sidewalks lineup was rounded out by bassist Don Summers, who had previously played with Ames in another group.

It would be more than four months before Mainstream decided to pass on releasing the single. Disappointed but not deterred, Ames released it in March 1967 on his own independent Tantara label, which was first established as a vehicle to release Neal Ford and the Fanatics singles but later allowed Ames to sign other bands. In the interim, the Moving Sidewalks had a heavy performance schedule in the Houston area, and the release of the single was followed by several appearances by the group on local television.

Despite that, Ames says that they received little support from the Houston rock scene. He explains,

> *Everyone pushed back on that record. I mean* everybody. *The feedback was that it was terrible, it has drug references. A deejay said, "That will never get any airplay, the singer can't sing, and it has terrible production." My*

brother said I ought to have the Fanatics play on their recordings. They all pushed back on it, and my response to that was, "I don't think that's right." And the more they pushed, I said, "You know what? I think this could be a number one record," and everyone was laughing about that and thought that I totally lost my mind.

As it turned out, Ames hadn't lost his mind. "99th Floor" rapidly climbed up the local radio charts, and on April 26 it was reported to be the number one song on both KILT and KNUZ, Houston's premiere Top 40 stations. New York–based record label Wand Records, which had released hits like the Isley Brothers' "Twist and Shout" and the Kingsmen's "Louie Louie," rereleased the single the following month based on the success. By the end of May, "99th Floor" had fallen out of number one on KILT, though the single remained in the station's top rotation for several more weeks.

While the song was a big hit in Houston, the single gained little traction outside Texas even after the Wand rerelease. Having a hit in Houston—especially for seventeen-year-old Gibbons—was an incredibly impressive accomplishment, but it failed to translate to wider success. However, in this era it was normal for musicians to have massive regional success in their home territory and yet be virtually unknown elsewhere—for example, a band could have a hit song on Dallas radio but receive no attention in El Paso. Perhaps most famously, rock musician Bob Seger had a massive following in his home market of Detroit in the late 1960s to mid-1970s—having multiple Top 10 singles in the city—but struggled with matching that popularity elsewhere. In the most notorious example, in July 1976 Seger performed before tens of thousands of fans at the massive Pontiac Silverdome outside Detroit but had played to just a few hundred people at the Chicago-area club B.Ginnings three nights earlier. The two venues might have been just three hundred miles apart, but they were in entirely different radio and promotional markets.

The Moving Sidewalks issued a follow-up single—a poppier side titled "Need Me"—in September 1967, and while it charted locally, it did not have the staying power or popularity of "99th Floor." What is clear is that the band was continuing to develop a significant following in Houston based on their active gig schedule, including regularly performing at the Catacombs Club, a popular Houston rock club in the late 1960s owned by Ames's older brother, Richard, and run by general manager Bob Cope.

The Moving Sidewalks tour dates are extensively documented by the Briscoe Center for American History in Austin, Texas, as part of the Richard Ames Music Collection, which includes calendars from Steve Ames during his time as manager of the Moving Sidewalks. Ames's calendars offer a wealth of information regarding just how busy the Moving Sidewalks were during this period, playing everything from regular bar gigs to private parties to high school dances. They document the band gigging extensively through Texas with a few out-of-state dates from October 1966 through December 1968, including many dates at the Catacombs Club, as well as a series of dates opening for Jimi Hendrix that would have a profound impact on Gibbons's guitar playing—and inspire countless questions about the link between the two musicians.

2
BILLY AND JIMI

Billy F. Gibbons was the favorite guitarist of guitar icon Jimi Hendrix.

It says so on the internet, so it must be true.

Don't believe it? Countless places on the internet state this fact with absolute certainty. Despite there being no clear source for this fact, Gibbons himself has leaned into it when speaking about his relationship with Hendrix, but he has also left a lot up to the mists of 1960s rock-and-roll legend.

When confronted with this "fact" in an interview in the early 1980s, Gibbons was elusive about its veracity in his response. He mentioned having heard that Hendrix had once said as much, noted that he had become friends with Hendrix on the road, and acknowledged that he had learned a lot from Hendrix's awe-inspiring ability to make a guitar sound as if it came from another planet.

Truthfully, it wasn't just that Gibbons had simply "heard" the story of Hendrix calling him one of his favorite guitarists somewhere along the line. The story was commonly repeated in ZZ Top's early press presenting the band as Texas' answer to the Jimi Hendrix Experience.

There's no denying that Gibbons and Hendrix met in Gibbons's pre–ZZ Top years while Gibbons was in the Moving Sidewalks and the band opened for Hendrix. There are even photos of Hendrix posing with the younger band, including Gibbons, reportedly taken backstage at the Will Rogers Auditorium in Fort Worth, Texas, on February 17, 1968. In more recent years, Gibbons has shared many anecdotes about his time spent with Hendrix backstage and in hotel rooms, learning new licks, painting, and listening to music together. These stories have given rise to the perception that Gibbons spent a substantial amount of time under the tutelage of Hendrix, who thereby unofficially anointed the young Houston guitarist as the next great guitar legend. It's not that Gibbons himself has said there was any sort of torch-passing moment between him and Hendrix, but it certainly makes for great copy for journalists writing profiles of Gibbons to paint it that way.

As can best be determined, Gibbons's pre–ZZ Top band, the Moving Sidewalks, opened for the Jimi Hendrix Experience for two dates in Texas on February 17, 1968, at the Will Rogers Auditorium in Fort Worth and on February 18, 1968, at the Music Hall in Houston, just a year and a half after Gibbons formed the Moving Sidewalks and just weeks after the US release of the Jimi Hendrix Experience's second album, *Axis: Bold as Love*. Interestingly enough, it was Richard Ames and Bob Cope at the Catacombs Club who had brought Hendrix to Texas. "Bob Cope was like a cross between James Bond and a big promoter," remembers Ames. "This guy was so cool, and he could talk the language of artists. He was the biggest connection we had to the industry, but it was mostly with concert promotion. We brought Hendrix on that first tour to Texas."

Hendrix's 1968 US tour with the Experience—consisting of Hendrix with bassist Noel Redding and drummer Mitch Mitchell—began with a series of dates at the Winterland and Fillmore Auditorium in San Francisco at the beginning of February. The Texas tour dates that they promoted started on February 15 at the Municipal Auditorium in San Antonio and ran through February 18 at the Music Hall in Houston. What might come as a surprise is that the Moving Sidewalks were not originally scheduled to open for Hendrix on the tour. "Apparently they were having a bad reaction to the people who were opening up and Bob Cope called me and said, 'You've got to get the Sidewalks together up here tomorrow night [in Fort Worth] to replace this other act immediately,'" shares Ames.

Opening for Hendrix, who was already gaining recognition as one of the most impressive guitarists in rock and roll, would have been a mind-altering experience for any young guitarist like Gibbons. "That was such a dynamic time for rock music," notes Hendrix collector and historian Mike Schuncke.

> Previously you had bands who were seen as strait-laced, who had a formula, played the hits, and performed the songs exactly like they are on the records. Then people like Hendrix came along and were improvising and writing songs about things that weren't being sung about up to that point. The way he played on stage was free-form and not constrained. Bands were breaking away from "keep it tight" and loosening up, so I imagine the excitement of Hendrix rolling into town and seeing him do something completely different that didn't sound like anything else on AM radio. No one had really witnessed that kind of combination of the way he played and his theatrics. When Billy was opening for him in 1968, that was when Hendrix was getting very comfortable with his bandmates and stretching out a little bit.

Gibbons would later tell the tale that the Moving Sidewalks made a bold move while opening for the Jimi Hendrix Experience: they played two of Hendrix's songs, "Purple Haze" and "Foxy Lady," since they were part of the Sidewalks' set at the time (naturally, both songs were also standard parts of Hendrix's set at the time too). Gibbons claimed that his band only performed Hendrix's songs because they did not know any other songs to fill out their opening set. There is no record of what the Moving Sidewalks were regularly performing in their set list at the time, but it is questionable as to why a band that had been performing regularly together for an extended period would have such a short repertoire to draw from. Regardless of the reason, according to Gibbons, Hendrix was amused by the Texas band's fearlessness (Gibbons would recount this story in the band's documentary ZZ Top: That Little Ol' Band from Texas).

Simply being around the Jimi Hendrix Experience had a profound impact on the Moving Sidewalks. "The name of the act was the Jimi Hendrix Experience, and being around those people was an experience," remembers Ames. "There was just an aura about them that was nothing like any other acts we had ever seen. It wasn't like a band, it was like three independent people, and even more bizarre was the band The Soft Machine, which was the act that was touring with them. That was huge for the Sidewalks playing those shows."

The Moving Sidewalks' brief time opening for Hendrix wrapped up the next night at the Music Hall in Houston on February 18, and afterward Hendrix headed east for dates in Philadelphia (February 21 and 22), Detroit (February 23), Toronto (February 24), and Chicago (February 25), while Gibbons and the Moving Sidewalks continued to play across Texas at any club, music hall, or even junior high prom that would have them. At most, Gibbons spent perhaps four days in Hendrix's company during those gigs in Fort Worth and Houston, though with a charismatic individual like Hendrix, a younger guitarist could likely learn a lot in just four days.

Nonetheless, perhaps too much of Hendrix's iconic showmanship and mind-set rubbed off on the younger band after their shows together. "After that, things were not quite the same with the Sidewalks," says Ames. "It disrupted everybody in the company, actually, because it was like, 'But we want to be like that!' when you can just randomly do your thing and hate the management. I guess in any other institution or world you're in, if you come across some people who are very successful and they're doing it in a totally different way, it kind of rocks the whole model that you have. 'This other way is better, and it's more fun for us,'" he adds with a laugh. "They were capable of doing this more free-form stuff, but musically [the Experience] certainly were way beyond everyone else."

In the months after the performances opening for Hendrix, the Moving Sidewalks opened for other rock-and-roll luminaries, such as the Doors (with one concert in Houston being the first time ZZ Top's longtime manager Bill Ham first saw Gibbons), the Jeff Beck Group, and Steppenwolf. But the Hendrix connection has been most highlighted in Gibbons's history, and with good reason. As the guitarist, singer, songwriter, and front man of a rock trio, Hendrix, along with Cream (whom ZZ Top inducted into the Rock and Roll Hall of Fame in 1993), provided a blues-based power trio format for ZZ Top to later emulate. More than just sonic innovation on guitar, Gibbons also learned about presenting a dynamic image and stage presence from Hendrix's example. Hendrix was one of the most prominent Black artists in a field that was becoming increasingly dominated by white artists. For example, Hendrix was one of a small number of nonwhite musicians to perform at Woodstock; he was the headline act for the festival, and he already stood out before his electric stage performance took effect on the audience. The Moving Sidewalks would soon adopt some flash on stage. By the time the group opened for the Doors for two dates at the Dallas Memorial Auditorium and Houston's Sam Houston Coliseum in July 1968, the Moving Sidewalks were incorporating flash bombs as part of their performances. The concerts occurred just days after the release of the Doors' third album, *Waiting for the Sun*, and right after their latest single, "Hello, I Love You," entered the *Billboard* Hot 100 (it would soon reach number one). Cope told the Moving Sidewalks that he may be able to arrange an opening slot for them on the national tour with the Doors. Perhaps hoping to impress the older, more established band, the Moving Sidewalks went overboard with the flash powder and allegedly damaged some of the Doors' amplifiers with explosive climaxes to their sets in Dallas and Houston. That put an end to any possibility of the band going on tour with the Doors—if it had ever been a possibility to begin with. During the summer of 1968, the opening bands for the Doors' US shows changed from concert to concert (or every other concert for shows in closer proximity that the opening act could travel to, like the Dallas and Houston shows), so the supposed opportunity may not have even been a realistic one.

As for Gibbons and Hendrix, the legend goes that Hendrix name-dropped Gibbons as one of the world's best guitarists when Hendrix appeared on *The Tonight Show Starring Johnny Carson* with guest host Flip Wilson in July 1969, nearly eighteen months after the shows he performed with the Moving Sidewalks. However, audio from the appearance shows that Hendrix said nothing about Gibbons. Of course, that didn't stop Ham, ZZ Top's manager, from later touting this "fact" in the press in the early 1970s. After all, Hendrix was no longer around to dispute its veracity, and few individuals would have had access to verify the content of the broadcast. By the time the internet came around, the anecdote had been repeated enough that it was widely accepted as fact. In defense of ZZ Top, they would be far from the only individuals involved in the late-1960s rock music scene to exaggerate the details of an experience with Jimi Hendrix.

And yet, as with most legends, the truth likely lies somewhere in between. Hendrix did think enough of the younger guitarist to gift him a pink Stratocaster that Gibbons still owns (though it reportedly went missing for several years). This certainly indicates that Hendrix and Gibbons developed a relationship during their short time together, as Hendrix could've easily made the guitar one of his many on-stage casualties. "At that time, Fender supported what he was doing as an artist," Gibbons recalled decades later. "He really didn't mind playing new, out-of-the-box guitars. Fender was sending out stacks of them; I remember he once got 17 different cartons from them. They were coming fast and furious at him with new guitars, but he had a few oldies and goodies. I acquired the pink one, a late-Fifties Strat, during our time together."[1]

No matter what truly transpired during the few days that Gibbons was in Hendrix's company, the ZZ Top guitarist has been clever to keep their encounter shrouded in mystery. In that psychedelic period of the late 1960s, just about anything could have happened, and Gibbons has shared stories of jamming with Hendrix backstage and painting with him in the hotels after the gigs. "We had seen his showman antics from older blues guitarists," Gibbons recalled in 2015. "But he had a vision and aura. I remember him tiptoeing across the hall at the hotel: 'Come in here. Do you know how this is done?' He was learning chops off Jeff Beck's first record, *Truth*."[2]

It's a fantastic story, but Beck's *Truth* was released in July 1968, five months after the Moving Sidewalks opened for the Jimi Hendrix Experience (most of the album was not even recorded until May 1968). However, Beck had recorded with the Yardbirds before 1968, and Hendrix could have been listening to one of those albums at the time. Or perhaps this occurred on another occasion—though there are very few details about other times Gibbons and Hendrix may have crossed paths after the Moving Sidewalks opened for Hendrix.

As the Hendrix example illustrates, Gibbons is known to play fast and loose with his personal history in the name of rock-and-roll mythmaking. Because he is a devotee of the blues, it isn't much of a surprise that Gibbons speaks of his past this way—the history of the blues is rife with legends, from the oft-repeated tale of Robert Johnson selling his soul to the devil at a crossroads to B. B. King running into a burning Arkansas dance hall to save Lucille, his beloved guitar. Much as "La Grange" would later borrow heavily from earlier blues recordings, Gibbons's anecdotes and yarns build on the tradition of the bluesman as a storyteller, though they cloud key details about a pivotal period of Texas rock-and-roll history.

Presumably, the last time Gibbons and Hendrix saw each other was when Gibbons attended Hendrix's April 26, 1969, performance at the Los Angeles Forum. The concert, which was one of the better professional recordings of the Jimi Hendrix Experience, marked something of a culmination of the band's live show just two months before their final performance. "If you go back to 1967's Monterey International Pop Festival when Hendrix first came on the scene, it was dynamic, raw, and still had some elements of showmanship from his days on the Chitlin' Circuit before the Experience," explains Schuncke. "I think in 1968 Mitch Mitchell and Noel Redding got into a groove, but by 1969 they were firing on all cylinders. Hendrix had a vision—especially with *Electric Ladyland*—of the kind of music he wanted to do, moving away from the pop of 'Foxy Lady' and 'Purple Haze' and burning his guitar. But people still wanted to see the theatrics and hear the hits."

A complete live recording of Hendrix's Forum concert was released in November 2022 under the title *Los Angeles Forum: April 26, 1969*. Gibbons provided liner notes for the archival release and promoted it with an appearance on the late-night talk show *Jimmy Kimmel Live!*, which is produced in Los Angeles. Gibbons performed Hendrix's "Foxy Lady" with the show's house band, Cleto and the Cletones, while playing the actual Gibson Flying V guitar that Hendrix played at the Isle of Wight Festival in 1970 (the guitar is part of Hard Rock International's extensive rock-and-roll artifact collection), creating something of a full-circle moment for a guitarist who was in such awe of Hendrix as a teenager.

The triumphant Forum concert occurred at a moment of endings and beginnings for both Gibbons and Hendrix. Just weeks later, both the Jimi Hendrix Experience and the Moving Sidewalks broke up. Hendrix, of course, would pass away a little over a year later in September 1970, never having the opportunity to play a concert with Gibbons and his then new band, ZZ Top. Hendrix would remain one of Gibbons's most-cited influences for the rest of his career, and since 2007 ZZ Top has regularly covered Hendrix's "Foxy Lady" in their live performances. Hendrix's sound had an obvious effect on Gibbons's guitar playing, which can be heard on the Moving Sidewalks' debut (and only) album, *Flash*.

Gibbons somehow managed to squeeze Hendrix's Forum concert in between Moving Sidewalks shows in Houston, including opening for bluesman John Mayall on April 28 at the Catacombs Club. Bill Ham was also acquainted with Mayall, who would stay at Ham's house while touring the area. During that gig, Gibbons and Ham met, and the seeds were planted for a new band that would succeed where the Moving Sidewalks had stalled.

3
WHERE THE SIDEWALKS END

Despite having a local hit in 1967 with "99th Floor" and opening for Jimi Hendrix, the Doors, and other major acts in 1968, the Moving Sidewalks continued to struggle in their attempts to gain popularity outside Texas. Wand Records dropped the band after "Need Me" failed to match the success of "99th Floor." Though the band would release two more singles on Tantara in 1968—a fuzzy, tripped-out cover of the Beatles' "I Want to Hold Your Hand" and the Steve Ames–penned "Flashback"—the drop from Wand marked yet another sign that the band's fortunes were on the wane.

On a much more positive note, in 1968 Billy Gibbons acquired one of his most prized possessions, which would have an incredible impact on his growing musical abilities. While Gibbons is known to be a guitar collector and has owned hundreds of guitars, including novel custom-built instruments that are both cosmetically unique (such as ZZ Top's famous fuzzy spinning guitars) and sonically powerful, he is forever linked with one particular guitar, a 1959 Gibson Les Paul Standard, which he has dubbed "Pearly Gates." Gibbons has said that he wanted that guitar ever since spying a photo of Eric Clapton playing a similar guitar while performing with John Mayall & the Bluesbreakers. According to Gibbons, he discovered the guitar was in the possession of a Houston-area rancher who had quit playing music to concentrate on his cattle. Gibbons said he paid for the guitar with $250 that he had earned after loaning his car to a friend who was an aspiring actress. He lent her the car because she needed to get to Hollywood for a screen test, though he warned her that it might not make the trek. When the car—a 1930s Packard—managed to miraculously survive the journey, Gibbons and his friends dubbed the old automobile "Pearly Gates." The actress managed to land some parts and, after deciding to stay in Los Angeles, offered to send the car back to Gibbons or sell it and send him the money. Gibbons instructed her to sell it, and his portion of the sale was the same $250 he used to buy the 1959 Les Paul, which in turn inherited the nickname "Pearly Gates." The guitar, which Gibbons has kept in its original condition, has earned legendary status, having been played in dozens of classic ZZ Top songs. To mark the fiftieth anniversary of the guitar in 2009, Gibson produced a limited-edition signature model of Gibbons's guitar, the Gibson Billy Gibbons "Pearly Gates" Les Paul Standard, but the original version is far more precious—Gibbons claims he has been offered as much as $5 million for it.

Meanwhile, the Moving Sidewalks were still gigging, recording, and trying to make it while the public's taste in rock music rapidly evolved. Gibbons's response was to go full-out Hendrix during the recording sessions that would yield the material for the Moving Sidewalks' only album, *Flash*. The album itself is a mix of different styles, but songs like "Pluto—Sept. 31st," which Gibbons cowrote, demonstrate an overwhelming Hendrix influence, with Gibbons even singing in an affected style that is reminiscent of Hendrix's own vocal stylings. Other pieces, like the combo that ends the album, "Eclipse" and "Reclipse," are bizarre montages of different sonic elements and effects that seem more like attempts at music-based comedy sketches rather than actual songs, but they hint at the irreverence of some of ZZ Top's more humorous aspects and lyrics.

Flash was largely recorded in late 1967 and 1968, but the album was not released until late 1969 after the Moving Sidewalks broke up. Unfortunately, time was not on the side of the Moving Sidewalks—the psychedelic rock of the 13th Floor Elevators and the Jimi Hendrix Experience was falling out of vogue as the end of the 1960s approached. With each passing week that *Flash* went unreleased, the Moving Sidewalks were missing their moment—if they were ever going to have one.

The frustration with the album's delay appears to have come to a head when the Moving Sidewalks blew off an important date at the Catacombs Club to take a sojourn to the Sunset Strip. One of the most notable concerts at the Catacombs Club took place on August 31, 1968, an event dubbed the First Annual Catacombs Pop Festival. Advertised on the bill were the Mothers of Invention, Country Joe and the Fish, Canned Heat, Neal Ford and the Fanatics, and the Moving Sidewalks. Forty years later, a *Houston Chronicle* blog post written by music journalist Rick Campbell recounted that period in the history of the Moving Sidewalks. According to drummer Dan Mitchell, the Moving Sidewalks skipped out on the performance to travel to Los Angeles—save for organist Tom Moore, who decided not to get out of bed—packing up their gear in Gibbons's Pontiac GTO and a U-Haul trailer. According to the post, Gibbons, Mitchell, and bassist Don Summers were in Los Angeles for several weeks and gigged regularly at the Sunset Strip's Galaxy Club before returning to Houston. Back home, Moore had to explain to Steve Ames that the rest of the band had bailed for the West Coast. The blog post contained a few additional wild stories about the mad tear in Los Angeles, including the trio living in a dilapidated motel and Gibbons speaking with a fake accent the entire time in an attempt to present himself as an Englishman. "That became the new thing," recalls Ames, "just to leave without telling anyone you were leaving and going to California to do your thing, and we'd be going, 'Oh, this is embarrassing, we've got these gigs booked.' There was a big disappointment, and with the Hendrix factor, it led to them saying, 'Screw this, we're just going to California,' without any real plan. I don't think it was a bad thing, but it was real insulting to us. Also, the emotional attachment—this was like your kids leaving home abruptly."

An oft-repeated part of Gibbons's history is his having briefly attended art school at the Warner Bros. studio in Burbank, California, the same studio whose record company would later sign ZZ Top. In a March 2020 interview on *The Trap Set with Joe Wong*, Gibbons mentioned that it happened when the Moving Sidewalks moved to California in late 1967 or 1968. Other articles and profiles have said that Gibbons went to the California art school as a teenager and formed his first bands out there, but Gibbons's early groups were based in Houston while Gibbons was attending Robert E. Lee High School (now Margaret Long Wisdom High School). Gibbons's book, *Billy F Gibbons: Rock + Roll Gearhead*, suggests that the Moving Sidewalks spent the summer of 1967 in Los Angeles. That is unlikely; not only does Ames's calendar document the group playing frequently in Texas during the summer, but at the beginning of the summer of 1967, "99th Floor" was on the charts in Houston and the band was performing concerts, making promotional appearances, and recording the follow-up single through July and August, all before their second single, "Need Me," was released in September. Perhaps most importantly of all, Gibbons was still a few months shy of eighteen in the summer of 1967, making a full-out move to the West Coast for the band, even a brief one, unlikely at that time, considering he had to be back in time for the start of his senior year of high school.

While the three members of the Moving Sidewalks did skip out on the First Annual Catacombs Pop Festival for a visit to Los Angeles, Ames's calendar does not align with a weeks-long stay in LA in the late summer of 1968 either. Stories abound that the trio version of the Moving Sidewalks at least performed at Sunset Strip's famed Galaxy Club in early September (Gibbons has recounted that the band simply pulled up in front of the club, loaded their gear onto the stage, and began playing) and may have also performed at Gazzarri's before returning to the Houston area. ("I don't know if they played out there," notes Ames, however. "I'm not real sure, but I don't think they played as a band. I think if they started to play out there, they wouldn't have come back.") Ames's calendar has the Sidewalks' first gig back in Houston on September 6, and the Moving Sidewalks were advertised to perform at the Safari Club in Baytown, Texas, the following day. They were also on the schedule at the Catacombs Club for September 13 and 14, as well as many other dates in their territory throughout the rest of the year. At other points, Gibbons has said that the Moving Sidewalks regularly drove back and forth between Houston and Los Angeles for gigs, which, while still unlikely, is at least more plausible than a onetime extended stay (though the dates and venues for such gigs are similarly unrecorded).

If that brief September 1968 visit was when Gibbons went to art school at Warner Bros., it was a stint of a single class or only a few days, not a full move to the West Coast. It seems far more likely that Gibbons attended Warner Bros. art school for a short period as a teenager, like when he briefly took percussion lessons in New York from Tito Puente. Other sources also say that Gibbons briefly attended the University of Houston (a possible explanation for why he was not drafted during Vietnam like others his age). Regardless of exactly when or how long Gibbons attended art instruction, his lifelong passion and eye for art and creative design are unmistakable and have been important assets in the imagery of ZZ Top.

In a bit of a pattern—highlighted by the Hendrix examples—Gibbons's statements in interviews about where he was in the early stages of his career do not match the Moving Sidewalks' and later ZZ Top's touring records. Another example is that Gibbons also once said he wrote the ZZ Top song "Just Got Paid" while living in Los Angeles and trying to figure out how to play Fleetwood Mac's "Oh Well." When exactly Gibbons could have lived in Los Angeles—the song was recorded in 1971, while ZZ Top was grinding out tour dates across Texas and the South—is unclear.

Similarly, Gibbons would later claim he spent three months in Europe in 1969 studying the Maharishi in northern Italy, presumably during the summer after the Moving Sidewalks disbanded and while the embryonic ZZ Top was still forming. Yet, in a 1976 interview with *Blast*, Gibbons said that he lived as an artist in Italy and Paris for three months in 1973. However, ZZ Top played at least one hundred concerts in the United States in 1973—possibly even double or triple that number since many were likely not recorded, including at least a few each month, making an extended European vacation by Gibbons that year also impossible. Whether Gibbons has been misremembering or conflating events or simply telling one-off tall tales of rock-and-roll mythology that do not line up with one another is difficult to determine.

Regardless of how much time the Moving Sidewalks spent in California, the visit to the West Coast did not change the band's fortunes. By mid-1969, their debut album was still unreleased two years after their first hit single, meaning that the group had completely missed any opportunity to capitalize on the local success of "99th Floor" and "Need Me" in 1967. In May 1969 the group and Ames went their separate ways, and the group itself disbanded after two gigs at the Houston club Love Street Light Circus Feel Good Machine on June 6 and 7, 1969. "There was that tension with them, and I made a lot of miscues along the way," recalls Ames. "We started the album and for some time were going through a lawsuit with a record company. But the nail in the coffin was that Tommy got drafted."

After Moore was drafted into the US Army, the Moving Sidewalks were left as a trio of Gibbons, Mitchell, and Summers. However, the three-man Sidewalks lineup was short-lived after Summers soon landed in the military as well. Weeks after the band disbanded, Ames's Tantara Records finally released *Flash* in August 1969 to almost no reaction: having been in the can so long, it was practically an oldie. "I don't know if we all sensed it, but I always had this thing about the 1960s where you sense that there's an urgency, and in retrospect, I think it's because bands didn't last long and eras of music didn't last very long," remarks Ames. "There's sort of this window of time. I think I had a sense of that but didn't know what to do except go as fast as I could. If you missed the trend, then you're really going uphill."

For Gibbons, the breakup of the Moving Sidewalks shortly after he met Bill Ham was impeccable timing. For all the band's talent, the organ-driven psychedelic sound of the Moving Sidewalks was already becoming passé by the time of the breakup. Additionally, Ham wasn't as interested in the Moving Sidewalks as he was in Gibbons, who by then had gained a reputation as one of the top young guitarists in the region. "Bill had a great eye for enthusiasm," said Gibbons in an interview after Ham's death. "We shook hands, and in fine fashion, he handed me a cigar and said, 'Son, I'm going to make you a star.'" Shortly afterward, Ham established Lone Wolf Productions to manage his new venture.[1]

The prototypical ZZ Top lineup was formed when Gibbons and Mitchell were joined by organist Lanier Greig, another veteran of the Houston psychedelic rock scene and former member of Neal Ford and the Fanatics. Greig had replaced former Moving Sidewalks manager Steve Ames as the organist in that group in 1966 and was adept at playing bass pedals as well. For this new group, the psychedelic connotation of the Moving Sidewalks name was retired in favor of a much more mysterious alternative: ZZ Top. The origin of the ZZ Top name was a closely held secret for the group once they became popular, and in interviews the members regularly pushed out alternate explanations (such as ensuring they would always be last in the record racks in music stores or that it was really "22 Top" and everyone kept misreading it) or shot down fan theories (that the name originated from Zig-Zag and Top rolling papers, or was inspired by the "ZZ" design of double barn doors, or was a nod to the letter designation of the back row in concert venues). According to Gibbons—the sole original member of the first lineup to have been present at the formation of the band—the true story is that he came up with the name after looking at blues concert posters on the wall of his apartment and focusing on the names of bluesmen B. B. King and Z. Z. Hill (Texas native Hill—real name Arzell J. Hill—was inspired to adopt "Z. Z." as his stage name by B. B. King). Gibbons combined the names to form "ZZ King," but decided that because the king is "at the top"—and probably because there were already several other famous bluesmen with the last name King besides B. B.—the band would use the name "ZZ Top" instead.

Robin Hood Brians, who is credited as an engineer on ZZ Top's first four albums, tells a different story about the reason for the name change from the Moving Sidewalks to ZZ Top that he heard from Dale Hawkins, the rock-and-roll pioneer who wrote the standard "Susie Q." Hawkins recorded at Brians's studio in Tyler, Texas (he even released a country album in 1969 titled *L.A., Memphis & Tyler, Texas*), and later become a record promoter and executive, which gave him a deep understanding of the legal intricacies of the music business.

"The first time they came was just because I was the only studio that was really recording hits back then," says Brians.

> *Their first session with me was the Moving Sidewalks. The first check I got came from [Ham's] bosses, the Daily Brothers down in Houston, who also owned Big State Records, a huge distributor in Dallas. Later on, Dale Hawkins—bless his heart—the last time he was in my studio before he died, he sat down and said "Hood, did I ever tell you about the name change on ZZ Top?" I said, "No." He said he got a call from Bill Ham one time, and he said, "Dale, I need some advice. I made a mistake. I've allowed my partners to have a piece of the action on this three-piece group I got, and they are going to be huge. I want to know how to cut them out and not get sued." Dale said, "Hood, I told him that here's the way you do it. You disband the*

group officially and announce that you're disbanding. Then you don't do any business whatsoever for 90 days. And then you form a new group with the same members, call that group another name, and go into business. You'll be clean in Texas and several other states you'll be fine." Sure enough, that's what he did. So when they came back, they told me they changed their name to ZZ Top. From then on, the checks came from Lone Wolf Productions, which was Ham's production company.

Ames, who owned the name Moving Sidewalks, has a different recollection of the purpose of the name change. "I think they wanted to continue with the equipment that I owned and the name I owned," says Ames. "I wasn't okay with that. I think that's what prompted them to change the name. I don't think it would've fit at all with what they were doing" (Houston's May 19, 1969, edition of the *Daily Court Review* shows the name "Moving Sidewalks" was registered as an "Assumed Name" by "S.C. Ames").

The business name "Z. Z. Top" was registered on June 20, 1969, by Mitchell, Gibbons, and Greig—listed in that order on the form—at the Harris County Courthouse, with the name appearing under the "Assumed Names" registrations in the June 24, 1969, edition of Houston's *Daily Court Review*. However, there may have been something to the story told to Brians by Hawkins—the October 13, 1969, edition of the *Daily Court Review* lists "Z Z Top" (no periods) under the "Assumed Names" registrations under the name "B. Hamm [*sic*]," and "Z. Z. Top" (with periods) in the same section under the "Withdrawals" headline with "L. Greig, et al" listed. These listings occur several weeks after Greig left the group and around the time that Mitchell also parted ways with ZZ Top. It's possible that at this point Ham took ownership of the band name under its slightly different spelling variation for legal reasons, though the band would eventually adopt "ZZ Top" (no periods and no space in the "ZZ") as the official band name.

Weeks before those registration changes, the group played their first concert as ZZ Top on July 4, 1969, in Houston at the Love Street Light Circus Feel Good Machine, where the Moving Sidewalks had hosted their final gigs less than a month earlier. This original trio recorded ZZ Top's first single, "Salt Lick," with the B-side "Miller's Farm," at two studios in Houston, Doyle Jones's Recording and Gold Star Sound Services.

Despite being released under the name ZZ Top, the two songs exist in a unique transitional space between the psychedelic rock of the Moving Sidewalks (both songs feature prominent organ) and the guitar-driven blues-rock of ZZ Top. Additionally, though ZZ Top was officially a trio, the single does feature bass guitar, which was also played by Gibbons over Greig's bass pedal. The single was self-released on a label of Ham's creation, Scat Records, and received some airplay on Houston's KILT, but attracted little notice elsewhere. Most fans of ZZ Top never heard the songs until they were released on the group's 2003 box set *Chrome, Smoke & BBQ*.

By the time the single was released in October 1969, both Greig and the organ had already left the group. The circumstances of Greig's departure are not clear, though it appears he exited for a career in acting. In a 2018 interview with *Shindig! Magazine*, Gibbons claimed that Greig headed to the West Coast and successfully auditioned to play Mork in the famed television series *Mork & Mindy* but ended up burning the opportunity and was replaced by comedian Robin Williams (he repeats this assertion in the band's official documentary, 2019's *ZZ Top: That Little Ol' Band from Texas*). It's a wild story but appears to have absolutely no factual basis because the character of Mork—a bizarre extraterrestrial from the planet Ork—first debuted on the popular sitcom *Happy Days* in an episode that aired on February 28, 1978, nearly a decade after Greig left ZZ Top (the *Mork & Mindy* series debuted later that year). In addition, none of the retrospective material about *Mork & Mindy* indicates that anyone other than Williams was offered the offbeat role. According to his obituary (he passed away in 2013), Greig worked as a session musician in Los Angeles after leaving ZZ Top, which seems a more likely explanation for his departure.

Greig was replaced in ZZ Top by Bill Ethridge, who was also an organist but wanted to play bass in the group. Ethridge had previously performed as a member of the Chessmen, a group led by blues guitarist Jimmie Vaughan, older brother of guitar legend Stevie Ray Vaughan. The Chessmen had previously played gigs with both the Moving Sidewalks and Dusty Hill and Frank Beard's band, American Blues. The move jettisoned the organ from the group's sound in favor of a power trio in the vein of Cream and the Jimi Hendrix Experience. However, since both of those groups had broken up, ZZ Top wasn't going to simply copy the sound of two defunct bands. Nonetheless, ZZ Top reached back to the music that had inspired Gibbons in the first place—the blues—to perhaps capitalize on the re-emerging popularity of the genre, which began to gain ground in Texas in the wake of the British electric blues revival prompted by guitarists like Eric Clapton, Peter Green, and Mick Taylor, who had all been featured in John Mayall's band the Bluesbreakers. Specifically, Gibbons has noted that he initially wanted ZZ Top to sound like the Jeff Beck Group, which at the time included Beck on guitar, former Faces member Rod Steward (vocals) and Ronnie Wood (bass), and Nicky Hopkins on keyboard. The Jeff Beck Group had recently released the album *Beck-Ola*, which reached number fifteen on the *Billboard* 200. While it may have been a trend, the blues certainly had demonstrated far more staying power than psychedelic rock, and the timely move was a stroke of brilliance by Gibbons and Ham that would define ZZ Top's sound for decades.

Mitchell left ZZ Top around the time of the release of the single, and the circumstances behind his ousting from the group are not clear. Even decades later in the *Shindig! Magazine* interview, Gibbons said he preferred not to discuss the reasons for Mitchell's departure but noted that they had made amends over the years (the two performed together again when the Moving Sidewalks reunited for a handful of performances in 2013). Gibbons's remarks seem to suggest that in the fall of 1969, he had already held auditions for a new drummer, who turned out to be Frank Beard, whom he may have thought a better fit for the sound he was trying to create with his new group. Beard has also insinuated in interviews that he wanted to be in a band with Gibbons and openly solicited to join ZZ Top (he later claimed he was so high on speed that he forced Gibbons into an eight-hour audition jam). Ham remained in possession of the group's name, and Gibbons chose to soldier on as ZZ Top with new performers.

Frank Beard, a veteran of the Dallas music scene, was hired by Gibbons and Ham as ZZ Top's new drummer at the suggestion of Ethridge, who had previously encountered Beard while they were both playing in Dallas. Beard, who had taken up the drums without any formal training after seeing the Beatles perform on *The Ed Sullivan Show*, had been drumming in bands in the Fort Worth area since the mid-1960s, playing in groups named the Hustlers and the Cellar Dwellers. The latter group may have gotten its name from a venue they frequently performed at, the Fort Worth Cellar, an underground strip club with a sister club in Dallas. Though a quarterback at Irving High School in the Dallas suburb of Irving, Beard was forced to drop off the team because he had married an older classmate whom he had gotten pregnant (presumably the high school administration didn't want a married teenager as the quarterback of the team).

Though separated by just under 250 miles, Houston and Dallas were completely distinct media markets and, as a result, had separate music scenes. Undoubtedly, Dallas had heard of the Moving Sidewalks (the Moving Sidewalks had opened for Hendrix in nearby Fort Worth, and the band later opened for the Doors at the Dallas Memorial Auditorium on July 9, 1968, among other concerts in the metro area), so it is still surprising that Beard and Gibbons, despite being the same age, did not cross paths earlier. Before joining ZZ Top, Beard's biggest success in music came as a member of American Blues, a band that combined a deep appreciation for the blues with the same wave of psychedelic rock that swept up the Moving Sidewalks and the rest of Texas.

American Blues had been born from the Warlocks, a Dallas group featuring guitarist-singer John Rockford "Rocky" Hill and his younger brother, bassist Joseph Michael "Dusty" Hill. Previously, the band also occasionally included female vocalist Mary Smith, with whom the act was promoted as Lady Wilde and the Warlocks. Smith, as Lady Wilde, was an English singer who had released a single, "Poor Kid," in Dallas in 1965 on ARA Records, which charted in Dallas (the Hill brothers possibly played on the single, a delightful piece of orchestral pop-rock). As Dusty Hill recounted in *ZZ Top: That Little Ol' Band from Texas*, having an English singer gave the group instant credibility on the scene since American audiences were so obsessed with British music. The Warlocks would perform gigs both with and without Smith, and in 1966 the Warlocks issued two singles, "If You Really Want Me to Stay" and "Splash Day," though by early 1967 Smith would leave the group permanently, and the band changed their name to American Blues.

Beard had known Dusty Hill since they were both teenagers growing up in the Dallas area. The Hill brothers, like Gibbons, came from a musical family—their mother, Myrl, was a nightclub singer and supported the growing interest in music that Rocky and Dusty developed. During their childhoods, the family briefly lived in Memphis, where Myrl worked as a waitress in a café frequented by a young Elvis Presley. She became a fan and brought several Presley 45s with them when they moved back to Dallas. Hill's mother introduced her children to the blues, a fact that Dusty later said made the family unpopular with other parents in the neighborhood because they did not want their children listening to Black music at the Hills' house. The

Hill boys quickly learned how to play instruments, with Rocky on guitar and Dusty on bass, and began performing live when Dusty was still in his early teens. Before long they were both frequently playing in Dallas clubs in both their own bands and as backup musicians for blues artists who came into town and needed a competent backing group for a gig. This meant that while still teenagers Dusty Hill (and later Frank Beard) had the opportunity to perform with Lightnin' Hopkins, Chuck Berry, Bo Diddley, and, most notably, Freddie King, with whom Dusty even said he had performed with at the famed Fillmore West in San Francisco. Dallas-born actress Morgan Fairchild, then known as Patsy Ann McClenny, who would later appear on the series *Dallas*, was acquainted with Dusty when her high school boyfriend played drums in a band with Rocky. Dusty (as a member of ZZ Top) and Fairchild were both honored by the Texas Film Hall of Fame in 2008, an honor presented by the Austin Film Society.

While Gibbons grew up the son of an established musician in an upscale neighborhood, both Beard and Hill came from more working-class roots. That included getting gigs wherever they could find them to make money. Among the bands that Beard and Hill had played in together was an ersatz version of the Zombies, the English group that recorded the hit songs "She's Not There," "Tell Her No," and "Time of the Season," a fact that writer Daniel Ralston uncovered in 2016 in an article for *BuzzFeed*. In 1969, a music management company named Delta Promotions put together two touring versions of the "Zombies" after the British group's "Time of the Season" became a hit single in the United States. Predicated on the fact that American audiences wouldn't know details about the actual group or even what they looked like because the song became a hit after the original Zombies broke up, Delta Promotions created two touring versions of the "Zombies" to perform across the United States. When asked for comment on how they had gotten involved in the fake group in the 2016 article, Beard declined to be interviewed, and Hill commented, "It was the '60s, man," and noted that Delta Promotions gave him the impression that the Zombies were a group manufactured in the studio, a not-uncommon arrangement in the era (with the early Monkees and the Archies as the era's most familiar examples). The "Zombies" ruse didn't last more than a few months, and Beard and Hill returned to more legitimate bands.

But American Blues was the primary vehicle of Beard and Dusty Hill, in which they were joined by Rocky and occasionally keyboardist Doug Davis. Despite what the name implies, the band's music was in the same vein of psychedelic rock as the Moving Sidewalks'. The band released an album, 1968's *American Blues 'Is Here,'* on a local record label, Karma, and also released a single from the first album, a trippy version of Tim Hardin's oft-covered "If I Were a Carpenter" that did not chart. Notably, the album was recorded at Robin Hood Studios in Tyler, Texas, owned by Robin Hood Brians, where ZZ Top would later record their first albums. Despite not drawing much attention after the first album, the band released a second album later that year, *American Blues 'Do Their Thing,'* which was released by UNI, a subsidiary of major label MCA.

The band's initial gimmick was that they performed in all-blue clothing and dyed their hair blue, a notoriously brash move for 1960s Texas, even in the music scene. Beard and Dusty Hill would later recall that they had trouble booking hotel rooms on the road because proprietors did not want the band members' hair dye rubbing off on the pillows. By the time they recorded their first album, they had stopped with the hair dye. The first album's producer, a Texas musician by the name of Scotty McKay who had previously recorded with rockabilly legend Gene Vincent, would later claim in the liner notes of a European reissue of the album (released under the title *Before ZZ*) that Jimi Hendrix performed on the album when he stopped in the studio during the session, a claim that has absolutely no factual basis.

Unusually, despite the Moving Sidewalks' occasionally playing in Dallas and the American Blues' occasionally playing in Houston, the two bands never shared a bill. With the American Blues going nowhere, the band broke up in 1969. Rocky Hill would return to playing blues and become a staple of the Texas blues scene, and though he opened for ZZ Top on occasion in the early 1980s and released the 1982 album *Texas Shuffle* and a 1988 self-titled album produced by Bill Ham, he never gained much notoriety outside Texas. He passed away in 2009 at the age of sixty-two.

Beard moved to Houston, where he encountered Gibbons and joined ZZ Top. The ZZ Top lineup of Gibbons, Beard, and Ethridge lasted for about three months before Ethridge left the band in January 1970. A 1996 retrospective article in *Texas Monthly* magazine claimed that Ethridge was fired for being a "bad influence" on Beard (decades later, Beard would open up about his substance abuse issues early in his career), though in a letter to *Texas Monthly* Ethridge denied that he was fired and said he instead left ZZ Top to return to Dallas to perform again with his former Chessmen bandmates guitarist Jimmie Vaughan and drummer Doyle Bramhall.

With ZZ Top again without a bassist, the band went through some temporary replacements. For a permanent solution, Beard suggested that his former bandmate, Hill, who had since moved to Houston, was an ideal replacement. Hill joined Gibbons and Beard for a rehearsal, where they jammed on a shuffle in C that lasted—depending on who is telling the story—anywhere from one to four hours (though the members have occasionally joked that they were still playing the same song decades later). That shuffle in C may have also later evolved into their version of "Thunderbird" by the classic Texas band the Nightcaps, a song that ZZ Top later recorded live for *Fandango!* and, controversially, would copyright despite not having written it.

With Hill, ZZ Top added not only an accomplished bassist to their lineup but also a soulful singer who could belt out both backing and lead vocals along with laying down the groove. Gibbons also immediately saw the advantages of working with a rhythm section that had already performed and recorded together. Though ZZ Top had a tumultuous first six months in terms of personnel, the Gibbons-Hill-Beard configuration would remain unchanged for fifty-one consecutive years, a rare example of consistency in a business where rock band membership is often constantly shuffling because of disagreements, deaths, or general inner band chaos.

Yet it wasn't just the fact that Beard and Hill had previously played together that kept the lineup intact for over half a century. "It would be hard to tie this incredible success and consistency to just one factor," says Matthew Wilkening, founding editor in chief of *Ultimate Classic Rock*. "Obviously talent is a big one. Chemistry, tenacity, and of course luck also play a part. I think the biggest thing with them is they knew what to change and what to hold on to."

4
BIG IN BEAUMONT

In its January 3, 1970, issue, *Cashbox* reported that London Recordings, the American arm of Decca Records—the UK record label that, while successful, infamously turned down opportunities to sign major rock acts, including the Beatles, the Kinks, the Who, and the Yardbirds, though it did have the foresight to sign the Rolling Stones, the Moody Blues, and the Zombies (the real band, not the bogus Frank Beard and Dusty Hill version)—acquired the master of the "Salt Lick" single, which London promptly reissued. The same issue of *Cashbox* contained a review of the single, describing ZZ Top as a "blues based underground teen act" and predicting that the single was "bound to attract FM welcomes and a possible AM/top forty showing." The prediction was off the mark, as the reissued single had no more success than the original release, and the new band (two-thirds of whom did not play on the debut single) forged ahead.[1]

The classic ZZ Top lineup of Billy Gibbons, Beard, and Hill made their live debut together on February 10, 1970, in Beaumont, Texas, in a show organized by Beaumont radio personality Al Caldwell, one of the first disc jockeys to play the band's music. Various stories about that gig persist—for example, some sources claim it was at a VFW Hall, others that it was at Knights of Columbus Hall—and an oft-reported tale holds that the group played to a single paying customer, whom they bought a Coke during a break in the set (Gibbons humorously noted in the band's documentary, *ZZ Top: That Little Ol' Band from Texas*, that the lone audience member still comes to their shows). Regardless of where the gig was or how many paying customers were actually present that night in Beaumont, the Gulf Coast area, including

Groves and Port Arthur, was one of the first markets to embrace the band with regular gigs and radio airplay. This early connection led to ZZ Top's being inducted into the Museum of the Gulf Coast Music Hall of Fame in 1998.

But being "big in Beaumont" would do little to bolster ZZ Top's fortunes across the landscape of Texas, let alone nationally. Much like the Moving Sidewalks and American Blues before them, ZZ Top ground out on the road with gigs almost nightly in Texas and occasionally other states in the vicinity. Part of manager Bill Ham's strategy to market the band on the road was to book ZZ Top to play gigs in the surrounding areas of a major city as a grassroots way to infiltrate that market without trying to break in by performing in the city itself. Between dates, ZZ Top would visit Robin Hood Studios in Tyler, Texas, to begin work on what would become their first album.

Under Ham's direction, the band also worked on developing their image. Ham had a strict edict that the band would not collaborate with musicians outside the group (some sources say that this was even contractually enforced) to keep the band firmly established as a trio. This decree lasted essentially for the first half of the band's career. "One time I had a call from Mick Jagger for Billy to come to Compass Point Studios in Nassau, Bahamas," shares Terry Manning, who would later engineer nearly every ZZ Top album from *Tres Hombres* to *Recycler*. Manning incidentally would own and work at Compass Point later in his career, but at this point he had not worked at the studio yet. At Compass Point, Jagger was recording his first solo album, 1985's *She's the Boss*, which featured several guest musicians, including Jeff Beck. "Jagger wanted Billy to guest. Of course, we had to run it by Bill Ham, who said, 'Absolutely not! I am not letting Billy out of what we do. I'm not letting him get out in interviews and pictures.'"

Along those lines, Ham also tightly controlled the band's publicity. For much of ZZ Top's career, the band played the fame game close to the vest.

Initially, the group did not speak to the press and posed for very few publicity photos. This was not through lack of interest but by design—Ham believed in keeping the group as mysterious as its unusual name. "So, he did have a tight control, but it was not really a bad thing necessarily because it worked for them," adds Manning. "It created a deep mystique of what is this band like. You had to go see them live to see them and you had to buy records to hear them. I think it was a bold tactic that Bill was using, and it really worked."

A few years into the band's career, Ham began promoting ZZ Top with the tagline "That little ol' band from Texas," forever closely linking the small group to their outsized home state and providing the group with a nickname that stuck for decades. But what Texas meant to the rest of the United States in the early 1970s was a different story. By the time ZZ Top was recording their first album, it had been less than a decade since President John F. Kennedy had been assassinated in Dallas and less than three years since the unpopular Texas-born Lyndon B. Johnson had announced that he would not seek reelection as US president. Outsiders' views of the state ranged from thinking of Texas as a cultural backwater to seeing it as a romanticized modern Wild West as captured in songs like Marty Robbins's "El Paso," even though the East Texas where Gibbons, Hill, and Beard had grown up was closer geographically to Memphis, Tennessee, than to the drier plains of West Texas. Meanwhile, inside Texas, the state was undergoing rapid change. Its economy—traditionally focused on farming and the petroleum industry—began growing in other sectors and attracting new residents. Texas' population rapidly grew over ZZ Top's prime years—in 1960, it was the sixth most populous state but leaped over Ohio and Illinois during the decade to become the fourth most populous in 1970. By 1980, it ranked third after having grown its population by 50 percent over the previous two decades.

But few Texas musicians embraced the iconography and larger-than-life stereotypes of Texas quite like ZZ Top, though it would be a little over a year into their career before they would fully wrap themselves in the imagery of the Lone Star State. Gibbons, in a then rare solo interview, spoke to the United Press International about the band's manufactured image in January 1977. "I guess you could say we're living the Texas myth—right up front for the world to see. I mean, we grew up with it and it seems natural—but it comes off differently in other places. We want to have the biggest—and the best—show there is. And if that's not the Texas image, nothing is."[2]

Without a formal record contract with London yet, Ham raised $12,000 from Daily Record Distributors of Houston, the promotion company he worked for, to fund the initial sessions at Robin Hood Studios in Tyler, situated two hundred miles north of Houston and one hundred miles east of Dallas. Robin Hood Studios was founded and is owned by Robin Hood Brians. A trained musician from an early age, Brians recorded a single, "Dis a Ittly Bit!" for Fraternity Records in Nashville at the famed Quonset Hut Studio as a teenager. The experience inspired him to build a recording studio in his parents' home to record East Texas musicians. Brians and his father later built a building for the studio in the backyard of the property; Robin Hood Studios opened in 1963 and has been operated by Brians for more than six decades. Ham agreed to split the band's profits with Daily in return for the loan to record the album (the agreement ended several years later in a lawsuit when Ham refused to pay Daily any more money after the band's third album—it was settled for $240,000).

While Ham may have hammered out the business and marketing for the band, he was also credited for producing ZZ Top's first ten albums and coproducing the following two with Gibbons. Though Ham had an ear for music, his technical know-how in the studio was limited, and he has often been the subject of humorous anecdotes about his directives. Ham had particular ideas on how the band should sound, but he did not always know how to execute those ideas. Ham decreed that the album could not feature any overdubs, a rule borne of a humiliating experience he once had. Brians remembers,

> When he was working for the Daily Brothers, he brought a group over there to San Antonio. They got on stage, and they didn't sound anything like the record. Come to find out, they had done a whole lot of overdubbing. That's when he made the hard fast rule that there would be no overdubbing if he produced a group. And then he brings me a set of drums, one guitar, and one bass. And I'm thinking to myself, "What's up with this?" That's when I got with Billy, and the third time they came up is when we pulled that little trip to the Country Tavern.

The "little trip to the Country Tavern" was a now famous instance when Brians sent Ham out to pick up food at the Country Tavern in Kilgore, Texas, over twenty miles away from the studio, so that he and the band could figure out the sound they were looking for without his meddling. Upon his return with the renowned barbecue from the Country Tavern, Ham was pleased with how the band now sounded. "Bill didn't really produce, he just ran the show," recalls Brians. "He was known as Atilla the Producer. I would've asked him for some points [on *ZZ Top's First Album*] since I created the sound, but he was so dictatorial that I just said, 'Leave it alone,' you know? Bill Ham was a very successful producer. He was tough, meaner than a junkyard dog when he needed to be, and business was business. I give him a lot of credit for their success. He put the hammer down when it came to protecting them."

"He was a different kind of producer than what you think of when you think of someone like Mutt Lange or another record producer," explains Manning, who worked extensively with Ham later on ZZ Top albums and recordings for other artists, including working on six albums for the rock group Point Blank, also managed by Ham.

He wasn't as deeply musical as some people might be as far as knowing the intricacies of musical notation or things like that. While we worked together, he just let me and Billy go at it, more or less, and then said what he liked or didn't like. He would have ideas too, of course. It was a bit like what you think of with a producer of a movie, the old-time producers who had gotten the people they wanted together. That was as much producing as sitting there and telling someone every note to play or something like that. It's getting the right combination. I worked with Bill very closely on ZZ Top and other albums as well as for several other artists. I spent many, many, many session hours, days, weeks, months, and years working with him, mostly at Ardent Studios but at other studios as well. I really liked Bill; he was almost like an uncle to me in a way. It's an odd thing to say because he was not that much older than me.

The album, uniquely titled *ZZ Top's First Album*, was recorded through the latter half of 1970 and released on January 16, 1971, by London Recordings. "The sessions were fun," remembers Brians.

I still haven't gotten an answer from Billy on one thing. When they recorded, the songs had no names and there was no singing. They were just groovy tracks, and it was Track No. 1, 2, 3, and 4. And then they came back, and they told me that they didn't write the melodies or lyrics until they already had the track cut. That's the way to control the groove, but I don't know. Some of the tracks just fit those lyrics so well that you just have to wonder. Maybe Bill Ham didn't let them sing the songs because he didn't want the hooks floating around. I can write a song called "Yesterday," or "Love Me Tender," or "Your Cheatin' Heart," and as long as I don't steal your melody or words, that's it. You cannot copyright a title, and the title is usually the hook.

Gibbons has said he wanted ZZ Top to sound like the Jeff Beck Group, and the band's first album is much in the English blues tradition filtered through the language of Texas with songs like "Somebody Else Been Shaking Your Tree" and "Backdoor Love Affair," as well as a blues song in the classic style, "Just Got Back from Baby's." Brians reveals that during the sessions Gibbons would have a process to mentally prepare for recording. "When we were recording, Billy Gibbons was into transcendental meditation," shares Brians. "Before he'd do his guitar tracks, he'd go back into my office, close the door, and sit there and meditate for twenty minutes. I got into TM because of him. I found a TM teacher locally, and I found it quite useful from time to time."

The band had jelled into a cohesive unit by the time the album was recorded. "There were never any conflicts at all in the studio," recalls Brians. "Everything was smooth, and it stayed that way. I loved working with them. They were professional, and I looked at it as a joy to get in the studio with them because I knew they were well prepared, had great equipment, and they knew what they were doing. Once we found that sound, it was great. It was fun."

In what would become a regular occurrence on most ZZ Top albums, Hill sings lead vocals on one song, "Goin' Down to Mexico," and Gibbons and Hill share vocals on another, "Squank." Also striking about the first album is its lack of lyrical humor, something that would become one of the band's trademarks. While most of the songs reflect standard blues lyrics, like "Brown Sugar," "Certified Blues," and "Backdoor Love Affair," there are some surprises, like "Squank," which is like a Stephen King science fiction / horror story come to life, and "Goin' Down to Mexico," with lyrics seemingly inspired not by Texas' southern neighbor but instead by the classic 1950 film *Sunset Boulevard*. Nonetheless, aside from changes to their sound via production flourishes, the band's first album firmly established the template for the rest of ZZ Top's career as purveyors of blues-based rock.

As part of Ham's image-making attempts for the band, the record sleeve has very few details about who or what ZZ Top is. The gatefold features several shots of the trio outside a ramshackle house looking more like subjects of Dorothea Lange's famed Dust Bowl photos than members of a 1970s rock band. The cover features an image of "Pearly Gates," Gibbons's treasured 1959 Les Paul, and the back features a watercolor of the three band members' faces by Bill Narum, a Texas counterculture artist and art director for Houston's *Space City News* underground newspaper. Narum would go on to play a prominent role in ZZ Top's art direction for the next two decades. Considering how much the band would lean into their Texas identity starting with their very next album, it is curious in retrospect that the album sleeve makes no reference at all to Texas or where this group may have come from (the only address listed on the original LP is London Recordings' New York City address).

The text on the back cover of the album—"In this day of homogenized rock, synthesized music, retakes, overdubbing, multi, multi-tracking, an honest recording by accomplished musicians is a rewarding pleasure"—reads like a prefabricated album review (in fact, it is framed as if it were from a media outlet named *abstract blues*) or a declaration of war on most other rock bands of the 1970s. The text, the brainchild of Ham, also became ironic in retrospect considering how much in-studio tinkering and use of synthesizers would feature in the group's later work. Another irony is that *ZZ Top's First Album* actually does feature overdubbing—for example, the rhythm guitar on "Just Got Back from Baby's" and "Certified Blues"—so the declaration was more feeling than fact.

ZZ Top's First Album just barely missed the charts, hitting number 201 on *Billboard*'s Bubbling Under the Top LPs chart listing the albums next in line for the *Billboard* 200, while the single, "(Somebody Else Been) Shaking Your Tree," failed to chart. Though the album didn't have a hit, the Gibbons-penned "Brown Sugar" was revived in ZZ Top's set lists in the mid-1990s and has continued to regularly appear as one of their "live" songs in concert that does not require the use of any backing tracks, unlike their later 1980s hits, which make up the bulk of the set lists. Humorously, in early articles about the band, Gibbons was sometimes mistakenly credited for writing the Rolling Stones' far better-known song with the same title, which was released three months after *ZZ Top's First Album*. It's likely Ham and Gibbons didn't mind the misappropriation, as having the young band's name linked with rock megastars like the Rolling Stones bought instant credibility.

ZZ Top's First Album gave the band more standing beyond the Houston and Dallas markets, and Ham was able to book them into new venues outside Texas. Still, the group was far from stardom. On February 20 and 21, 1971, ZZ Top played a two-night stand opening for Canned Heat at the Warehouse in New Orleans and slept on the dressing room floor between gigs; they couldn't afford hotel rooms as it was the weekend before Mardi Gras. However, the gigs were successful, and ZZ Top would regularly perform at the Warehouse through 1974, returning in 1979 and 1982. Two months after sleeping on the floor in New Orleans, ZZ Top would make their debut in Memphis—a city that would later become their second home—as part of a blues festival featuring Delta blues legend Bukka White as a headliner. ZZ Top was also able to land some choice opening slots for bigger bands at arena shows in Texas, including Quicksilver Messenger Service, Ike and Tina Turner (with Ike reportedly giving Gibbons some poor advice on what to wear on stage), and, most notably, the Allman Brothers Band. ZZ Top opened for the Allman Brothers Band for a few shows, including on September 17, 1971, at the Mid-South Coliseum in Memphis and September 26, 1971, at the Sam Houston Coliseum in Houston, just weeks before guitar icon Duane Allman died in a motorcycle accident at the age of twenty-four. Gibbons would later speak about Allman as a musician and the brief time he spent in his company with nearly the same reverence as he did Jimi Hendrix.

On stage, Gibbons and Hill soon developed a second-to-none rapport. Though their performances would become far more choreographed starting with the 1980s tours, even in the early years the guitarist and bassist would often play while standing no more than a few feet apart directly in front of Beard, even on very large arena or stadium stages. This not only kept the band's energy centralized during the performance, with all eyes at center stage, but also projected the close-knit image of the band.

While ZZ Top was making progress on the road, they returned to Robin Hood Studios in the fall of 1971 to record their second album. By that time, Gibbons, Hill, and Beard had been performing together for nearly two years and had developed a live repertoire that reflected their growing strength as a musical unit. Playing live in various set lengths also lent to the band expanding the length of their songs; though both *ZZ Top's First Album* and the band's second album, *Rio Grande Mud*, feature ten songs, the latter album is more than five minutes longer.

Unlike *ZZ Top's First Album*, *Rio Grande Mud* embraced the band's Texas upbringing much more clearly. Its title, *Rio Grande Mud*, possibly references the mud of the Mississippi Delta that birthed blues legends like Muddy Waters. On *Rio Grande Mud*, ZZ Top began demonstrating more of the band's eccentric personality, with a heavy helping of the blues—some of it traditional ("Mushmouth Shoutin'" is very derivative of "Can't Hold Out Much Longer" by blues harmonica legend Little Walter, and "Apologies to Pearly" is a tip of the hat to Freddie King's "The Stumble," although it features Gibbons playing slide guitar). Other blues pieces on the album are uniquely ZZ Top, like the soulful seven-and-a-half minute "Sure Got Cold after the Rain Fell," which is also the longest song the band ever recorded, as well as more straightforward rock, like "Francine" and "Chevrolet," and even some more offbeat experimental work like the bizarrely structured "Ko Ko Blue" with its tendency to veer into unconventional arrangements and flourishes. Gibbons also had the opportunity to show off his impressive skill on the harmonica, which went unheard on *ZZ Top's First Album*. "Mushmouth Shoutin'" also includes a rare credit on a ZZ Top album to an outside musician, Pete Tickle on acoustic guitar, one of ZZ Top's earliest associates.

The album's cover art, again designed by Narum, depicts the members of ZZ Top emerging from a mud bath in the Rio Grande, the river that forms the border between Texas and Mexico. The back cover features a photo of the band performing live at the Sam Houston Coliseum on June 6, 1971, one of the nights that the band opened for the Allman Brothers Band and Quicksilver Messenger Service. The photo shows that the band was still working out its image. Hill is depicted with a large, wide-brimmed hat, while Gibbons is still beardless and wearing a loose-fitting shirt, reflecting the transition from counterculture psychedelic rockers to good ol' Texas cowboys in just a few short years.

The album was promoted with a single, "Francine," by far the most pop-driven song on either of the band's first albums. The composition originated as a song demo by the Children, another Texas-based band that at one time was signed to ATCO Records, a subsidiary of Atlantic Records. Though the band released an album, *Rebirth*, in 1968 and even appeared in filmmaker Robert Altman's bizarre 1970 Houston-based comedy film *Brewster McCloud*, a combination of the usual pitfalls of the rock-and-roll lifestyle—bad management, drugs, and inner turmoil—dampened the band's once-promising fortunes. Gibbons was acquainted with the members of the Children and filled in for the band's guitarist, Kenny Cordray, for at least one concert, in Huntsville, Alabama, opening for B. B. King after Cordray sustained an injury. That introduced Gibbons to the song "Francine," which was written by Cordray and Children front man Steve Perron, a highly regarded songwriter with a history of drug addiction that had impacted the Children's career.

On the original back cover of *Rio Grande Mud*, the song was credited to Perron-Cordray, but on the LP label, the credit reads "S. Perron; K. Cordray; Gibbons," which is how it was credited on the single and all subsequent releases and also how the song is registered with BMI. However, the two versions of the song are extremely similar, and it seems likely that Gibbons was granted (or demanded or co-opted) a cowriting credit for ZZ Top's recording the song—a not-uncommon arrangement in the music industry. There could be even more to the story: on both April 9, 1978, and May 17, 1978, the *Port Arthur News* reported in stories that a Port Neches, Texas, musician named Joseph Matte had written "Mexican Blackbird," "Francine," and "Neighbor, Neighbor" and sold them to ZZ Top. The inclusion of "Francine" on the list makes the claim especially dubious since the song originated with the Children, so while artists selling songs to more established artists is not unheard of, this particular claim is unconvincing.

"Francine" became ZZ Top's first single to chart, reaching number sixty-nine on the *Billboard* Hot 100. However, just days before the release of *Rio Grande Mud*, *Rolling Stone* published a lengthy article about Perron with a sensationalist title ("Steve Perron: A Guitarist Who Almost Made It—Then Came Smack"). Perron at that time was hospitalized in an attempt to finally kick his drug addiction. Sadly, he would pass away the following year. The entire situation with ZZ Top covering the song and having to potentially pay royalties to individuals outside the band was allegedly too much for Ham, who reinforced his edict forbidding his band to collaborate with outside musicians to avoid such complications. Except for covers, no outside songwriter would be credited on a ZZ Top album until 1996's *Rhythmeen*.

More recently, "Francine" raises eyebrows for another reason: it is an ode to the title girl, who toward the end of the song is identified as only thirteen years old. With that in mind, it's worth noting that Cordray was only about fifteen years old when he cowrote the song. Humorously, the lyrics also make a reference to "Stevie P."—who is Steve Perron, the song's other cowriter (the original demo features Perron singing "Billy G." instead, likely a reference to Gibbons himself).

While *Rio Grande Mud* also did not feature any major hits, the album peaked at number 104 on the *Billboard* 200 and hung in on the chart for ten weeks. Still, it left a lasting impression on the band's fans. The upbeat "Just Got Paid" could be considered ZZ Top's first classic as it has remained a standard in the band's live show, and both "Francine" and "Chevrolet" have been revived in concert on occasion. Meanwhile, "Bar-B-Q" was eventually adopted into the live extended version of ZZ Top's later hit "La Grange" and thus became recognizable even to ZZ Top fans who don't know that bit of the jam originated as another song.

Less than two weeks before the release of *Rio Grande Mud*, ZZ Top promoted the album by making their first appearance outside the South or Southwest with a five-night stand at the famed Whisky a Go Go on the Sunset Strip in Los Angeles from March 22 to 26, 1972. The concerts were meant to introduce the band to the lucrative and press-saturated Southern California market. London Recordings sent limousines to ferry the local press to the venue. The reviews of the show indicated how badly ZZ Top needed industry exposure. The write-up in the April 15, 1972, edition of *Billboard* not only panned the performance, noting ZZ Top as little more than a tribute to Cream and the Jimi Hendrix Experience, but also identified the band as "English." Nonetheless, after the release of the album, ZZ Top was able to extend their influence into new markets and were now regularly visiting venues in Tennessee, North Carolina, Mississippi, Alabama, Missouri, Oklahoma, and even as far north as Ohio and Illinois. Their popularity in Texas was still growing as well, and the band staged a sold-out performance on July

21, 1972, at the Dallas Memorial Auditorium. ZZ Top returned to California at the end of the year, though much farther north, performing at two shows at the famed Winterland Ballroom in San Francisco in December.

Just weeks after the Winterland concerts, ZZ Top had their first performances outside the continental United States after the Rolling Stones hand-picked the trio to open their January 1973 concerts in Hawaii. ZZ Top was selected to open the Stones' Hawaii shows on the recommendation of Barry Fey, a Denver promoter who was one of the first to book ZZ Top outside Texas or the Southeast. Fey had booked ZZ Top's tour opening for Ten Years After at the Denver Coliseum on November 29, 1972. The Stones' London Recordings connection—London released the band's records in the United States through 1971—may have helped as well. Texan Bobby Keys, who played saxophone as part of the Stones' touring party and was a close friend of Rolling Stones guitarist Keith Richards, also vouched for his fellow Lone Star State musicians.

The Rolling Stones' 1973 Pacific Tour, which was in support of their landmark *Exile on Main St.* album and followed the band's wildly successful 1972 American Tour, kicked off with a benefit concert at the Los Angeles Forum before the band headed to Hawaii's Honolulu International Center. The visit to the fiftieth state for three shows—one on January 21, two on January 22—was meant to be a stopover for a five-night stand at Tokyo's famed Budokan, which would be the Stones' first-ever shows in Japan. However, the Tokyo dates were eventually canceled when Japanese authorities refused to let Rolling Stones lead singer Mick Jagger into the country because of his prior drug convictions. Planned dates in February in New Zealand and Australia were on the cusp of cancellation as well, but they proceeded as planned.

As a result, the Stones booked Hawaii dates to ensure that the band would have a Pacific base of operations while these legal issues were being sorted out. The Honolulu International Center was already in the news because the

Rolling Stones concerts occurred just one week after Elvis Presley's famed Aloha from Hawaii concert, which was broadcast internationally via satellite. ZZ Top were determined to make a grand impression on both the Stones and the Hawaiian audience. The band members arrived more than a week early in Hawaii, using the time for rehearsals and a well-deserved break from the road.

To that end, Ham did not want his group mixing too much with the notoriously hard-partying Stones and their entourage. After the first night, Ham put the band on a two-drink limit at the hotel bar. Luckily for the band, they discovered that the bar served an oversized novelty cocktail called "Chimp in Orbit" that was served in a glass so tall that it would be placed on the floor with a long straw. Therefore, the band could have "two drinks" and still have an enjoyable time in the Aloha State.

The Stones gigs went very well for ZZ Top and sparked a long-running admiration among the bands, particularly with Keith Richards, since the members of ZZ Top and Richards shared many of the same musical influences and reverence for American blues. In 1981, ZZ Top opened the Stones' stadium shows in Houston and Dallas, and in 2003 they opened a Rolling Stones concert in Finland. The following year, Richards inducted ZZ Top into the Rock and Roll Hall of Fame, humorously noting that when he first met them, he thought, based on their long-bearded look, that they were in the Witness Protection Program but that their disguises were not going to work.

Of course, Richards first met them before ZZ Top had long beards, but as with Billy Gibbons, one should never let the truth get in the way of a good Keith Richards quip.

5
MANNING AND MEMPHIS

Shortly after the Hawaii concerts, ZZ Top returned to Texas and began work on their third album at Robin Hood Studios. Though *ZZ Top's First Album* and *Rio Grande Mud* are full of songs that fans of the band think of as early classics, the lack of chart success or radio airplay meant that they were largely unknown to the general public despite ZZ Top's growing reputation through relentless touring regionally. While songs like "Brown Sugar" and "Just Got Paid" hinted at what was to come from the trio, ZZ Top came into their own with *Tres Hombres*. Several important developments helped the band reach a new level of success with their third album, which has held a lofty position in the band's catalog above all the other albums except perhaps *Eliminator*. Indeed, to this day songs from *Tres Hombres* remain staples of the band's live show. They have performed three of them, "Waitin' for the Bus," "Jesus Just Left Chicago," and the standout "La Grange," the most in concert, and other songs from the album, like "Beer Drinkers and Hell Raisers" and "Precious and Grace," also have occasionally appeared in set lists and are fan-favorite tracks.

Tres Hombres was the first of seven ZZ Top albums engineered by Terry Manning. Manning had grown up in El Paso and played in several local bands, including occasionally performing with early Texas rock-and-roll hero Bobby Fuller. He made his major impact on the industry upon moving to Memphis, where he began a career as an engineer and producer, recording and mixing dozens of classic albums for Stax Records. He was the primary engineer working with the Staple Singers on their hits but also worked on recordings by the likes of Isaac Hayes, Ike and Tina Turner, Booker T. & the M.G.'s, Sam & Dave, and Leon Russell, among many others. Manning

moved on to Ardent Studios in Memphis, joining many other younger producers and engineers in creating one of the most renowned music studios
in the world. He also worked as the mixing engineer on *Led Zeppelin III*,
the powerhouse band's 1970 album. By 1971, Ardent had established a new
location in Memphis on Madison Avenue, just four miles from Beale Street.
Both Ardent and Manning would become essential components of the ZZ
Top sound and the band's success over the next fifteen years. Manning recalls,

> *The very first time I had heard ZZ Top was when I was coming home from*
> *a session in Memphis about midnight one night. Back in those days, at night*
> *FM radio would play album cuts or long cuts, like fifteen-minute songs or*
> *whatever. This new song came on the radio that I had never heard, and it*
> *just blew me away. I just loved the singer's voice and the guitar playing. The*
> *song was "Sure Got Cold after the Rain Fell." I was just so taken with it that*
> *it was one of those few moments where you actually pull off the road and*
> *stop so you can hear the song. I just loved the sound of the group, but Billy*
> *was the key feature in that.*

Manning, hearing the group's potential from the track, was determined
to work with ZZ Top. "I started thinking, 'Who is this group? I have to find
this group. I'd love to work with someone like that,'" he remembers. "It just
so happens that right about that same time the *Led Zeppelin III* album had
come out, which I did the mixing and mastering on, and Billy had heard that
on the radio and thought, 'Why can't ZZ Top sound a little more like this
technically?' So he started hunting me down while I was hunting him down.
It really was an odd twist of fate."

Though the band recorded the tracks for *Tres Hombres* at Robin Hood
Studios, as they had their first two albums, the call was made for a change
of scenery, and ZZ Top followed Manning to Ardent Studios in Memphis to
finish the album. "They came to Memphis and played a gig in a place called

the Warehouse that's long gone," says Manning. "It was kind of a dump—a big, old, dusty warehouse, literally. I knew they were playing there, and I had a friend take a note backstage. Billy found out about it and sent me a note, and we ended up with phone numbers exchanged. We got together, and he talked Bill Ham into coming to Memphis to work with me. The very first thing we did was a B-side remix of one of the songs on the second album."

Tres Hombres was brought to Ardent in Memphis after it had been tracked at Robin Hood Studios for overdubs and all the mixing and mastering. Memphis soon became a second home for ZZ Top; the band would go on to record or finish the music for every ZZ Top album through *Rhythmeen* at Ardent, and while recording they would typically set up shop at the Peabody Hotel, a historic luxury hotel in Downtown Memphis. "I know Billy was very enamored with Memphis," shares Manning. "I'm from Texas and so is the band, and Texas is everything to all of us. But he always said that Memphis is an extension of Texas in a way. It had that deep, soulful thing, and especially in those days and before those days, it had so much musical soul coming into and out of Memphis. But Billy just really enjoyed it. We didn't go Stax or Sun all of a sudden, but I think there is some of the soul in there. Certainly, he was probably feeling it and thinking about it."

Manning also notes a humorous story recalling how Billy Gibbons once prepared himself for a challenging vocal session. "I remember for one of the later albums, when he was going to do a vocal, he said, 'Ah, my voice isn't quite right.' It was wintertime, and he took his shirt off, went outside, and ran around the lot twice while screaming in the cold weather. He came in saying, 'Now my voice is all right!' Maybe Memphis contributed to that somehow." Because of the band's long history of recording in Memphis, ZZ Top was one of the inaugural inductees into the Memphis Music Hall of Fame in 2012 alongside some of their musical heroes, like B. B. King, Howlin' Wolf, and, of course, Memphis icon Elvis Presley.

During the time that Manning was mixing *Tres Hombres*, he made some production decisions in conjunction with Gibbons that had an enduring impact on both the album and the band's history. The first two songs on the record, "Waitin' for the Bus" and "Jesus Just Left Chicago," segue into one another with only a fraction of space between them, linking the songs together forever. The two songs are typically played back-to-back on rock radio, and ZZ Top always performs them together in concert. Over the years, the short gap between the songs has been noted incorrectly as a sequencing mistake, but Manning says that wasn't the case.

> *When it was time to sequence the album, they had given me an order—I can't remember if it was Billy or Bill Ham—so I was putting the songs together in that order on a quarter-inch Scully tape machine. When I got done with the first song and it was time for the next song, I thought, "Wow, the keys work together here. What about the timing?" I thought I'd put them together as if they played it as one big, long thing. Timing wise and key wise, it all worked out. When everybody heard it, they all said, "Yeah, that's it." So I will take credit for that. There are a lot of things that I'm proud of, and that would be one of them.*

The funky "Waitin' for the Bus" is deceptively complex, featuring several key changes as Gibbons sings about a long wait for public transportation at the end of a workday. "Jesus Just Left Chicago" is one of the band's finest blues tunes and creates a unique visual placing Jesus Christ on a journey between Chicago and New Orleans, taking stops in Mississippi (turning muddy water into wine, naturally) and, in a bizarre route, California. Linked together, the two songs offer a six-and-a-half mini-suite that demonstrates two very different sides of ZZ Top, and they have been inseparable ever since. "I think it really made a difference to the spread of ZZ Top at that time with that album because radio would play them together, so you got what they later called a 'twofer,' a double play, automatically from that," adds Manning. "I think it may have helped a little bit with the promotion. It didn't hurt that the songs are fantastic."

The album's single, the blues-boogie blast "La Grange," was released a few weeks before *Tres Hombres*, and it peaked at number forty-one on the *Billboard* chart dated June 29, 1974, a month before the album was even released, though it fared better on the less authoritative *Cashbox* (number twenty-four) and *Record World* (number thirty-three) charts. Because "La Grange" has since ascended into the pantheon of classic rock songs, it has given the retrospective impression that it was a much bigger chart hit than it actually was at the time. While it didn't have the *Billboard* numbers, "La Grange" has permeated pop culture, being heard in commercials and feature films, most notably the 1998 blockbuster *Armageddon*. It has been included on nearly every ranked list of top rock songs of all time and is seemingly in the repertoire of every bar band across the globe.

In the blues tradition, the basic track of "La Grange" borrows liberally from John Lee Hooker's "Boogie Chillen'" (which later became the subject of a lawsuit) and Canned Heat's eleven-minute opus "Fried Hockey Boogie" from 1968's *Boogie with Canned Heat* (the "haw, haw, haw, haw" vocal line is a nod to another Hooker song, "Boom Boom"). The few lyrics in the song, which are sung by Gibbons in an affected tone that makes many of them difficult to decipher, refer to a notorious century-old brothel, the Chicken Ranch, outside the city of La Grange, Texas, that was famed throughout the state and even allegedly supplied prostitutes to Texas-born president Lyndon B. Johnson. Coincidentally, the Chicken Ranch was in the news at the time the album was released after Houston's ABC affiliate, KTRK-TV, ran an exposé on it in July 1973. The unwanted publicity forced the Chicken Ranch to close later that summer. Because of the timing, many—including occasionally ZZ Top members themselves—have attributed the closure of the Chicken Ranch to "La Grange" increasing the profile of the illegal institution. In reality, the exposé originated at the end of 1972 when the Texas Department of Public Safety began surveilling the Chicken Ranch, and law enforcement tipped off Marvin Zindler, the KTRK-TV reporter who broadcast the story, about the investigation. ZZ Top's "La Grange" obviously brought more attention to the Chicken Ranch in its final weeks of operation, but it certainly didn't precipitate the closure.

Nonetheless, "La Grange" helped popularize the Chicken Ranch so much that potential customers were still showing up to the site years after it had closed. The story of the Chicken Ranch was later dramatized in the 1978 musical *The Best Little Whorehouse in Texas*, which had a Tony Award–winning run on Broadway and inspired a 1982 feature film adaptation starring Dolly Parton and Burt Reynolds.

The final track was shaped during mixing, which included removing some of Gibbons's vocals. Manning recalls,

> *Billy had done some ad-libs and things as an overdub, and when we came in to mix it, we were trying to choose which of the ad-libs to put in, the "haw haw haw haw" and "They got a lot of nice girls." I remember that there were several other ad-libs that we put in that, for whatever reason, Billy wanted to be taken out. One was "Going halfway around the world and back again." I'll never forget that. But it was so exciting because the guitar-work is so fantastic and his singing—well, what singing there is on that song because it is almost an instrumental—was so different from anything else you'd hear on the radio at the time.*

Almost a year after the release of the single, *Broadcasting* magazine likened the enthusiasm for "La Grange" to a breakthrough for the group, noting that the single was receiving heavy airplay in Houston and Seattle, though it also received significant airplay in Atlanta (where it was a top request on WQXI), Hartford, Charlotte, Los Angeles, and other major markets. It almost seemed like it was ZZ Top's appointed time to finally release a popular song. "They had been steadily building up a following with nonstop touring, so they were due to be rewarded with a hit on some scale," explains Matthew Wilkening, founding editor in chief of *Ultimate Classic Rock*. "Another *Tres Hombres* song could have been a smaller breakthrough, 'Jesus Just Left Chicago,' for example. But they were lucky or smart enough to have the perfect career-defining song ready at exactly the right time."

Of course, *Tres Hombres* offers so much more than just its three most familiar songs. Other standout songs include the chugging, straightforward bar rock of "Beer Drinkers and Hell Raisers," the funky groove of "Shiek," and one of ZZ Top's most narrative-driven songs, "Master of Sparks," purportedly based on a true story about Gibbons and his friends welding together a circular steel cage with a seat and seat belt inside, finding a volunteer to crawl inside, placing it on a pickup truck bed, and rolling the ball cage off the bed as the truck sped on a moonlit highway outside Houston. The ensuing sparks from the daredevil experiment, with the cage crashing and burning rather than rolling, inspired the title "Master of Sparks." *Tres Hombres* might be ZZ Top's most narrative-driven record, with stories touching upon the supernatural ("Precious and Grace") and the sacred ("Hot, Blue and Righteous") depicted across the Texas landscape. In addition, even more so than the first two albums, Gibbons lets his personality shine with his varying vocal tone on songs like "Master of Sparks" and "La Grange."

In keeping with the Tex-Mex theme of the album's lyrics, the gatefold photo inside the album features a bountiful, colorful feast of food from Leo's Mexican Restaurant in Houston, which continued to tantalize taste buds for nearly thirty more years (unfortunately, Leo's, which would eventually feature ZZ Top memorabilia on its walls, closed in 2001). The album's back cover features the tagline "In the Fine Texas Tradition . . ." to indicate that ZZ Top was now fully embracing its home-state roots.

And yet, despite all its power, *Tres Hombres* is a leaner, meaner record than its predecessor—clocking nearly ten minutes shorter than *Rio Grande Mud* despite again featuring ten songs. "That whole album really got into my soul as we mixed it," says Manning. "I can just picture myself back at the console and hearing them, especially the guitar solos. It's just amazing how good [Gibbons] was at all that." Following the success of *Tres Hombres*, the production team of Bill Ham as the credited producer, Terry Manning as an engineer, and Billy Gibbons working uncredited on the production side as well would help drive the success of the band for almost the next two decades. "Bill Ham called Billy, him, and me at the console the 'triumvirate' at one point," remembers Manning.

While *Tres Hombres* has since stood the test of time, many critics were not won over by the album or ZZ Top. Later that year, the *Tres Hombres* review in *New Musical Express* called ZZ Top's latest album derivative of the Doors' *L.A. Woman* album and the Rolling Stones, noting them as obvious influences on the material (specifically citing "Shake Your Hips" from the Stones' 1972 album *Exile on Main St.* as yet another forerunner for "La Grange"). Nonetheless, the review concluded that while the songs might riff on material by more famous bands, the album was well produced and featured strong guitar and vocal work by Gibbons.

In addition, though *Tres Hombres* was by far the band's biggest album, it would not hit its sales peak (number eight on the *Billboard* 200) until August 1974, over a year after its release. This was an obvious sign that ZZ Top was building an audience and growing in popularity. In the meantime, ZZ Top again returned to the road, this time adding new markets to perform in. The expansion was not always a rousing success. On July 16, 1973, ZZ Top was penciled in to play their first concert in Manhattan as part of the annual Schaefer Music Festival at Wollman Rink in Central Park to support hard rock band Blue Öyster Cult, but plans changed, and ZZ Top was instead on the West Coast on that date. This included performing as support for the Doobie Brothers and guitarist Mike Bloomfield at a concert at Los Angeles's Palladium on July 10, with *Los Angeles Times* reviewer Richard Cromelin dismissing the group's performance as "Texas rock 'n' raunch."[1]

The change of plans may have been a precautionary move after a concert that ZZ Top was supposed to perform with hard rock pioneers Deep Purple a month earlier at Cornell University in Ithaca, New York (about two hundred miles north of Manhattan) ended chaotically when ZZ Top halted their performance after two songs because of stormy weather and Deep Purple never took the stage. Unfortunately, the crowd became rowdy when no announcement was made as to why the concert was ending early or if it would be rescheduled. Both Deep Purple and ZZ Top had trekked from a performance at the Cobo Arena in Detroit the previous night—a distance of four hundred miles by way of Canada (the tour canceled a concert in Cincinnati to make the potentially much more lucrative date at Cornell work)—and were forced to postpone a concert scheduled for two days later at the Omni in Atlanta because of water damage to their equipment. ZZ Top had already stepped up to a bigger role on the tour when the previous main support act, the Billy Preston Family, broke up following the tour's June 8 stop in Evansville, Indiana. The tour reconvened for a concert in Jacksonville, Florida (over one thousand miles away from Ithaca), just three days after the Cornell debacle, so sticking around to see how the weather turned out in upstate New York was not a realistic option for either group. ZZ Top continued with the Deep Purple dates at Tampa Stadium (June 16), Palm Beach International Raceway (June 17), and the rescheduled Omni concert (June 18). At the time, Deep Purple was arguably at the height of their popularity in the United States, so being on a bill with them on a tour of large venues was a boon for the Texas trio.

ZZ Top faced another bad omen in the New York City market that summer. A scheduled concert on August 17 at the Singer Bowl in Queens, supporting progressive hard rock band Uriah Heep and Irish guitarist Rory Gallagher, was canceled because of low ticket sales and crowd-control concerns after a July 12 concert headlined by the Edgar Winer Group at the same venue attracted low sales, gatecrashers, and vandalism. However, ZZ Top played support for Uriah Heep for numerous other dates that went forward that summer in the Northeast. Several other concerts on that tour had crowd incidents, including the August 27 concert at the Allentown Fairgrounds in Allentown, Pennsylvania, after a few thousand gatecrashers caused a near-riot at the venue, making front-page news in the local papers.

Yet some critical reviewers were beginning to take the group seriously. Steve Simels from *Stereo Review* saw the band at a hometown show in Houston, calling them "a local phenomenon on the verge of becoming a national one" and saying, "[ZZ Top] won me over, not by any particular qualities of originality, but by the sincerity and unpretentiousness of what they did."[2]

While ZZ Top was grinding it out gig by gig on the road, London Recordings was claiming to be doing its damnedest to build sales. "We're merchandising wherever ZZ plays," Bob Small, who worked in advertising at London, told *Radio & Records* during the Tres Hombres Tour. "We're hitting radio in all markets, progressive particularly, even in areas where they haven't yet appeared, in the hopes of building up at least some familiarity on the audience's part for when the band does appear. Once they come into town, we coordinate the radio spots and retail displays in an all-out promotional effort." However, it would soon become clear to Ham that London was unable to keep up with local demand for product during ZZ Top tours.[3]

By that time Ham was firmly tying the group to its Texas roots and persona without any hesitation. "ZZ Top's music comes from the seedy, raw underbelly of Texas," read Ham's statement as part of the band's marketing materials. "It's driving down dust roads 100 mph, beer in hand, looking for the ever-elusive, good-time type of music. ZZ Top draws on a rich tradition of Texas music, stamps it with our own identity, and pounds out the most progressive blues-rock around." Naturally, the band's concerts in Texas were among their biggest sellouts, with *Variety* noting that ZZ Top's September 22, 1973, concert at the Tarrant County Convention Center in Fort Worth was sold out, grossing $76,541.[4]

Though ZZ Top opened for many bands in the six months after the release of *Tres Hombres*, the headliner who had the biggest influence on the group was the shock rock band Alice Cooper. In December 1973, ZZ Top opened a string of concerts for Alice Cooper, concluding with a New Year's Eve show in Buffalo, New York. In that period, Alice Cooper was still a five-piece rock band whose lead singer (born Vince Furnier) adopted the band's name as his own stage name (in 1975, front man Cooper would split from the band and take the name with him). At the time, Alice Cooper was riding on the big success of the group's number one album *Billion Dollar Babies*, released earlier that year, and its Top 40 singles "Elected," "Hello Hooray," and "No More Mr. Nice Guy" (however, the tour with ZZ Top immediately followed the less successful release of the band's subsequent album, *Muscle of Love*). By that time, Alice Cooper had also become infamous for their wildly entertaining show involving stage effects, including a simulated decapitation, designed by famed magician James Randi. The gimmicks, as well as Cooper's blood-stained stage costumes, drew controversy and complaints as well as sold-out performances. Though the teaming of the premiere purveyors of shock hard rock with a Texas boogie trio might seem incongruous on paper, just over two years later, ZZ Top would note that despite Cooper's outrageous on-stage antics, Billy Gibbons, Dusty Hill, and Frank Beard felt that in the markets they toured together, including the Northeast, the Midwest, and dates in Toronto and Quebec, northern audiences perceived *them* as the freaks. "He had such a weird act to begin with, and the combination with our thing it really clicked," Gibbons told *Creem* in 1976. "The music—he got down with some pretty hard and heavy stuff sometimes, and we were just out there pickin'. They really couldn't figure it out. They'd think, 'What are these guys doin' with this other guy?' But it was really a magical combination. 'Cause here we were singing 'bout the idea of Texas and . . . well, it was just as weird as what he was doin' to a lot of the people up East" (Beard then interjected in the interview, "It was weirder probably").[5]

But the experience on tour with Alice Cooper helped bring home to ZZ Top that while they were less visually shocking, they were also selling an image perceived as foreign to most audiences, and it was more in tune with the mythic Wild West of outlaws, whisky, and whores than the reality of 1970s Texas. Not that those things did not exist in contemporary Texas, of course, but ZZ Top's music amplified the caricature of Texas that existed outside—and, in some cases, inside—the state. Based on their experience touring with Alice Cooper, ZZ Top felt it was about time for the band's image to catch up to the music. Gibbons would later credit the tour with Alice Cooper as the inspiration for ZZ Top to try a similar show business presentation in their live shows, though with ZZ Top's own spin on the concept. While the blues had gotten a reputation for being serious business in the wake of the English revival, rock and roll had seemingly robbed it of its flair for showmanship pioneered by Howlin' Wolf and others, and one thing they could certainly draw from their Texas roots was showmanship.

At that time, ZZ Top was typically lumped together in the press with the emerging southern rock scene and bands like the Allman Brothers Band, with whom ZZ Top toured in 1971, and the Marshall Tucker Band, with whom ZZ Top played a few dates during breaks in the schedule of the Alice Cooper tour. But Texas and its vast landscape were perceived by people as quite different from the rest of the South, with most of the southern rock bands hailing from eastern states. Texas, as well as ZZ Top's version of Texas that it was bringing to the world, had its own identity and rhythm, its own rich musical heritage, and, perhaps most importantly, its own visual trade-marks. While the Nudie suits—brightly colored, rhinestone-covered West-ern suits designed by noted tailor Nudie Cohn of Nudie's of Hollywood that reportedly cost the band $1,300 apiece—worn by the band around this time may have been unusual for a rock band of the 1970s, the look was not unique in the music business and perhaps confused people who thought ZZ Top was a country music trio. To continue growing beyond the southern rock label, ZZ Top would need to be about more than just Western wear and songs about Texas.

6
THE WORLD'S LARGEST BARN DANCE

It became apparent as the months went on that ZZ Top was still having trouble breaking into new markets. On the 1974 tour ZZ Top made their debut at Madison Square Garden, opening for Ten Years After on May 13, though it would be almost a decade before the band would perform at the venue again. The concert drew 15,620, a few thousand less than a full house. Just two months later, ZZ Top returned to New York City to play the Schaefer Music Festival at the Wollman Skating Rink Theater in Central Park, this time headlining over Brownsville Station. However, *Variety* noted that ZZ Top drew poorly (reporting that the concert grossed just $7,750 of its $15,500 potential, one the lowest-drawing concerts of the season at Wollman Rink) and that the fans who did attend were hostile to Brownsville Station (however, the review gave both bands positive notices).

Of course, the 1974 legs of the Tres Hombres Tour were not without incident. A concert scheduled for June 4, 1974, at the Iowa State Fairgrounds ended in a rain-soaked riot that caused $4,000 in damage when the concert was postponed because of the inclement weather. ZZ Top ended up performing on June 7 but received a horrible concert review in the *Des Moines Register* the following day, with the unsigned review stating, "There was a story once about a fella who killed himself by drilling holes in his skull with an electric drill. He probably would have enjoyed the ZZ Top concert Friday at the Iowa State Fairgrounds in Des Moines," also calling the group "about as enjoyable as a visit to the dentist."[1]

With the constant touring by ZZ Top, the occasional bad reviews did not stem from a lack of effort. The following week, Billy Gibbons injured his finger before a concert in Denver but still took the stage, and during a concert that ZZ Top headlined at Memorial Stadium in Charlotte on July 13, a police officer was shot in the parking lot (ZZ Top donated $1,000 for the officer's medical bills). The relentless touring schedule helped spread the news about ZZ Top to rock fans, but to reach a new level of popularity, the band needed to do something bigger to attract national attention. Ham had an idea to create one of the biggest concerts in the history of Texas. To celebrate the success of *Tres Hombres* and to demonstrate the band's growing popularity to the media, ZZ Top announced that it would hold a party in grand fashion by hosting "ZZ Top and Friends' First Annual Texas Size Rompin' Stompin' Barn Dance and Bar-B-Q" on September 1 at the University of Texas, Austin's Memorial Stadium. The billing for the Labor Day weekend event also boasted Bad Company, Joe Cocker, and Santana in what is thought to have been the largest one-day music festival in Texas history up to that point. While ZZ Top had played stadium shows and festivals before, this was the first one they had organized themselves and served as something of a victory party on their home turf. Initial plans to surround the stadium date with several other gigs in Texas were put on hold to focus on the Barn Dance and Bar-B-Q so it could be promoted in ads as the band's only Texas appearance in 1974 (though ZZ Top had played a concert across the state in El Paso on May 31 earlier in the year).

One of the more incredible feats of the Barn Dance and Bar-B-Q was that Bill Ham was able to get several of the country's biggest rival music promoters, including famous West Coast promoter Bill Graham, to assist in the production and promotion of the concert festival. Some proceeds were earmarked for the university's student government, which also helped organize the concert.

To fully embrace the gimmick of the festival's name, barbecue was sold at the concert for $2.50 a plate. Unfortunately, the Texas Attorney General's

Office's Consumer Protection Division later got involved when audience members filed complaints that the advertising did not make clear that the barbecue was not included in the price of admission. It was also originally planned that the concert would feature an actual barn with livestock, and while that detail didn't make it to the festival, the concept would figure into the band's Worldwide Texas Tour, which would launch twenty months later.

In the lead-up to the Barn Dance and Bar-B-Q, ZZ Top crisscrossed the country to play concerts in Las Vegas (August 18); Bakersfield (August 23) and Long Beach (August 24), California; and Atlanta (August 30). The Long Beach concert got a strong write-up in the *Los Angeles Times*. "ZZ Top seems to have snuck in through the back door when no one was looking," wrote reviewer Richard Cromelin. "Without a superstar buildup, its picture gracing the cover of few if any magazines, the three-piece outfit (which sold out the huge Long Beach Arena on Saturday) shows signs of becoming the most successful 'people's band' since Grand Funk." The Atlanta concert at the Omni Coliseum was also reported by *Variety* to be a sellout. Going into the Barn Dance and Bar-B-Q, momentum was on ZZ Top's side.[2]

In terms of attendance, the Barn Dance and Bar-B-Q could not have gone better. ZZ Top played to a capacity stadium crowd of seventy-five thousand, who braved ninety-degree heat, with temperatures on the field hitting triple digits. Led Zeppelin guitarist Jimmy Page joined Bad Company for their encore as a surprise guest. ZZ Top didn't hit the stage until around 9:30 p.m., more than ten hours after the concert began. While reviews were generally good, attendees criticized the festival for not having adequate concessions, security, and facilities for such a large crowd (Ham would later place the blame for those failures squarely on the university's student government). The total gross was $630,000, with over $21,000 given to the student government. However, several fans suffered sunstroke, and nearly three hundred attendees were arrested by local police, including for vandalism. Parts of the stadium were damaged, including two entry gates and plumbing, and holes were burned into the stadium's brand-new Astroturf field when attendees set off flares, infuriating the football team's legendary coach Darrell K. Royal, a College Football Hall of Fame inductee whom the stadium would be named after in 1996. Repairs had to be completed in just twenty days before the Longhorns had their first home game of the 1974 season. Though there were initial plans for a second and third annual Barn Dance and Bar-B-Q, the event remained a one-off, and it would be more than twenty years before another concert (the Eagles in 1995) was allowed at Memorial Stadium. It would also be eight years before ZZ Top played a concert in Austin again, this time at the university's Frank C. Erwin Jr. Center on the El Loco-Motion Tour. The concert was reportedly filmed by ZZ Top after Ham turned down offers to broadcast it on ABC's *In Concert* and NBC's *Midnight Special*, but footage from the festival has never materialized aside from a few seconds of amateur footage of the massive crowd preserved by the Texas Archive of the Moving Image.

The publicity from the concert, including negative stories about the vandalism, made headlines in football-loving Texas, and the damage to the field likely didn't win the band any fans with older Texans, but for the purposes of getting their name out there, it was certainly not bad press. By the end of October, ZZ Top returned to touring the Northeast, followed by a tour in the Midwest through the end of the year. After a short break for the holidays, the group was back on the road early in the new year. ZZ Top would play nearly one hundred concerts in 1975, one of the band's busiest years on the road to date. In the months after the Barn Dance and Bar-B-Q's success, ZZ Top continued to pull high grosses on tour. Their March 31, 1975, concert at the Civic Auditorium in Grand Rapids, Michigan, drew a $19,600 house, and an April 26 date at the Metropolitan Sports Center in Bloomington, Minnesota, sold out at $41,088.

Between concerts, ZZ Top worked on the band's fourth album, *Fandango!*, which featured an unusual concept: side A was a live recording from ZZ Top concerts at the Warehouse in New Orleans, while side B contained new studio recordings of six songs, mostly quick numbers of less than three minutes each. As with *Tres Hombres*, the studio recordings were tracked at Robin Hood Studios and mixed and mastered at Ardent Studios, with Terry Manning mixing both the live and studio sides of the album. The live side featured three tracks—"Thunderbird," "Jailhouse Rock," and the group's "Backdoor Medley," featuring "Backdoor Love Affair" from the group's first album, Willie Dixon's "Mellow Down Easy," and John Lee Hooker's "Long Distance Boogie." The album also included an aerial photo of Memorial Stadium filled to capacity for the Barn Dance and Bar-B-Q (captioned "With 80,000 friends") to demonstrate the band's drawing ability.

The half-live, half-studio concept behind the record was the brainchild of Ham, who believed the band's arduous road schedule following the release of *Tres Hombres* wouldn't leave them enough time to record a proper studio album. "That was Bill Ham's idea to do something radically different," recalls Manning. "Nobody had ever done a half-and-half album that I know of. I thought it was a little odd when he mentioned it, but it really does work because they're great in the studio. But by the time we were doing that album, we were doing more overdubs and technical things. So, Bill wanted to give the pure live experience but not have a live album come out, which at the time, unless you were Peter Frampton, was almost a waste." While Manning credits Ham with the concept for the album, Gibbons was undoubtedly familiar with the 1965 album *Having a Rave Up with the Yardbirds*, the group's second American album. The first side of the album features studio recordings featuring Jeff Beck, including some of the band's most familiar songs, like "Heart Full of Soul" and "The Train Kept A-Rollin'," while the second side includes live recordings featuring Eric Clapton. Two of Clapton's later albums with Cream, 1968's *Wheels of Fire* and 1969's *Goodbye*, also were similarly split between studio and live recordings, so the concept wasn't completely novel.

Engineer Terry Koehn, who later became the audio engineer for the Louisiana Superdome, recorded the band on a sixteen-track, two-inch tape machine for the live side at the Warehouse in New Orleans. It was most likely recorded during one or both of ZZ Top's concerts at the Warehouse on April 12 and 13, 1974. In *Billy F Gibbons: Rock + Roll Gearhead*, Gibbons claims that the live side was recorded at the Warehouse on June 5, 1971, during a concert that ZZ Top opened for the Allman Brothers Band and Quicksilver Messenger Service. However, that date is too early for the recording, and it is unlikely that the band would be releasing a live performance that, at the time of the release of *Fandango!*, was nearly four years old. Gibbons's book also says that the June 5, 1971, Warehouse concert took place in the aftermath of a hurricane, but there is no record of a hurricane taking place around the date of that particular concert. Gibbons was likely conflating ZZ Top's Warehouse concert with the Allman Brothers with another concert that ZZ Top played at the Warehouse later that year on September 18, 1971, during which the band opened for bluesman Taj Mahal. Hurricane Edith made landfall in Louisiana on September 16 of that year and moved east across the South over the next several days.

After its April 1975 release, *Fandango!* reached number ten on the *Billboard* album chart (just two spots shy of the peak set by *Tres Hombres*), becoming the group's second consecutive Top 10 album; it was certified gold just two months after its release. More importantly, the album's lead single, a short Dusty Hill–sung rocker titled "Tush," would be ZZ Top's first Top 40 hit, peaking at number twenty on the *Billboard* Hot 100. The song had been written in mid-1974 during a soundtrack and added to the band's live repertoire shortly afterward, so it had been well seasoned by the time the group recorded it for the album. Most of the other songs on the studio side of *Fandango!*—"Nasty Dogs and Funky Kings," "Blue Jean Blues," "Balinese," "Mexican Blackbird," and "Heard It on the X," a tribute to border-blasting radio stations—quickly became concert favorites by the time the album was released. Several of the songs remained regulars in ZZ Top's set lists for decades, particularly "Tush" and "Heard It on the X." The new tunes helped make *Fandango!* a long-term success for ZZ Top. According to the band's publicity materials, the album was still selling fifty thousand copies a week six months after its release. The album also became ZZ Top's first international number one album after it topped Canada's *RPM* Top Album Chart for two weeks on September 20 and September 27, 1975 (the band would score another number one on that chart ten years later with *Afterburner*). *Fandango!* became a certified gold record in both the United States and Canada before the end of 1975 (it eventually went platinum in Canada).

The studio side of the album demonstrated Gibbons's vocal ability to shift into new characters on "Mexican Blackbird," where he adopts a heavy hillbilly Texas drawl in a humorous character-building song. Despite his being a native Texan, Gibbons's upbringing demonstrates he was far from a hillbilly, and audiences outside the Lone Star State probably couldn't otherwise distinguish between a Texan from the affluent Tanglewood neighborhood of Houston and a cattle rancher from West Texas.

In addition, the studio side of *Fandango!* marked the first time in which all songs were credited to Gibbons, Dusty Hill, and Frank Beard, a three-way credit that would appear on every ZZ Top song for the next fifteen years. While songs weren't always penned in a group setting (especially as Gibbons was the band's main songwriter), the credit was a business arrangement that would help keep the band on equal footing behind the scenes and, arguably, one of the major reasons why ZZ Top did not encounter the personnel issues faced by nearly every successful rock band.

Likely helping that prolonged success were the strong reviews for *Fandango!*, even in the international press. The review in the UK magazine *Sounds* claimed that ZZ Top would "tear this country apart" when they crossed the Atlantic for their first UK tour, praising the album as "potent as moonshine whisky and as wild as a rampant coyote on heat with a boil on its bum" and "the toughest Southern music that you're ever gonna hear."[3]

By the release of *Fandango!*, the band's growing popularity was hard for even their harshest credits to ignore. ZZ Top would return to Madison Square Garden—at least the downstairs room—when they performed at the Felt Forum on May 23, 1975 (the Felt Forum, now known as the Theater at Madison Square Garden, is a smaller venue located beneath the Garden). At that time, London Recordings was supporting *Fandango!* with promotional posters in New York City's subway system and late-night television spots in several top markets. The venerable *New York Times* gave ZZ Top a few column inches after their concert at the Felt Forum, a review that halfheartedly praised the group's performance but dinged ZZ Top by noting that the venue was only half filled. (*Variety* reported that the concert grossed $16,500 of its $33,000 potential. Ham later claimed that the concert had low attendance because it was Memorial Day weekend, rightfully noting that many New Yorkers typically flee the city for the holiday weekend.) The band received a much harsher review for the concert in *Billboard*, claiming that ZZ Top had "a minimum of performing ability" and that its music consisted of "two-dimensional exercises" with "an inability to define endings for the songs," noting that it was no surprise that 40 percent of the venue's capacity stayed home.[4]

As such, ZZ Top still had trouble filling venues in the Northeast despite their huge regional success in other parts of the country. The UK magazine *Melody Maker* noted this disparity in its write-up of the Felt Forum concert: "South of the Mason-Dixon line ZZ Top are among the biggest rock attractions on the road, drawing enormous crowds to their hellzapoppin rock shows. Up East they're relatively unknown—a classic case of territorial ups and downs, and one which seems to have bugged ZZ since their career began in 1970." As evidence, ZZ Top's 1975 summer dates throughout the country were far more successful, including two headlining festival performances, the Summer Festival of Rock at Diablo Stadium in Tempe, Arizona, on June 21 and the Florida Jam at the Tampa Fairgrounds in Tampa, Florida, on July 5, the latter drawing over thirty thousand. It appeared to be a purely Northeast bias—a mid-June swing through the West Coast, including concerts in Seattle (June 14) and at the Los Angeles Forum (June 19), were nearly sellouts. However, the Los Angeles gig caused the band a prolonged legal headache because they had canceled a performance at the Sahara in Las Vegas two nights earlier, citing an injury that Hill suffered after falling off the stage during the show in Seattle for the need to postpone (the night before the Seattle concert, the band also played a rowdy gig at the Tri-City Raceway in Richland, Washington, that led to the city considering banning rock concerts). However, the group played another concert the night after the Seattle show in Spokane. Whether Hill legitimately sustained an injury or the band simply needed a night off during a lengthy West Coast tour, the promoter of the Vegas show, Gary Naseef, sued the band in March 1976 for $7 million, alleging that ZZ Top had failed to offer a rescheduled date, and he was unable to provide refunds. The legal issue dragged on for years and may have been the reason why ZZ Top did not go back to Las Vegas for over a year, finally returning on September 22, 1976, for a concert at the Las Vegas Convention Center during the Worldwide Texas Tour, though it would be almost another four years after that before ZZ Top would perform in Las Vegas again.[5]

And yet, it appeared that while riding the success of *Fandango!* and "Tush," the Northeast bias soon dissipated. ZZ Top's August 9 concert at the Convention Hall in Asbury Park, New Jersey, a beach town with a rich musical history located less than sixty miles south of the Felt Forum, was a sellout.

ZZ Top continued playing concerts in the fall, including sellouts and record-breaking concerts in Atlanta (September 13) and Nashville (September 20), followed by a successful return to the Northeast, including shows in Syracuse, New York (September 25); Bangor, Maine (September 26); and Albany (September 27), as well as sellouts in Waterbury, Connecticut (September 29), and Boston (October 3). The band's late-1975 concerts were putting up almost unbelievable numbers. The September 13 concert at the Omni in Atlanta broke the venue's concert-attendance record set by the Rolling Stones earlier that year, and the September 20 concert at Nashville's Fairgrounds Speedway broke Elvis Presley's attendance record for any concert crowd in Nashville. The group also broke various concert-attendance records in Kansas City, New Orleans, Oklahoma City, and Tulsa, in addition to racking up at least twenty sold-out performances. But perhaps sweetest of all, the band returned to the Felt Forum in New York for a November 22 concert. Just six months after receiving poor reviews for playing in a half-filled theater, the band sold out the venue (followed by a glowing review in *Variety*), and while in town, they received their gold records from the Recording Industry Association of America for *Tres Hombres* and *Fandango!* There was no longer any doubt that ZZ Top had arrived.

The group once again returned to Texas to close out the year and celebrate their success, playing six concerts in five days across the state, including a Thanksgiving double-header at The Summit in Houston, a brand-new arena built to serve as the new home of the Houston Rockets, a National Basketball Association team that had moved to Houston in 1971 but did not have a home arena. ZZ Top was just the second artist to perform at the arena after the Who had held a concert there the week before. Harkening back to the previous year's Barn Dance and Bar-B-Q, Ham said in his statement to the press, "Last year, Texas came to ZZ Top. This year, ZZ Top is going out to play for the friends and neighbors who made them what they are today, and what better time to do it than a Thanksgiving weekend." Tickets for all shows sold out in hours, grossing at least $500,000, including all thirty-six thousand tickets to the two shows at the brand-new Summit (the band grossed at least $10 million on the road in 1975 alone).[6]

The year-ending Texas concerts also previewed the band's next major concert publicity stunt. By the 1975 Texas shows, ZZ Top had begun experimenting with stage ornamentation featuring cacti, tumbleweeds, cattle skulls, and even a pair of live vultures, which previewed the stage design of their much more elaborate Worldwide Texas Tour the following year. The tour would become part of rock-and-roll legend as one of the most ambitious extravaganzas in the history of live rock concerts.

7
TAKING TEXAS TO THE PEOPLE

ZZ Top opened 1976 with a dozen arena dates, including the group's first proper tour of Canada, but this was simply a warm-up for what was to come later in the year. Notices began appearing in the press in mid-May 1976 that ZZ Top was planning something big—literally. The band announced that they would be launching a tour with the largest stage ever constructed for a rock tour (sixty-three feet by forty-eight feet), weighing thirty-five tons, and designed in the shape of Texas. The stage was pitched at an angle of four degrees so it would give audiences a full view of the Lone Star stage for what the band called the Worldwide Texas Tour (subtitled "Taking Texas to the People"). Pretour press revealed that the stage took a crew of forty people seven hours to construct per show and featured as ornamentation both flora and fauna hailing from Texas, including a longhorn steer, a black buffalo, two vultures, two rattlesnakes, and tarantulas (though the tarantulas were soon were sent back to Texas early in the tour because their diet of live crickets was too challenging to coordinate day to day). The band spent $140,000 to hire an animal wrangler for the tour and spent about $4,000 a week to care for the animals.

The caravan for the rock-era version of Buffalo Bill Cody's Wild West Show included over a half dozen forty-foot semitrailers painted with murals by Bill Narum depicting the varied landscapes of Texas. Despite the tour's name and pretour announcements that the "worldwide" tour would visit Europe, Japan, Australia, and Mexico, the massive undertaking never left the United States, likely because of the immense costs of bringing even a slimmed-down version of the presentation overseas.

To promote this wild excursion, Bill Ham's publicity machine went into overdrive by sharing the raw numbers of the trek with anyone who would listen—and even the same listeners multiple times. "One thing you become resigned to when you commit yourself to doing a story on ZZ Top is that you will receive press releases five times a week thereafter running over these same facts and anecdotes and phone calls approximately twice a week with the same information," rock critic Robert Duncan wrote in *Creem*.[1]

For a band whose Nudie suits were their flashiest stage effect up until then, one might wonder why ZZ Top would go to such expense, particularly for the livestock, which only appeared on stage for less than a minute before the band's scheduled encore. The fact was that ZZ Top was not immune to trends as a touring attraction. Groups like Alice Cooper (whose lead singer, also named Alice Cooper, had recently gone solo) and KISS, both of whom ZZ Top had toured with, had been grabbing headlines and attention for their effects-filled stage shows. Even the Rolling Stones embraced showmanship more than previously for their 1975 Tour of the Americas, featuring stage props like a giant inflatable penis. With groups as wide-ranging as Pink Floyd and Blue Öyster Cult employing light shows and other visual effects in their concert productions, ZZ Top figured they would need to tap into the special effects trend to appeal to their growing arena audiences. However, they were determined to do it in their own Texas fashion. From a headline perspective, the ploy worked. Many national outlets felt compelled to report on a tour that was bringing the Lone Star State experience (or at least a prefabricated version of it) across the country, and the sheer pageantry of the tour attracted a June 20 profile in the *New York Times* looking at the growth of southern rock, even if ZZ Top did not quite fit the definition of the genre.

Quite the contrary, ZZ Top's increasing notoriety in providing stage flash along with their pounding rhythms was in some ways the antithesis of the southern rock aesthetic, in which most bands spent little more time thinking

about the on-stage presentation beyond selecting what T-shirt to wear that
night and how high to hang the Confederate flag behind the drum riser. The
carefully orchestrated color schemes and mythic depiction of Texas was something a group like Black Oak Arkansas or the Marshall Tucker Band or their
management would have little interest in. In that sense, the spectacle truly set
ZZ Top apart. The Worldwide Texas Tour was as much of a traveling circus
as an Alice Cooper or KISS tour but was rooted in a presentation that would
be more palatable to wider audiences than shock rock by building on decades
of Western mythology—more Gene Autry than Vincent Price, more *Eyes of
Texas* than *Texas Chain Saw Massacre*.

The band and crew spent a week at the Astroarena in Houston rehearsing
the show and its various stage effects (including getting the animals accustomed to the loud music and arena atmosphere). The tour kicked off at Grove
Stadium at Wake Forest University in Winston-Salem, North Carolina, on
May 29, following several days of storms and tornado warnings. Joining ZZ
Top at the first show were Lynyrd Skynyrd and Point Blank, the latter another
band managed by Bill Ham that occasionally opened for ZZ Top from 1975
to 1982. The wet conditions prevented the animals from making their stage
debut, and only about twelve thousand fans were in attendance, less than
half of the stadium's capacity. But the trial-by-fire nature of that first concert
proved that the outlandish concept was workable, and what followed was
an eighteen-month mission of bringing Texas to arenas and stadiums across
the country. Opening acts on the first leg of the tour rotated on and off
depending on the market and varied across the rock spectrum; they included
Aerosmith, Blue Öyster Cult, the Marshall Tucker Band, Elvin Bishop, Ted
Nugent, Bob Seger, the J. Geils Band, and REO Speedwagon, among others.

Of course, with so many moving parts the tour was not without its issues.
The seventh show took place on June 12 at Pittsburgh's Three Rivers Stadium, home of the National Football League's Pittsburgh Steelers and Major

League Baseball's Pittsburgh Pirates. The concert occurred several weeks into the beginning of baseball season while the Pirates were on the road from June 11 to 18, and under normal circumstances that would have been adequate time to load the show in and out. A retrospective article written in 2009 in the *Pittsburgh Post-Gazette* recalled it as the "hands-down winner for the city's craziest show ever." There were over two hundred reported injuries (though that number was later halved by authorities because many were very minor), and two women were found dead after the concert (one had drowned in one of the rivers in the vicinity; another was killed in a hit-and-run far from the venue). Even the bison got loose at one point, though it was safely wrangled. The Pirates' physician at the time, Dr. Joseph Finegold, called the worst injuries at the concert "the most horrible thing I have ever seen since World War II," and the raucous event led to lawsuits, including one by a sixteen-year-old female concertgoer who alleged severe injuries sustained after a firecracker landed on her lap. Following the concert, the city decided to bolster the police presence at subsequent rock concerts throughout the region. Despite the chaos of the Pittsburgh concert, it still drew over forty-eight thousand (many thousands more if gatecrashers are counted) and grossed more than $450,000. Thankfully, a vast majority of the concerts on the tour did not suffer from the same level of violence, though arrests were common, particularly in larger markets.[2]

The tour alternated between stadium and arena shows, and ZZ Top continued to break records along the way. The June 30 concert at the Charleston Civic Center in Charleston, West Virginia, was among the many sellouts. The July 17 concert at Tulane Stadium in New Orleans set a new rock concert attendance record for the city with over fifty thousand attendees, though aggressive policing was subsequently blamed for a dozen reported injuries. The New Orleans City Council voted to institute a rock concert ban in Tulane Stadium following complaints (however, a similar ban on rock concerts in any of the city's public parks did not pass). Humorously, San Diego issued a ban on any further rock concerts at San Diego Stadium, another professional football and baseball venue, to take effect after ZZ Top's August 9 concert because of concerns about potential unruly crowd behavior. However, the concert went on without any major incidents, and the ban was short-lived (concerts at the venue resumed the following summer).

Unsurprisingly, as the tour extravaganza rolled across America, many rock critics who were already familiar with musician gimmicks from David Bowie to Alice Cooper didn't buy ZZ Top's over-the-top Texas image. "Onstage they look like nothing but a bunch of dumb shits from Texas, three boys who just walked off the set of *Bonanza* and are heading out after the show to eat three sirloins apiece," wrote critic Jon Tiven in a mostly insulting article in the short-lived rock magazine *Blast*. "But when Big Billy Gibbons throws down his two-ton spurs and ten-gallon hat, takes off his stacked cowboy boots, and removes his padded Nudie suit, behold this rock 'n' roll shrimp. He doesn't even look big enough to hold a flute, never mind play the heaviest guitar made by Gibson, the Les Paul."[3]

For his part, Billy Gibbons was open about the band's music and image as selling a persona about Texas. "The message is expressing the sense of adventure one would experience in the Southwest," Gibbons shared in an interview with the *Albuquerque Journal* in advance of their August 4 concert at the Tingley Coliseum. "It's a sense of adventure that many people don't know about. And there isn't that much adventure left in the world anymore. This is part of ZZ Top's success—the message of adventure and what we whee [*sic*] when we were growing up in the Southwest. A lot of people are looking for the same things we were, and still are."[4]

In an interview with *Creem*, Gibbons expanded on what the band's image meant to its fans, especially those who weren't natives to the Lone Star State or anywhere south of the Mason-Dixon Line.

I was really amazed at the reception we've been getting in Boston, New York, all these cities so far culturally removed from where we came from. But I think that now when you drive from New York to LA, you can eat the same food, stay on the same road from coast to coast if you want—I think everything has become so standardized that the idea of Texas with its vast wide-open spaces, the last place you can hop in your car and drive a thousand miles an hour, drink as much beer as you can consume, and drive off the road and still keep going—I think that's got some kind of magnetic quality for people who are, say, up here where it's a little more confining. That may be the reason why they like what we're talking about.[5]

Nonetheless, despite the tremendous success of the tour, ZZ Top was still regularly being disparaged by rock critics, even in a tongue-in-cheek fashion. "ZZ Top is sort of like Communism," wrote Robert Duncan in *Creem*. "Apparently there's about eight million of their fans out there but you can't really tell who they are and it can make you feel a little weird. I mean, chances are something like one in three that your next-door neighbor is a ZZ Top fan. So how come he never mentioned it? Is he ashamed? Is he afraid? You see what I'm talking about. It sounds like the Commies." Though Duncan later admits in his article to being won over by the band after interviewing them, he remarks, "This is what I concluded in advance about ZZ Top: That they were probably the dumbest motherfuckers in existence who could only punch desultorily and inaccurately at their instruments whereupon they produced the most loathsome throbbing squat noise this side of Black Oak Arkansas and that they were probably being completely sold down the river by heartless management abetted . . . by the most hard-sell publicity robot in the biz."[6]

And how did Texans feel about the band's "Tex-ploitation" tour? The Worldwide Texas Tour first came "home" for two concerts at The Summit in Houston on November 25 and 26, 1976, and two concerts at the Tarrant

County Convention Center in Fort Worth on November 27 and 28. If sold-out concerts are any indication, Texans by and large loved it. But some members of the Texas press saw ZZ Top's image as a load of, well, manure. "Many people think of Texans as good ol' boys with burr haircuts who drill for oil, raise cattle, and talk with a twang that you could cut with a knife," wrote Jeff Davenport in the *Houston Daily Cougar*, the newspaper of the University of Houston. "The new image that ZZ Top helps to perpetuate is that of a buffoon with long hair who has his hand wrapped around a longneck. . . . But this isn't just exploitation of the Texas mystique, it is exploitation of rock music fans (the latest in a continuing series). It has become a contest to see which group can play the loudest. And the crowds just eat it up. They keep putting down good money to hear ZZ Top and their contemporaries play mindless noise."[7]

The first leg of the Worldwide Texas Tour ended on August 14 with a concert at the (appropriately named) Cow Palace outside San Francisco, a concert that involved around three hundred fans tossing bottles at police outside the arena when they were unable to get tickets to the sold-out show, though no major injuries were reported. During the one-month break (the tour would resume on September 10 in Waterloo, Iowa), the band put the finishing touches on their next album, *Tejas*. "It's still in the preparation stage—we're taking a full month off to rehearse," Gibbons said in a mid-1976 interview. "The tunes are things we've been working on individually which we've toyed with in hotel rooms and at sound checks but still have a few bugs to work out." Unlike the four previous albums, which were recorded at Robin Hood Studios, *Tejas*, named for the band's home state, was ironically entirely recorded outside Texas at Memphis's Ardent Studios, like all their ensuing albums through *Antenna*.[8]

The album's title is the Spanish pronunciation of *táysha*, a word meaning "friends" in the language of the Caddo tribe native to what would become

Texas (the word later morphed into "Texas," which was adopted as the name of the territory). The title was intended to coincide with the theme of the ongoing tour. *Tejas* is often the most forgotten of ZZ Top's 1970s albums, and yet it was the band's most musically adventurous record so far, serving as an aural passage through mythical Texas landscapes from Narum's dreamlike pastel painting of grazing longhorns and bison through its final track. Though it did not contain any hits, it features underappreciated gems like Dusty Hill's powerhouse vocal on "Ten Dollar Man" and the gorgeous instrumental "Asleep in the Desert."

ZZ Top canceled three concerts (November 14 in Augusta, Maine; November 17 in Passaic, New Jersey; and November 19 in Syracuse, New York) in advance of the new album's release, returning to the stage with back-to-back Thanksgiving concerts at The Summit in Houston on November 25 and 26. By the end of 1976, the Worldwide Texas Tour had already sold over seven hundred thousand tickets.

Released on November 29, 1976, *Tejas* failed to hit the sales level of *Fandango!*, and its three singles—"It's Only Love," "Arrested for Driving While Blind," and "Enjoy and Get It On"—did not follow in the success of "Tush" ("It's Only Love" was the highest charting of the three, peaking at number forty-four). Despite being released at a pivotal time in the group's history, *Tejas* is a largely forgotten entry in the band's catalog, though "Arrested for Driving While Blind" has made appearances in the group's set lists in later years. The reviews did not help the album sales, with *Tejas* spending twenty-four weeks on the *Billboard* 200—half as many weeks as *Fandango!* For example, the *New York Times*, which still considered ZZ Top a band popular only "in its own narrowly circumscribed geographical area" despite sold-out concerts across the nation, called *Tejas* "a determinedly boring record, with the same dogged formulas worked over and over again. Rock at its best can be basic, but this is ridiculous."[9]

Though some of the concerts struggled with attendance (the second leg opener in Waterloo, Iowa, was only about half full), others (like the one the following night in Minneapolis) were sold out. There were also still a fair number of unruly crowds. For example, concertgoers who couldn't get into the sold-out October 16 concert at the Charlotte Coliseum in Charlotte, North Carolina, caused $500 in damage to entry doors and windows when they were denied entry, and riot police were called in for crowd control (the building manager noted that it was the worst disturbance at the venue "since the old days when fans got involved with the hockey players," but dismissed it as a minor incident overall).[10]

After breaking for December and January, the Worldwide Texas Tour resumed in Madison, Wisconsin, for its third leg on February 16, 1977. Nonetheless, the group's concerts were still facing crowd trouble, with sixty-one arrests total at the March 16 and 17 concerts at the Boston Garden and nearly fifty arrests at the Lincoln, Nebraska, show at the Pershing Auditorium (the arena reportedly spent $2,700 on security, considered an industry high at the time). But there was no denying the returns: by the time the third leg ended with a concert on May 7 in Lawrence, Kansas, the tour had grossed $8.76 million, and at that point the band was still considering bringing the tour to Japan and Australia. They returned to the road on June 7 in Albuquerque for a series of West Coast dates, including visiting Honolulu in early July, which may have demonstrated to the band how challenging bringing the full-scale tour overseas would be. The proper Worldwide Texas Tour wrapped up with a show on July 10 in Rapid City, South Dakota, but the band returned to the road later in the year for a final set of five dates in Shreveport, Louisiana, and across Texas at the end of December, including a New Year's Eve show in Fort Worth and a New Year's Day show in Amarillo, both opened by blues icon Muddy Waters. These last shows of 1977 featured a scaled-back presentation—after all, following eighteen months on the road,

ZZ Top really didn't need to bring Texas back to Texas. During these dates ZZ Top debuted a cover of the Sam & Dave soul classic "I Thank You" as a duet between Gibbons and Hill, a song they would record for their next album, which was released two years later. The smaller jaunts served as a support tour for the release of *The Best of ZZ Top (10 Legendary Texas Tales)*, featuring songs from the band's first four albums, which quickly went gold (it was eventually certified double platinum in 1994). The compilation was released by London just four months after the release of *Tejas* without input from Ham or the band. *The Best of ZZ Top* did not contain any songs from *Tejas*, with London likely hoping to avoid cutting into the sales of that album by including recent singles like "It's Only Love" or "Arrested for Driving While Blind" on the compilation. Fitting in with the Worldwide Texas Tour imagery, the album cover is designed to look like a cowboy pulp magazine, with the song titles serving as the content of the issue (the subtitle *10 Legendary Texas Tales* also fits that theme). However, it was the band's first album cover not designed by Bill Narum, likely because ZZ Top and their management were not involved with the release. The unauthorized compilation was reportedly a sore point for Ham and was a contributing factor in ZZ Top's not signing a contract extension with London. Other sources say that London executives already suspected that ZZ Top would not be signing a new contract, and that led to the release of the compilation because Warner Bros., the band's subsequent label, released *The Best of ZZ Top* in most territories outside North America.

At the end of the road, the Worldwide Texas Tour sold over 1.2 million tickets and netted a reported profit of $11.5 million. Of course, the costs of the tour—particularly on the earlier legs with the full production—were enormous (the $11.5 million figure came from more than $100 million in ticket sales). While that would still be a marked success by just about any measure, and the tour's extravagance has since entered rock mythology, in reality it seemed that the band's popularity had hit its peak with the rock audience.

While rock groups like the Eagles, Queen, and even ZZ Top's former tourmates Aerosmith were racking up Top 40 singles, ZZ Top still could not get a break on the pop charts outside the brief popularity of the "Tush" single. Though many ZZ Top fans have since embraced *Tejas* for its different approach to the band's tried-and-true formula, it just wasn't the right album to capitalize on the success of the tour.

In the late 1970s, it was standard for a rock band to release a live album after a tour of such magnitude. But Ham and ZZ Top were already known for not doing anything standard; perhaps they felt that *Fandango!* already gave enough of a taste of ZZ Top's live show, and any more servings of live recordings might cut into what was really making the band money: concerts. In short, ZZ Top found themselves at a critical juncture in their career after becoming one of America's biggest concert attractions. The next question was what they should conquer next.

8
THE LONE WOLF HORNS
PLAY THE BLUES

Unsurprisingly, ZZ Top was exhausted after the Worldwide Texas Tour, even if they never had the chance to take the tour outside the United States. The band had been on the road constantly in the nearly eight years since Dusty Hill's first show with the group in February 1970, with only the occasional few weeks off between tour legs, and even those periods were full of recording and other band-related obligations. They decided that after such a massive undertaking, it was time to take a lengthy hiatus, which, according to the band, was initially only supposed to last three months. The band's absence would spark rumors, from the entire group dying in a plane crash to the members retreating to a Tibetan monastery, which ZZ Top was perfectly fine with the press fanning in their extended offseason. Virtually nothing factual about ZZ Top was reported in the press for nearly a year, though behind the scenes Bill Ham was cashing in on the band's obvious popularity.

Once again, shrewd management by Ham led ZZ Top to an extremely lucrative deal. In the summer of 1978, Ham negotiated the release of the band from London Recordings, including securing the rights to the band's master catalog. Shortly afterward, ZZ Top signed with Warner Bros. Records. Ham told the *Hollywood Reporter* that the deal represented a substantial upgrade in support for his band. "Can you imagine selling out concerts for 60,000 people and not having product in the store? We've been living under that cloud for years." For example, J. W. Williams, who worked with Ham at Lone Wolf Productions and was ZZ Top's tour manager for many years, has related that there were times when ZZ Top was playing a particular arena and no record stores in the vicinity had their albums in stock. London's unauthorized release of *The Best of ZZ Top* was also a major factor in the decision. Warner Bros. acquired the rights to the band's back catalog from Ham and by early 1979 had reissued all five previous studio albums plus *The Best of ZZ Top*, though the label would not release a new compilation of the group's previous material until the controversial 1987 box set *The Six Pack*.[1]

Various accounts, including those from the band members themselves, describe ZZ Top's post–Worldwide Texas Tour break as lasting three or four years, though that is inaccurate. The group played its final show before the hiatus on January 1, 1978, and began sessions for their next album in mid-1979, so the break lasted at most a year and a half. The band members have since given various accounts of new experiences and misadventures encountered during the hiatus—enough that it probably felt like it lasted three years. Famously, Hill spent time working as a baggage handler for a few weeks at the Dallas Fort Worth International Airport to get grounded, while Billy Gibbons appears to have spent a significant amount of time in France and England, intending to experience the latest sounds of punk and new wave (which, he later said, were far more interesting to him than the disco songs then dominating the charts in the United States), though the lengths of his stays in Europe and what he was up to tend to fluctuate depending on the telling. In an interview with the band in the July 1982 issue of rock magazine *Kerrang!*, Gibbons also said he spent some time during the hiatus hanging out in Jamaica with Bob Marley.

Most importantly, though they wouldn't come forward with this information until much later, the band and Ham felt the break was necessary for Frank Beard to get clean after he developed addictions on the road during the grueling tour. The full extent of Beard's addictions was not fully acknowledged by the band until the 2019 documentary *ZZ Top: That Little Ol' Band from Texas*, in

ZZ Top performing, ca. 1974. *London Recordings / Photofest © London Recordings*

ZZ Top performing live in the 1970s. *London Recordings / Photofest © London Recordings*

Billy Gibbons on stage at Monsters of Rock 1983 at Castle Donington, United Kingdom, on August 20, 1983. *John Atashian / Alamy Stock Photo*

Billy Gibbons posing with a Chiquita travel guitar in Dortmund, West Germany, in May 1982. *dpa picture alliance / Alamy Stock Photo*

ZZ Top enjoying leisure time in Dortmund, West Germany, in May 1982. *dpa picture alliance / Alamy Stock Photo*

ZZ Top in 1983 with the Eliminator coupe, Billy Gibbons's custom 1933 Ford. *Warner Bros. Records / Photofest © Warner Bros. Records*

ZZ Top perform on the United Kingdom's *The Tube* on November 18, 1983. *Pictorial Press Ltd / Alamy Stock Photo*

As Warner Bros. recording artists, ZZ Top increasingly embraced wearing coordinating outfits to unify the band's image. *Warner Bros. Records / Photofest © Warner Bros. Records*

ZZ Top taking a break during the filming of the "Velcro Fly" music video in 1985. From left to right: Frank Beard, Dusty Hill, Ty Reveen (designer of the Afterburner World Tour stage), unknown, and Billy Gibbons. *Courtesy Ty Reveen*

Concept art for the Afterburner World Tour stage. As it was originally designed for a pitch to the Canadian rock band Loverboy, the art features more than three musicians on the stage. *Art by Milo Duffin, concept by Ty Reveen, image courtesy Ty Reveen*

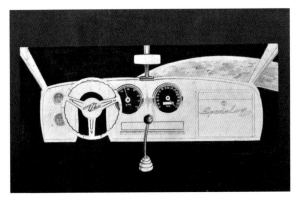

Concept art for the Afterburner World Tour stage. *Art by Kerin Shelbourne, concept by Ty Reveen, image courtesy Ty Reveen*

ZZ Top recorded the song "Doubleback" for the Universal Pictures movie *Back to the Future Part III* (1990) and filmed a cameo during the film's dance scene set in 1885. *AMBLIN ENTERTAINMENT / UNIVERSAL PICTURES / Ronald Grant Archive / Alamy Stock Photo*

ZZ Top performs during the Recycler World Tour in 1990. *INTERFOTO / Alamy Stock Photo*

ZZ Top in 1992 in a promotional photo for the "Viva Las Vegas" single from *Greatest Hits*. *Warner Bros. Records / Photofest © Warner Bros. Records. Photographer: Bill Reitzel*

Dusty Hill and Billy Gibbons performing at New York City's Beacon Theatre on November 10, 2005. *Photofest*

ZZ Top performing during the 2004 Rock and Roll Hall of Fame Induction Ceremony at the Waldorf Astoria in New York, New York, on March 15, 2004. *Nicolas Khayat / ABACA / Alamy Stock Photo*

Billy Gibbons performs with his 1960s band the Moving Sidewalks at the 2013 Austin Psych Fest on April 26, 2013, the second of three reunion performances the band played during that year. *WENN Rights Ltd / Alamy Stock Photo*

ZZ Top performs with Jeff Beck on August 12, 2014, at the Mountain Winery in Saratoga, California, during the Beards 'N Beck Tour 2014. *Jerome Brunet / ZUMA Wire / Alamy Live News*

Dusty Hill, Billy Gibbons, and Frank Beard during a break from filming the Gruene Hall jam session for the 2019 documentary *ZZ Top: That Little Ol' Band from Texas* in Gruene, Texas. *Photo by Ralph Chapman*

Billy Gibbons and wife Gilligan Stillwater attending "An Evening Honoring Billy Gibbons and Butch Trucks for Their Contributions to Art and Culture," an Adopt the Arts event held at The Roxy, Los Angeles, 2015.   *WENN Rights Ltd / Alamy Stock Photo*

which Beard revealed he spent his first major royalty check (totaling $72,000) completely on drugs. He was able to overcome his addictions as part of the Palmer Drug Abuse Program (PDAP), a rehabilitation program founded in Houston in the early 1970s. After successfully completing the program, Beard decided to give back, and in 1979 he became the first member of ZZ Top credited with an outside project after he produced an album, *Off the Streets*, by a band called Freeway, which was a collaboration among individuals involved with the PDAP. The project was organized by Bob Meehan, a cofounder of the program who had helped Beard in recovery (in 1980, Meehan was removed as the head of PDAP for a variety of reasons, including expenditures for the rock band project, after exposé reports on news programs *60 Minutes* and *20/20*). Notably, Beard became extremely interested in playing golf while in recovery and later moved to a house adjacent to a golf course, where he spent significant amounts of his time when not playing with ZZ Top.

Another oft-told tale of the band's hiatus is that when they reconvened after the break, Gibbons and Hill were surprised to discover that, unbeknownst to one another, each had grown a chest-length beard, which soon became the band's most identifiable visual trademark. While it's probable that the band-mates didn't consult each other on the length of their facial hair before returning to work, footage from the band's December 31, 1977, performance at the Tarrant County Convention Center in Fort Worth, the penultimate show on the Worldwide Texas Tour and before the band's hiatus, shows both Gibbons and Hill sporting already lengthy beards, and even Beard—ironically the member often noted as not having a long beard—wearing lengthier whiskers than he typically did. Regardless of how much planning went into the coordinated beards, they obviously were a huge contribution to the band's image and arguably its most recognizable trait—even people who can't name a ZZ Top song still recognize Gibbons and Hill's look, one of the most distinctive of any group in rock history.

Ultimately, the band's hiatus lasted about a year, and in early 1979, ZZ Top began recording their next album, *Degüello*, a Spanish idiom meaning "no quarter" or "no surrender"; the name borrows the title of a bugle call, "El Degüello," used by the Mexican Army at the Battle of the Alamo in 1836. Once again, the band convened at Ardent Studios in Memphis, fueled by Gibbons's musical discoveries during his time in Europe.

Demonstrating their growing interest in experimentation, *Degüello* is an album that embraces a variety of sounds and sonic innovations. For example, all three members learned to play saxophone (Gibbons on baritone sax, Hill on tenor sax, and Beard on alto sax) for songs like "She Loves My Automobile" and "Hi Fi Mama." While the group didn't master the instrument, they learned enough that Terry Manning could splice together a convincing "horn section" for the two songs, and the album sleeve features a photo of the trio dressed in their best swing jazz attire and holding their saxophones, with the caption identifying them as "the Lone Wolf Horns." The members also filmed a video of themselves playing the saxophones in this attire that would be projected during concerts when they performed these songs live during the supporting tour.

The horn parts were just one of the sonic innovations that Gibbons was exploring on *Degüello* with the assistance of his bandmates and Manning. "Billy wanted to expand," recalls Manning.

He, of course, never, ever wanted to lose the core of what ZZ Top is based on, which is Texas blues. He never wanted to get away from that, but he loved other things as well. There were other groups that might have been called at the time new wave that had a much different sound. He wanted to incorporate different sounds into the core of the Texas blues. As we went along, we kept progressing. Billy always liked to move ahead and do something new, but never lose what they had. We were experimenting with different

amplifiers, different guitars, different recording techniques, different over-
dubs. I remember sometimes he wanted to do something on guitar that took
more than two hands to do. I play guitar—not like Billy, of course—and he
would have me hold a certain fret or do a certain thing at a certain time by
reaching over while sitting at the console as he played the lead or rhythm part
we were doing, so it was actually things you couldn't do with two hands. We
were going in all kinds of wild directions.

In fact, the album features numerous instances of Gibbons's guitar being processed in various ways to produce unique sounds reminiscent of synthesizers
or keyboards.

Perhaps the wildest track featured on *Degüello* is "Manic Mechanic," a
bizarre, two-and-a-half-minute narrative about an auto race featuring heavily
processed vocals and guitar over a funky beat and several mid-song stops and
starts. "I think 'Manic Mechanic' is probably the ultimate in that direction,"
remembers Manning. "You can't really call it Texas blues, but it is. That was
nuts."

The vocal effect on "Manic Mechanic" was created with a voice manipu-
lator that Manning had heard being used on a daytime talk show.

Billy wanted a different sound on the voice and at the time I had watched
a Phil Donahue show. They had a guest on that didn't want to be known,
so they had him in shadow and manipulated his voice. They had this wild
vocal sound on it. I just went nuts, saying, "What is that vocal sound?" I
actually called up The Phil Donahue Show, *spoke to their engineer, got*
them to tell me what little box they had used, ordered one, and brought it in
for some of those crazy voice sounds. We would do whatever it took to have
fun and go wild in the studio and accept that people would like it. We did it
because we liked it, and we hoped that other people would like it.

Despite a heavy reliance on studio effects, ZZ Top figured out how to reproduce them live and played the song on the tour supporting *Degüello*, and the band has regularly revived it in their set lists over the past decades.

But *Degüello* wasn't all experimentation. For two cover songs, ZZ Top reached back into their influences. The Sam & Dave soul song "I Thank You," a 1968 number nine hit on the *Billboard* Hot 100 for the duo, which ZZ Top debuted live during their final shows before the hiatus, was the album's first single. ZZ Top also recorded a cover of the blues standard "Dust My Broom," which was credited on the original album to Elmore James, the blues legend who recorded a version of the song in 1951. However, "Dust My Broom" actually predates James, and on subsequent releases of *Degüello*, the song has been correctly credited to blues pioneer Robert Johnson, who originally recorded the song as "I'll Believe I'll Dust My Broom" in 1936 (though, like many blues songs, its rhythm and melody predates Johnson's recording). In addition to James's version, Gibbons was undoubtedly also familiar with the version recorded by Fleetwood Mac on their 1968 album *Mr. Wonderful*.

While "I Thank You" returned ZZ Top to the Top 40 for the first time in nearly five years since "Tush" (it peaked at number thirty-four on March 15, 1980, nearly four months after the release of the album), the more enduring song from the album is "Cheap Sunglasses," a funky ode to the benefits of wearing inexpensive eye protection. Though it only spent two weeks on the *Billboard* Hot 100 (peaking at number eighty-nine) despite the band's spending a significant amount of money on promotional sunglasses, "Cheap Sunglasses" became one of the band's signature live songs, quite possibly because they were so often seen in public appearances wearing cheap sunglasses. The album also featured another concert favorite, "I'm Bad, I'm Nationwide," a walking blues song whose lyrics have become something of a bravado-fueled mantra for ZZ Top, as well as "A Fool for Your Stockings," a somber, bluesy song that has occasionally appeared in the band's set lists over the decades.

Neither single was overly successful, and *Degüello* ultimately peaked at number twenty-four on the *Billboard* 200, seven spots lower than *Tejas*, which was considered a major disappointment. However, *Degüello* spent almost twice as many weeks on the chart as *Tejas* did. Though eventually certified platinum by the Recording Industry Association of America in 1984, *Degüello* was the lowest-charting ZZ Top album since *Rio Grande Mud*. Still, the numbers were consistent with the group's preceding albums, though not the success that the band might have expected now with the weight of Warner Bros. Records behind them.

Fully recharged twenty-three months after their last concert, ZZ Top returned to the road with the Expect No Quarter Tour kickoff in Shreveport, Louisiana, on November 20, 1979, just after the release of *Degüello*. The tour would last over a year and consist of over one hundred dates in the United States, with a small number in Canada and Europe (a planned Australian tour never materialized). The Shreveport concert would mark ZZ Top's first live performance since the end of the Worldwide Texas Tour on New Year's Day 1978. ZZ Top almost completely abandoned the Western aesthetics of the Worldwide Texas Tour for the new tour, dressing in more contemporary clothing (Gibbons often wore a smaller-brimmed hat or even a trucker hat, while Hill frequently opted for a beret). The standard set list also underwent a major overhaul, losing almost all the songs from the first two albums in favor of more recent singles and album cuts.

The band spent the rest of 1979 touring the South and Midwest, celebrating New Year's Eve with a show at the Omni in Atlanta. The tour continued throughout 1980, with the band playing straight through the year except for the month of June (there were a few other short breaks from the road), concluding with another New Year's Eve concert, this time in Dallas. ZZ Top finally took another break from touring at the beginning of 1981, though the band went into the studio to record their next album and hit the road again in May 1981.

The band's years away from the stage appeared only to make fans all the wilder during their concert appearances. A *Variety* review of the February 3, 1980, concert at the Sportatorium in Hollywood, Florida, noted that the crowd "became a stagefront crush before the band's opening note." The review was almost entirely negative, calling the volume "tiresome" and the band's cover of "I Thank You" "funkless," declaring the performance "a show for hard-core fans only. The curiosity seeker is likely to be bored—or worse," while noting that the local sheriff's office claimed that the concert became out of control.[2]

Yet the group continued to play high-grossing shows. *Variety* reported that ZZ Top's concerts at Long Beach Arena (February 15), St. Paul's Civic Center Arena (March 2), and Philadelphia's Spectrum (March 29) were sell-outs, and the band moved a lot of tickets in other major markets as well. ZZ Top was also the first rock band to play the Riverfront Coliseum in Cincinnati on March 21 after eleven people died during a stampede at a Who concert in December 1979. Despite the group's reputation as a raucous act, the Riverfront Coliseum concert went forward without a major incident (though perhaps because of fans taking caution after such a horrific incident, only 11,700 of the arena's 18,000 seats sold out). The sold-out May 4 show at the Capitol Theatre in Passaic, New Jersey, aired live on *King Biscuit Flower Hour* and has since become one of the band's most heavily bootlegged live performances.

But something funny happened on the way to *Degüello*: after a decade of largely dismissing ZZ Top as a discordant heavy metal trio (a reputation they never deserved), major critics started—believe it or not—to express admiration for the group. In the *New York Times'* review of the concert at Long Island's Nassau Coliseum on May 2, Robert Palmer noted it "wasn't just loud and kinetic; the band was worth listening to" and praised Gibbons, writing, "He organizes his guitar solos intelligently and varies his sound and attack so frequently one doesn't grow impatient with the music's restricted melodic range," though he also remarked that Gibbons is "no Otis Rush or Buddy Guy."[3]

The review of *Degüello* in *Audio* magazine raised a prophetic question about the continuing evolution of ZZ Top: "What other band in their position has actually become *hotter* players over the years, gotten weirder in a funny sort of way, and still managed to bring out the animal in every teenage audience they encounter? Not many, and on their new LP—their first in about four years or so—these guys seem to be as fiery and farcical as when they first started to catch the public eye."[4]

In an interview with John Rockwell of the *New York Times*, Gibbons called the album's music "Gulf Coast rhythm and blues" and attributed its new sound to the music he heard while in Europe during the band's hiatus. "In Europe, there's this tradition to accept what is good as good for all time," he remarked. "In America, people try to be new for newness's sake."[5]

A major development in ZZ Top's live performances debuted with the Expect No Quarter Tour and would go on to fuel the band's concerts for the rest of their career. ZZ Top's use of backing tracks for instruments and vocals during concerts over the last four decades has been something of an unspoken component of the live show. The use of backing tracks is obvious (as talented as he is, Gibbons cannot possibly play multiple guitar tracks at the same time, as is often heard during live performances of songs like "Gimme All Your Lovin'") but rarely acknowledged. As the band's studio recordings became more technologically complex with *Degüello*, involving parts that could not conceivably be performed by three musicians alone in a live setting, ZZ Top incorporated those advanced techniques in concert to reproduce the songs as closely as possible. In a 1990 interview with *Musician*, Gibbons attempted to be vague in answering the question of whether or not the band played with a keyboardist.

Umm . . . there's a great furor right now about what's being labeled "canned music." We did our fair share of experimenting with different sequencers and with different approaches to just being entertainers, and I don't think the jury's back in on that one yet. . . . We prefer to do it live. It's no different than being an auto mechanic. If the tire jack breaks, you can't fix the tire. If the keyboard decides to blow a fuse, you can't do it. But as long as the equipment's there, we'll take a stab at it.[6]

Of course, by the time of that interview, ZZ Top had been using backing tracks in their live performances for over a decade. The practice began on the Expect No Quarter Tour to provide the saxophone sounds for the songs from the new album. The effect was made possible by some backstage wizardry by Terry Manning, who recalls,

I made this device for them called the Tap-A-Top-22. That way it had a sort of backward "ZZ" and "Top" in it. It had eight buttons on it, which meant it was your eight favorite notes. I would choose the eight notes that they needed the most for the songs, and it had an eight-track tape machine because that was the biggest TASCAM tape machine that you could get then, connected to my box with the eight buttons. They were kind of like keys on a keyboard, and you would have eight notes you could play. They would have a musically proficient tech person who learned to play the notes off the Tap-A-Top-22 live. Of course, sometimes things would break down or wouldn't work, but they did that a lot. Later, when computers came in it was much easier to have what used to be called "tape assist," and of course, almost every group does that now. You want to play live, but you want to give the audience a taste of what it's like on the record.

Especially during the *Afterburner* and *Recycler* support tours, reviewers consistently noted the band's use of backing tracks in their live performances, as if audiences were too oblivious to notice the obvious use of prerecorded accompaniment (few critics, however, noted this as a detraction, except in the sense that it robbed the concerts of the potential for spontaneity). Despite the wide use of backing tracks in the entertainment industry in live performances over the last several decades, at times ZZ Top became a major target by other musicians for using them, perhaps because it seemed to some to be contradictory to the longtime insistence that the group was the "same three guys, same three chords." After getting kicked off the Recycler World Tour as the opening act for rallying against the tour's corporate sponsor, Miller Lite, Rich Robinson of the Black Crowes criticized ZZ Top for using backing tracks, causing Hill to respond in a 1992 interview, "We don't cheat, we just use a few triggers," though that statement was an oversimplification of the backstage wizardry required for a ZZ Top concert.[7]

Four years after announcing that the Worldwide Texas Tour would travel to Europe, the Expect No Quarter Tour finally featured ZZ Top's first shows on the Continent. Immediately after their April 14 concert at the Birmingham-Jefferson Civic Center in Birmingham, Alabama, ZZ Top jetted to London to tape their appearance on *The Old Grey Whistle Test*, a popular late-night music program that aired on BBC2. The performance featured ZZ Top performing "I Thank You" and "Cheap Sunglasses" from *Degüello*. Four days later, ZZ Top performed in Grugahalle in Essen, West Germany, with the entire concert filmed for the music program *Rockpalast*, which aired the following day. Then two days later, ZZ Top performed at Pavillon Baltard, Nogent-sur-Marne, in Paris, France, in another concert that was also professionally filmed for broadcast. The group finished their European tour with a concert at London's famed Hammersmith Odeon on April 24. While breaking with Ham's long tradition of not letting the band perform on television, these recordings served as a way to introduce the group to European audiences instead of building an audience show by show as they did in the United States, since it would have been impossible for ZZ Top to organically grow their audience that way in Europe without spending months abroad.

While not releasing video footage of the band's live performances and avoiding appearances on shows like *Saturday Night Live*, *The Midnight Special*, and *Don Kirshner's Rock Concert* may have helped maintain the band's mystique in the United States at the time, it meant that ZZ Top had little to release as archival live material in later decades. Whereas artists like the Rolling Stones, Bruce Springsteen, and the Who have been able to occasionally get a sales pop from their devoted fan bases with live album releases of concerts from their earlier years, ZZ Top is severely limited by what it has available. In recent decades it would be unthinkable for a band not to record spectacles like the Worldwide Texas Tour or the Afterburner World Tour for posterity, but for ZZ Top's first four decades, this was a brand strategy to sell as many concert tickets as possible.

As a result, the German performance has become one of the most viewed documents of the pre-*Eliminator* era of ZZ Top. It was released in 2009 as both a CD and DVD and serves as a crucial document of the group's live performances in light of how little professionally recorded footage of the group from before the MTV era exists publicly.

While *Degüello* did not sell as well as *Tres Hombres* or *Fandango!*, just looking at the album as an experiment in expanding what ZZ Top could sound like proved to be a successful endeavor. Gibbons saw that he did not have to continually rely on the blues and boogie that made the group famous. The success that ZZ Top had on the road demonstrated that audiences would follow them even if they strayed from the sounds of "La Grange" and "Tush." It served as a welcome invitation for ZZ Top to push their sonic experimentations even further with their next album.

After finally putting the brakes on the Expect No Quarter Tour with a January 3, 1981, concert at the Mid-South Coliseum in Memphis, ZZ Top again entered Ardent Studios to record a new album with Manning.

Most of the tracks from the band's first album of the 1980s, which they would release under the title *El Loco*, took a highly energetic tone. "Tube Snake Boogie," featuring a lyrical analogy that nobody really needed to explain, is perhaps the album's most famous track as its second single and mixes a funky groove with some boogie guitar by Gibbons and a Howlin' Wolf–inspired vocal, seemingly intended to be a strip club anthem. If the lyrics of that song were too obvious, "Pearl Necklace" was even more blatant, a guitar-driven pop classic with another echo vocal effect on Gibbons's voice. Following the amusing "Manic Mechanic" on *Degüello*, *El Loco* features several songs in which Gibbons again demonstrates the range of his voice, such as "Ten Foot Pole," with a deep soul growl, and "Heaven, Hell or Houston," a mix between an R&B song and what sounds like an answering machine message of Gibbons speaking in an affected accent. But the album was not all about experimentation—songs like "Don't Tease Me" and "Party on the Patio" are the straightforward ZZ Top rock that fans became accustomed to, with both songs featuring powerful vocals from Hill.

The album's experimentation wasn't just limited to vocal and guitar effects to create a cleaner, more polished (not to mention contemporary) sound. On *El Loco*, ZZ Top attempted its first true pop ballad, "Leila," which was released as the album's first single. Its country and western love ballad influences are obvious. The song, which features a rare appearance by an outside musician, Mark Erlewine, who plays pedal steel guitar, was unlike any other the band had previously attempted.

Erlewine is the longtime owner of Austin's Erlewine Guitars, one of the most renowned guitar repair and custom guitar shops in existence. In addition to building custom guitars for Gibbons and other musicians like Paul

McCartney, Albert King, Joe Walsh, Don Felder, Johnny Winter, and Mark Knopfler, Erlewine has for decades had the almost holy responsibility of repairing Willie Nelson's famous guitar, Trigger, and has refurbished guitars for countless other professional musicians.

Gibbons and Erlewine first crossed paths when Gibbons came into Erlewine Guitars in the 1970s. Erlewine remembers,

> *I had my guitar shop here in Austin right down the street from the Austin City Limits Studios. I had been in business probably four years, and one day a guy came in with a beret on. It was Billy Gibbons. I didn't know him because I didn't follow ZZ Top. As an apprentice, I helped my cousin Dan build the Flying V for Albert King, called Lucy, and I think that's where he had heard about me. We struck up a conversation and became friends. He's such a guitar nut, so we fit right in with each other. We started hanging out and traveling together while coming up with different guitar ideas, and I would do my best to execute them.*

One of Gibbons's most frequently used guitars built by Erlewine is the Automatic, which drew influence from two of the most popular guitars in rock and roll. Erlewine recalls,

> *We designed one which we called "The Automatic," which is basically a Strat body shape but built like a Les Paul with a carved maple top on mahogany. It went through various peghead iterations. I built him a couple of double-neck Automatics for the Degüello tour. There's a cover of Guitar Player magazine, February 1981—Billy is on the cover in my blue denim shirt that he borrowed for the shot while playing the double-neck that I built him. The top neck has "Reverend" inlaid in pearl and the bottom neck has "Willy G." I have to say it was a nice guitar. I also built a number of guitars with various inlays for him, but most of them were the Automatic style.*

Gibbons can be seen playing the guitar on the *Degüello* song "Lowdown in the Street" in the footage from ZZ Top's 1980 *Rockpalast* performance.

However, perhaps the most famous guitar collaboration between Gibbons and Erlewine is the Chiquita travel guitar, just 27.5 inches long and 4.25 pounds, which Gibbons held in promotional photos for *El Loco* and occasionally used on stage, most notably when performing the *El Loco* track "Groovy Little Hippie Pad." Erlewine recalls,

> *Billy was always having to buy a ticket on a plane for his guitar if he was taking a special one with him because he wouldn't check it. I think that's what got him thinking about creating an FAA-friendly travel guitar that you didn't have to check and you could just put in an overhead bin and pull it out to practice while you were flying. We worked on that by coming up with different designs and scales, and then I started making prototypes until we found one that seemed to work pretty well. We started a company named the Chiquita Guitar Company, and I went to Japan to start production on those. We had a very rough start. The first factory did a horrible job—it took a long time to get them and most of them were unusable. I had to go back to Japan to a different factory that finally got it right. It was a long process, but it was worth it in the end—I've carried the torch ever since.*

The Chiquita guitar got additional exposure when featured in the opening scene of the hit 1985 film *Back to the Future*. "That was a shock to me," says Erlewine. "A customer came in one day and said, 'A movie just opened yesterday, and I think it has one of your guitars in it.' I had no idea."

When it came to performing on "Leila," Erlewine was selected for the job because of his proficiency in playing pedal steel guitar. He remembers,

> *Pedal steel is my instrument, and Billy messed around with pedal steel while he was trying to get ready for a new album. He would come to the shop and*

say, "I want you to play something on this tune." That particular song was
"Leila." I wrote a part to it thinking he was going to learn it. But I got a
call from Billy in Memphis, and he said, "Load up your steel—I want you
to come to lay this track." That was an awesome experience though it scared
the hell out of me. I was at Ardent Studios with Bill Ham and Terry Man-
ning in the control room looking at me through this big plate glass window.
I was all alone in this big studio with my headphones on, and they rolled
the tape and told me to play my part. An integral part of pedal steel is the
volume pedal for sustain to create that nonending note. I was so scared that
I was just fluttering on the volume pedal. When they rolled it back to me,
they said, "Ah, this is fantastic! Thanks for your help." I heard what I had
done and said, "No, no, no!" so we cut it again, probably a few more times.

While "Leila" was another example of Gibbons's attempts to expand ZZ
Top's sound, it was not particularly successful as a single, peaking at number seventy-seven, and perhaps hurt album sales since it was a very different
sound for ZZ Top and didn't sound anything like the rest of *El Loco*. Per
Ham's edict that ZZ Top and only ZZ Top would be credited for performing
on their albums, Erlewine was not credited on the album.

Of all the album's tracks, the one that most points to the future direction
that ZZ Top would take is the synthesizer-heavy "Groovy Little Hippie Pad,"
an upbeat song with humorous lyrics about a hippie finding his place in
the consumer-driven 1980s. Decades later, Gibbons credited the inspiration
for "Groovy Little Hippie Pad" to seeing the new wave band Devo doing a
soundcheck in a Houston "country and western bar" and observing one of
the members playing a Minimoog. When this could have taken place is hard
to guess unless Gibbons is fuzzy on the details. Before the release of their
debut album in August 1978, Devo largely performed in the vicinity of Ohio,
where the band formed, as well as in a handful of cities in the Northeast,

including New York and Philadelphia, and in California and on a tour of Europe. By the time the band started touring nationally, it was playing theaters, including the Texas Opry House in Houston on July 31, 1979, and the University of Houston's Cullen Performance Hall on August 6, 1980, neither of which fit the definition of a "country and western bar." Regardless, Gibbons was inspired by the sound. "One of the guys in the band was playing a Minimoog, and he did this figure on it," he remembered. "He was just noodling around. But it was enough. What came out of that was 'Groovy Little Hippie Pad'—same figure. It was a direct derivative of punk. Devo was a big influence on that album—and the B-52s as well. They had that song 'Party Out of Bounds.' Our song 'Party on the Patio' was an extension of that. [The critic] Lester Bangs played it for some punks in New York, and they dug it. It proved we weren't just a boogie band. We had this new wave edge." The band even featured the song on tour as the opening number, a sonic blast that alerted audiences that the group was fearless in treading new ground.[8]

Though "Groovy Little Hippie Pad" may have been inspired by Devo and new wave, the basis for the track was Gibbons's desire to expand ZZ Top's sound beyond what could be performed by three musicians on traditional musical instruments, adding more sonic depth to their recordings. As with "Leila," there was an uncredited contributor to the development of "Groovy Little Hippie Pad." Linden Hudson, an associate of the band who had become adept at creating music with still-emerging synthesizer technology, worked closely with Gibbons on the synthesizer track for the song. Like Erlewine's steel guitar part, Hudson's contribution to the album would go uncredited, and it marked the beginning of a collaborative relationship between Gibbons and Hudson that would expand for ZZ Top's next album, *Eliminator*, in contentious fashion.

The album cover for *El Loco* depicted the three members of ZZ Top wearing stained blue jumpsuits and large sombreros while being busted by a

lawman in the desert for smuggling what appears to be large sacks of marijuana. It marked the first album since *Fandango!* in which the band members
were depicted on the album's cover art, but it was the first to feature Gibbons's
and Hill's long beards and all three members wearing sunglasses and coordinating outfits, a visual depiction that would become standard for the band
moving forward.

ZZ Top only took a four-month break after the conclusion of the Expect
No Quarter Tour before launching into their next tour, titled the El Loco-
Motion Tour, in May 1981, in advance of the June release of the new album.
Once again, the band followed a rigorous schedule, playing nearly 150 con-
certs from May 1981 through January 1983.

While *El Loco* broke tremendous new ground creatively for ZZ Top, its
sales did not reflect success. The uncharacteristic "Leila" stalled at number
seventy-seven on the *Billboard* Hot 100, and the raunchy "Tube Snake Boogie" failed to chart (though it did reach number four on the then new Rock
Albums & Top Tracks chart, which later became the Mainstream Rock chart,
reflecting the song's popularity on radio). Though the album charted higher
than *Degüello* by peaking at number seventeen on the *Billboard* 200 versus
Degüello's peak position of twenty-four, *El Loco* ended its run on the *Billboard*
200 after twenty-two weeks, about half as many weeks as *Degüello* spent on
the chart, which showed that the band's audience wasn't growing respective
to their ambitions.

For example, after having a sellout at the Philadelphia Spectrum on the
Degüello support tour, the group only hit two-thirds of its gross potential at
the same venue on the *El Loco* support tour just eighteen months later. ZZ
Top took a brief break from their tour to open four Texas shows for the Rolling Stones, two at the Astrodome (October 28 and 29, 1981) and two at the
Cotton Bowl (October 31 and November 1), a decade after the trio had first
opened for that band in Hawaii. ZZ Top performed another New Year's Eve

show, this time at the Mid-South Coliseum in Memphis to ring in 1982. Of course, the band continued to sell out shows in its home territory, including an April 16, 1982, concert at the University of Texas, Austin. The tour ran straight through 1982, breaking for a few weeks from mid-April, then traveled to Germany and the Netherlands for a few dates and an appearance on Germany's *Rockpop in Concert* recorded at Westfalenhallen in Dortmund, with ZZ Top playing a ten-song set (including "Groovy Little Hippie Pad" and "Ten Foot Pole" from the new album). The group took another break from the road for the summer of 1982, returning for more North American dates in September, then launching yet another leg at the end of the year (including another New Year's Eve concert, this time in Phoenix) and playing a small number of dates at the beginning of January 1983.

But the fact that *El Loco*, the second album on ZZ Top's contract with Warner Bros., underperformed obviously concerned Gibbons. The singles "Leila" and "Tube Snake Boogie" could not have been more different—a soft country ballad and a bawdy boogie—as if the band was shooting wide to see what would hit better in the market. Yet neither single caught the attention of mainstream audiences (while "Tube Snake Boogie" has become a staple of ZZ Top concerts, "Leila" has not made its way onto the band's set lists).

Still, album sales aside, by most other measures ZZ Top was one of the most popular bands in the country. The group had already shown their mettle as a concert draw hundreds of times, even if music sales didn't reflect that. But the box office numbers were immaterial when it came to the band's giant record deal with Warner Bros., a corporate conglomerate that could drop ZZ Top from its balance sheet without much red ink. Warner Bros. expected a hit album. More importantly, Gibbons wanted his band to have a hit album. He would get that opportunity, though it would come as the result of an incredible number of stars aligning just at the right time for ZZ Top.

9
DRIVEN TO SUCCEED

August 1, 1981, marked the launch of MTV, which almost overnight changed the landscape of the pop music industry and, a year and a half later, the trajectory of ZZ Top's career. MTV initially debuted as a twenty-four-hour music network targeting teenagers, with a substantial amount of its programming devoted to music videos. Though only airing in about 2.5 million homes in New Jersey at launch, in a short time the cable network became a national phenomenon following a hugely successful and vigorous marketing campaign, "I Want My MTV," which encouraged viewers to demand the channel on their airwaves (or that their parents get cable television). By 1989, the channel was available in nearly fifty million households and vastly expanded the popularity of cable television.

As the channel expanded into new markets, record executives noticed that exposure on MTV led to substantial record sales boosts for featured artists in the regions that aired MTV. This included several new wave and British bands that were not getting significant airplay on American radio but were getting exposure on MTV. Executives soon noted that MTV was an invaluable tool to market music to teenagers, and a flashy music video could make or break an artist's career even more than radio, because while radio was still regional and singles had to be promoted market by market, MTV had a growing reach across the United States. Promotion on the channel could truly bring a pop star national recognition overnight, setting in motion the decline of regional radio airplay as a primary factor in star making.

While an artist's visual image was essential to success in pop music even before bobby socks became a cultural fad, MTV became a pop culture game changer in the promotion of mass entertainment and firmly linked the importance of music and image in the recording industry. A creative music video, or even just a video featuring an attractive artist, could become a hit on the channel and, as a result, make a career. Shortly afterward, success on MTV became an almost essential component of a successful career in pop music as record executives used popularity on MTV as a measure to determine which artists to promote in record stores, on radio, and through concert tours. While not everyone was able to satisfy their "I Want My MTV" pleas, either because cable television or the channel itself was not available in their city or region (or simply because of the cost), other music video programs on local and network channels were launched to follow MTV's success, including the syndicated series *MV3*, debuting in 1982, and NBC's *Friday Night Videos*, launching in July 1983, which gave music videos an even wider exposure.

In its earliest years, MTV's content primarily focused on white pop, rock, and new wave artists from the United States, Canada, and the United Kingdom. Other genres of music—most notably, country and the burgeoning rap and heavy metal genres—were almost entirely ignored. There was also a strong focus on younger artists who would appeal to teenagers.

Of course, ZZ Top did not fit into many of those categories. Besides the fact that the group had never created a music video, by 1981 its members were over thirty and entirely too old-school "Texas" for a channel devoted to hot youth culture. While *El Loco*, released just weeks before the launch of MTV, incorporated some new wave influences, "Tube Snake Boogie" and "Leila" were far from the typical music heard on the channel, and three hombres who looked like ZZ Top weren't exactly poster children for a channel dominated by much younger, beardless faces.

However, while MTV's library of music videos available at launch primarily consisted of artists lip-synching to the recorded track, the growth of the channel encouraged artists to create more conceptional videos incorporating narrative elements, actors, animation, and other techniques that would bring more visual flare to the network.

While the members of ZZ Top did not have pop idol looks by the launch of MTV, they did have a signature look that stood out. On top of that, what ZZ Top had that contemporary bands like 38 Special and Molly Hatchet did not was their inherent humor. Billy Gibbons, Dusty Hill, and Frank Beard weren't afraid to look ridiculous or approach an interview with levity, something that most rock musicians seemed very adverse to.

But before ZZ Top could think about music videos, they needed to think about a new album. In 1982, ZZ Top returned to Ardent Studios to record the follow-up album to *El Loco*, which would eventually become *Eliminator*, by far the most successful album in ZZ Top's catalog. *Eliminator* has accounted for nearly half of the group's total album sales worldwide in the decades since its release and is one of the most successful rock albums of the 1980s. Yet for the first twenty-five years of its existence, there was virtually no thorough explanation of how it was crafted in the studio beyond the album's limited liner notes. Still today, more than four decades later, many details about exactly how these songs, heard by hundreds of millions of ears, were written and recorded are shrouded in mystery. Any attempt to tell the story of the making of *Eliminator* runs into the issue of Gibbons's vagueness, occasionally supported by equally vague comments by Hill and Beard, about how it was developed and produced.

The one question that raises little dispute is the why—why ZZ Top so radically changed their sound and image for *Eliminator*. The answer is obvious: Gibbons, like most pop musicians, wanted ZZ Top to have an unstoppable hit record. It wasn't just the pressure of the Warner Bros. record deal. By 1982, it had been seven years since ZZ Top's last Top 10 album, *Fandango!* (which hit number ten) and their last (and still up to that point, only) Top 20 single, "Tush" (which hit number twenty). While the band could sell out concerts across the United States, they still sold far fewer records than most of their contemporaries, and they still had very little traction outside the United States and Canada.

Over the last four decades, Gibbons has told various stories about what inspired the radical sound of *Eliminator*. One story focused on his frustration over *El Loco* not having a hit single, considering that the Rolling Stones, a band with a few years on ZZ Top, had a Top 10 single in several countries with the 1980 dance song "Emotional Rescue." He wondered how ZZ Top could create songs that would similarly appeal to the pop and new wave audiences while still being recognizably in ZZ Top's oeuvre. He has also cited the influence of punk and new wave bands, as well as electronic synth-pop bands like Orchestral Manoeuvres in the Dark.

"That album was just radically different from anything that they had done before," recalls Terry Manning, who once again was credited as the engineer for *Eliminator* but played an even larger uncredited role in its creation.

Part of that was because they had taken some time off between albums and would go do other things, which is a good thing for people to get fresh insight into other worldy ideas. Billy had been traveling through Europe and checking out clubs. He had come to me before we started Eliminator *and said, "You know, I go to clubs and they'll play all this dance music and as soon as a certain beat comes on people jump up and start dancing and you just see the excitement and feel they have for it. Because I'm there at that club that night, they'll be very kind and play 'Tush' or 'La Grange' or something, but I notice that while people love it, they don't really get up and dance to it like they do for the dance music. Is there any way we can incorporate the excitement of what would make people dance into what we do?"*

Manning was also intrigued by the possibilities of danceable rhythms on a ZZ Top album, which required utilizing a drum machine instead of Beard as the driving backbeat of each song. "I never would talk about it for years, but it's become known, especially because of the documentary [2019's *ZZ Top: That Little Ol' Band from Texas*], that Frank was having some troubles, and his troubles kind of bled into his playing abilities at the time in the studio," shares Manning. He continues,

> *Billy said that another thing that he wanted to deal with was the rhythms, we had to keep the rhythms especially if we wanted the songs to be danceable. To my horror, I went out to a few dance clubs, and I would take a stopwatch and time everything to see what beats people were dancing to the most. I made lists of it and we actually sequenced that album starting at a certain beat with "Gimme All Your Lovin'" at one certain tempo and the next song is that tempo plus a beat or two faster ["Got Me Under Pressure"], and the next one is that second tempo plus a beat or two faster ["Sharp Dressed Man"] before we drop down later in the sequence ["Need You Tonight"], as you have to—you can't keep going up, you have to bring it down then bring it back up. So it was actually all planned very carefully, and we got our machine to keep the timing exact. It was recorded quite differently from any other ZZ Top album we had done prior to that.*

In addition to a new approach to the way ZZ Top constructed music, central to the album's presentation was Gibbons's customized 1933 Ford coupe, a striking-red hot rod that Gibbons had built by California's Buffalo Motor Cars and dubbed the Eliminator coupe. Cars have figured in the lyrical content of rock and roll since even before Chuck Berry ("You Can't Catch Me" and "No Particular Place to Go"), the Beatles ("Drive My Car"), and the Beach Boys (who had several hits about cars, including "Little Deuce Coupe," written about a 1932 Ford coupe, and "Fun, Fun, Fun"). "Rocket 88," the 1951 song released under the name Jackie Brenston & His Delta Cats (the "Delta Cats" were actually Ike Turner and his band, Kings of Rhythm) that some critics consider the first "rock and roll" song, is about the Oldsmobile Rocket 88. With all three members of ZZ Top having an interest in cars, it was natural that the band would also regularly record songs about automobiles, from "Chevrolet" on *Rio Grande Mud* to "She Loves My Automobile" on *Degüello*, among many others. But *Eliminator* was the first instance where ZZ Top used a car as the concept for an album, with the title as a reference to elimination automobile races. The Eliminator coupe was featured not only on the cover art of the album but also prominently in the band's new music videos and merchandising. Wisely, because Gibbons used the car for business purposes, he was able to get a tax deduction that helped resolve the outstanding balance he had on the customization bills (Gibbons's original Eliminator coupe now resides at Cleveland's Rock and Roll Hall of Fame, potentially allowing it to have been yet another tax deduction).

While Gibbons and Manning were the primary architects of *Eliminator* once the album got to the recording stage at Ardent, the name of another major contributor to the early stages of the album is listed nowhere in the credits. A former acquaintance of the band, Linden Hudson, played a significant role in the preproduction of the album. His contribution is now widely known and accepted, particularly since Hudson has in recent years been speaking openly about his involvement in the early stages of *Eliminator* in interviews, most recently in a profile in the summer 2023 issue of the revived *Creem* magazine. His insight into the creation of *Eliminator* has also served as a rare firsthand account of how the individual members of ZZ Top and management often worked independently, despite the public image of unity and fraternity.

According to Hudson, he first encountered ZZ Top early in their career when he was a DJ at KLOL, a Houston FM station that had adopted a free-form rock format in 1970. Gibbons was a guest on his program, and Hudson regularly played ZZ Top's early songs during his show. Eventually

Hudson left the station and Houston, while Gibbons and ZZ Top went on to superstardom, and the two fell out of touch. By the late 1970s, Hudson was back in Houston and had gained a reputation as something of a studio wizard with an ear for new synthesizer technology. Beard hired Hudson to build a recording studio in his new home in Houston, and he soon became a frequent houseguest of Beard, watching his home while Beard was away and keeping the studio maintained (as well as serving as an all-around handyman). The studio was meant to be a spot for Gibbons, Hill, and Beard to demo new music, though, according to Hudson, it was mostly he and Gibbons who recorded in the studio, bonding over their shared interests in new recording technology.

One of Gibbons and Hudson's first collaborations resulted in the synthesizer track for "Groovy Little Hippie Pad" on *El Loco* and the backing track that the band would play to on tour. After working on the synthesizer parts for *El Loco*, Hudson began a fruitful collaboration with Gibbons in which the pair worked on demos for the next ZZ Top album. In Hudson's recollection, Beard and Hill had very little involvement in these demo sessions as Gibbons and Hudson experimented with synthesizers and sequencers to record demos for ZZ Top's next album, working together often without the participation of Hill and Beard and without the knowledge of Bill Ham. In fact, in Hudson's version of the events, it was he who utilized a stopwatch to determine the most popular beats in contemporary pop music and shared that information with Gibbons.

Hudson's version of the creation of the album's demos is not without merit. Hudson claims and has posted recorded evidence online to support his assertion that he was involved in the preproduction demo recordings (and perhaps even the composition) of at least "Got Me Under Pressure," "I Got the Six," "Dirty Dog," "Legs," "Thug," "TV Dinners" (originally titled "Troubles"), and "Sharp Dressed Man"—in other words, at least seven of the album's eleven songs. However, Hudson receives no acknowledgment for his contributions anywhere on the *Eliminator* album. He claims that when he tried to raise the issue with Gibbons or anyone else associated with the band, he became persona non grata in the ZZ Top camp.

In a few retrospective interviews in recent years, Gibbons has acknowledged Hudson's involvement in the preproduction of *Eliminator* but, as is his nature, has been vague about the details. Gibbons spoke most openly about Hudson's contributions to the album in a 2013 interview with MusicRadar in which he shared some history of each ZZ Top album. When it came to *El Loco*, Gibbons said, "We had befriended somebody who would become an influential associate, a guy named Linden Hudson. He was a gifted songwriter and had production skills that were leading the pack at times. He brought some elements to the forefront that helped reshape what ZZ Top were doing, starting in the studio and eventually to the live stage." Gibbons did not mention Hudson in his comments about *Eliminator* in the same article. A year later, a CNET reporter asked Gibbons a more direct question about Hudson's involvement in the album: "Sound engineer Linden Hudson was described as a high-tech music teacher on your highly successful *Eliminator* album. How much did the band experiment with electronic instruments prior to that album, and what did you learn through that experience?" Gibbons's response didn't mention Hudson directly, instead comparing the band's change in sound to one of their musical heroes going electric ("We had always been open to technology and what it had to offer, and, as a matter of fact, so did our forebears. Muddy Waters went electric when resources and circumstance allowed him to do so, and we went 'electronic' when we had that opportunity").[1]

Finally, in 2016, Gibbons and Beard both spoke somewhat more openly about working with Hudson in a retrospective on *Eliminator* in *Classic Rock* magazine. "Linden was quite an influential, inspirational figure," Gibbons said. "He was right there with us when some of the material was developed and brought forward some production techniques that were then valuable. I still treasure the moments that he and I spent together. There was quite a bit of time that the two of us sat behind a mixing console discussing new ways to go about making popular music." As for Beard, he was more remorseful than reflective, adding, "The whole thing was a particular disappointment to me. Basically, Linden was kind of a house-sitter for me. He looked after my home when we were out on tour. What happened with him was a real drag. But you have to move on."[2]

Fans who have learned about Hudson's involvement in the creation of *Eliminator* are often stunned by the revelation that the seemingly fun-loving "little ol' band from Texas" may not have been on the up and up when it came to giving credit where credit was due. In that case, it is worth exploring the convoluted history of ZZ Top's songwriting credits.

With popular music in general, songwriting can often be as much a contractual exercise as a creative one. Regarding the Beatles, one of the first examples of significant pop musicians who wrote the lion's share of their own music, most of the band's songs were credited to Lennon-McCartney, even if John Lennon and Paul McCartney did not extensively collaborate on a particular song. The partnership has been so distinctive that it later became a legal issue with Lennon's estate when McCartney chose to reverse the credit to "Paul McCartney and John Lennon" for the nineteen Beatles songs featured on his 2002 live album *Back in the U.S.* Similarly, Mick Jagger and Keith Richards of the Rolling Stones established the Jagger-Richards songwriting partnership early in the band's career and would continue to credit all band compositions to the partnership even when the duo was barely on speaking terms and writing music almost completely independently. Mick Taylor, who played guitar with the Rolling Stones from 1969 to 1974, has said that he quit the band in part because he did not receive writing credit on several

"Jagger-Richards" songs that he believed he should have. Similarly, Taylor's replacement in the band, Ronnie Wood, has said in numerous interviews over the past four decades that he had to fight for the handful of cowriting credits he has received as a member of the band.

Legal battles over songwriting credits became increasingly common as writing credits became more valuable with music licensing in film, television, commercials, and other media. In 1992, Mike Love of the Beach Boys sued his bandmate and cousin, Brian Wilson, to receive writing credit and royalties for seventy-nine Beach Boys songs that Love believed he should have received cowriting credit for. After a 1994 trial, Love received writing credit for thirty-five of the songs in question. More significantly, pianist Johnnie Johnson, who worked with Chuck Berry extensively from 1953 to 1973, sued Berry in 2000 with the claim that he should have received cowriting credit for several of Berry's biggest hits, though the case was dismissed because the statute of limitations had run out. Had the case proceeded, it may have changed the entire historical perception of Berry as the universally acknowledged "father" of rock and roll. Curiously, the Beach Boys and Chuck Berry also were involved in a songwriting dispute with one another. Berry was not originally credited for cowriting the Beach Boys 1963 hit "Surfin' U.S.A.," even though it is a cover of Berry's 1958 hit "Sweet Little Sixteen" with new lyrics.

In many ways, ZZ Top's various songwriting controversies parallel those of another popular 1970s blues-based rock band, Led Zeppelin. During the group's recording years, Zeppelin borrowed liberally from blues music, as dozens of other blues rock bands did in the 1960s and 1970s. Chiefly because of Zeppelin's inconsistent history of crediting the original artists (and, of course, the band's immense popularity and financial success), the band later became a frequent target of plagiarism suits, including for the songs "Babe I'm Gonna Leave You," "Boogie with Stu," "Bring It on Home," "Dazed and Confused," "The Lemon Song," "Whole Lotta Love," and, most recently,

"Stairway to Heaven." These legal proceedings have led to amended writing credits for songs on half of Zeppelin's studio albums, most notably giving credit (and financial settlements) to blues luminaries like Willie Dixon and Howlin' Wolf. Zeppelin was far from the only band of that era that claimed to be following the "blues tradition" of interpreting the music of their blues forefathers, but they are certainly the band that has been sued the most for it, likely because they are one of the most popular bands of all time.

ZZ Top faced a similar plagiarism lawsuit over the similarities between "La Grange" and the 1948 John Lee Hooker song "Boogie Chillen'." The publisher, producer, and copyright holder of "Boogie Chillen'," Bernard Besman, sued ZZ Top in 1992, citing Hooker's recording of the song with blues rock band Canned Heat on the 1971 album *Hooker 'n Heat*, which was released just two years before "La Grange," as the closest version to ZZ Top's later song. Hooker, who no longer had any ownership of the song, was not involved in the lawsuit and publicly supported ZZ Top as part of the blues tradition. In response, ZZ Top's legal team acknowledged the influence of "Boogie Chillen'" on the band's hit song but noted that they believed the song was in the public domain because Besman did not properly file a copyright registration for the work when it was first released (incidentally, later that year ZZ Top sued car manufacturer Mitsubishi for using a knock-off version of "La Grange" in television commercials without compensating ZZ Top). Though the verdict in the "Boogie Chillen'" suit was in ZZ Top's favor (and the US Supreme Court declined to hear the case), the affair ended with a confidential settlement in October 1997. The case ended up triggering a revision of US copyright law that passed Congress with bipartisan support the following month to protect earlier recordings that may not have been properly copyrighted.

As one of the most successful rock bands in American history, ZZ Top is no stranger to similar cases of disputed writing credits, and these issues mostly stem from the group's earliest albums. Ham released a self-penned doo-wop single "Dream On" under the name Bill Ham and The Van Dels in 1958 for Dot Records, and he is credited for cowriting half of the songs on both *ZZ Top's First Album* and *Rio Grande Mud*, though he never received another writing credit on any of the band's studio albums for the rest of his tenure as their manager and producer. From *Fandango!* through *Recycler*, nearly all the group's songs (apart from covers) were credited to Gibbons-Hill-Beard, in that nonalphabetic order.

While many have questioned why Gibbons received writing credit for "Francine" on *Rio Grande Mud*, the band's first single to chart, because the ZZ Top recording is so substantially similar to the original demo recording by the Children, much more egregious is ZZ Top's handling of the song "Thunderbird." ZZ Top had been performing the boogie song "Thunderbird," frequently as a set opener, as early as 1971 (for example, it is the first song performed in one of the earliest-known live recordings of the group from a 1971 show in Pensacola, Florida). However, it was not released on a ZZ Top album until *Fandango!*, where it serves as the opening track on the live side of the album. On the album, "Thunderbird" is credited to Gibbons-Hill-Beard, the band's standard songwriting credit. However, the song was not composed by ZZ Top. It had been written and recorded by a Texas group called the Nightcaps and released as a single in 1960, before Gibbons had even learned how to play guitar. The song became popular in Dallas in the early 1960s, and the band was revered in the local scene, even inspiring the name of the Texas-based blues rock band the Fabulous Thunderbirds. However, the Nightcaps never registered for a copyright for the song. Fifteen years after it had been originally released, ZZ Top copyrighted the song with Gibbons-Hill-Beard listed as the songwriters, despite their version of the song being virtually lyrically and musically identical to the Nightcaps' version. Though the Nightcaps sued ZZ Top for claiming the song outright in 1992, there was little that they could do from a legal standpoint. The case was ultimately dismissed in 1995 because the statute of limitations had long expired, giving ZZ Top a legal victory but certainly not much of a moral leg to stand on. ZZ Top has continued to periodically perform the song live throughout their career, including for the 2022 album *Raw*, the soundtrack of the band's documentary *ZZ Top: That Little Ol' Band from Texas*, where it remains credited to Gibbons-Hill-Beard.

There are stories on internet message boards regarding other songs that ZZ Top recorded in the early 1970s that may have originated with outside writers. Evidence for these claims ranges from scant to compelling, but it is difficult to determine what may be the truth with any certainty all these decades later, as many of the principals involved have either passed or are relying on recollections from fifty years ago. Other ZZ Top songs have obvious influences; for example, "Beer Drinkers and Hell Raisers" from *Tres Hombres* is very similar to R&B singer Robert Parker's 1966 single "Barefootin'," a song ZZ Top would later cover in concert on occasion—but they are different enough to escape all but minor criticism.

Hudson, however, had registered a copyright for the song "Thug," which he says that he initially recorded as a demo himself when he realized that Gibbons had taken an interest in the song. According to Hudson, he was taken completely off guard when he discovered that the song was rerecorded and included on *Eliminator*. He told Beard that he intended to sue the band for copyright infringement, which led to Hudson moving out of Beard's home.

In 1986, Hudson received a settlement of $600,000 for "Thug," but the credits were never altered on the album to acknowledge his contribution. *Texas Monthly* also reported that his attorney and publisher took two-thirds of the settlement. Hudson says it is the only money he has earned for his work on *Eliminator*.

Hudson's possession of the copyright for "Thug" is clear evidence that the Gibbons-Hill-Beard credit that ZZ Top used for much of their career was bunk in at least some instances, and it is generally acknowledged that the members of ZZ Top had an agreement during this period to share credit for all songs on their albums as a matter of long-standing policy in a similar arrangement to Lennon-McCartney or Jagger-Richards. That obviously would not excuse the band for not crediting Hudson at all in any form on *Eliminator* but may suggest why so much of this information has been ignored, glossed over, or (as some have argued) suppressed by the band over the decades. The fact that Gibbons eventually acknowledged Hudson's involvement in retrospective interviews (though remained completely vague about the specifics of his contributions) gives further credibility to Hudson's crucial role in the development of *Eliminator*.

Yet that continues to raise questions. Is it possible that Gibbons did not view Hudson's contributions to the songs, outside "Thug," as songwriting? After all, not all musicians present at the time of the development of a song are determined to be songwriters. Or did Gibbons, in his desire to continue fostering the "same three guys, same three chords" image of ZZ Top, choose to willfully ignore Hudson's contributions to the degree that the released album makes no mention of him? Or was the decision to deny credit to Hudson up to Ham and out of the band's hands? Others who have worked with the band have generally accepted their contributions will not be credited or acknowledged, but few have claimed to have had a hand in developing over half the songs on a particular album, let alone one that has sold over ten million copies in the United States alone.

But the story behind Hudson's involvement in the creation of *Eliminator* is just one of the album's major mysteries. Obviously, any listener could tell you that the album's musician credits—simply listed as Billy Gibbons on guitar and vocals, Dusty Hill on bass and vocals, and Frank Beard on drums—are absurdly wrong based on all the extra instrumentation heard on the album (Gibbons would later remark that Ham decided to keep the credits succinct). For one, there is no mention of synthesizers anywhere in the credits despite their unmistakable presence. Long before the Hudson stories came to light, ZZ Top faced criticism from purists for the substantial change in their sound, particularly the heavy use of synthesizers, on *Eliminator*, given that the band once prided themselves on doing it all with just three instruments on stage. Gibbons has generally been dismissive of such criticism, noting that pop music naturally evolves.

Unsurprisingly, the band members are often as vague about recording the album as they have been about writing it. In a March 2023 interview on Redbeard's *In the Studio* radio program, Gibbons and Beard were asked why they thought *Eliminator* was so successful compared to their previous albums. Beard answered with a detailed explanation of how the band experimented with new sounds, creating a blueprint for Gibbons to expand upon, but followed it up with, "Then again, that all could be bullshit," while laughing.[3]

That kind of response harkens back to the band's irreverent MTV interviews during the height of their popularity—answers that entertain but don't actually address the question. In other instances, Gibbons or Hill have spoken about recording *Eliminator* together all in the same room because they didn't like recording separately on *Degüello* and *El Loco*. But that is also misleading, as the trio obviously couldn't have possibly recorded the songs live with all the obvious overdubs and extra electronic instrumentation. Some fans have even speculated that Hill's bass and Beard's drumming are not on the album at all.

Whether there are other contributions by either Hill or Beard on the final album is subject to endless debate and speculation, with former ZZ Top organization member David Blayney writing in his 1994 book *Sharp-Dressed Men: ZZ Top Behind the Scenes from Blues to Boogie to Beards* that Beard was initially upset when he instantly realized that he was not drumming on the opening bars of "Gimme All Your Lovin'." That would suggest that Beard played enough at Ardent Studios to believe that he had recorded most of the album, however, before being replaced by a drum machine.

Most commentators have determined that the released version of *Eliminator* was primarily recorded by Gibbons and Manning, with backing vocals by session singer and future Survivor lead singer Jimi Jamison. Jamison would continue singing background vocals for the band on the next two albums, *Afterburner* and *Recycler*, and up to his death in 2014, Jamison's media releases would tout that Gibbons once referred to him as "the fourth member of ZZ Top" for his essential background vocal contributions to their biggest hits. In addition, Hill sang lead vocals on one song, "I Got the Six." Tellingly, Beard and Hill were not present for most of the recording sessions in Memphis, and Manning has shared that he recorded parts of the album, including nearly all of "Legs," on his own at his home studio.

Despite its substantial long-term sales, *Eliminator* was not a smashing success out of the gate, but the album had (no pun intended) legs. It's worth noting that despite its massive sales success, *Eliminator* peaked on the *Billboard* 200 at number nine—one spot behind the peak position of *Tres Hombres*. However, whereas *Tres Hombres* spent a still-impressive 81 weeks on the *Billboard* Top 200, *Eliminator* spent 185 weeks and didn't hit its chart peak until November 1983, more than six months after it was released. *Rolling Stone* reported that in February 1984, almost a year after the album was released, *Eliminator* was still selling more than one hundred thousand units a week. In fact, "Legs" was not issued as a single until May 1984 and became the band's biggest chart hit after the conclusion of the Eliminator Tour and during the time the band was working on their next album. The album has kept on selling ever since. "They picked up on synth-rock and new wave at exactly the right time, and of course turned out to be an unlikely perfect match for MTV," notes Matthew Wilkening of *Ultimate Classic Rock*. "As the decades have rolled on though, the most impressive thing about *Eliminator* is its re-listenability. Every song is composed and arranged so perfectly, with Gibbons's extensive soloing serving like a second or third lead singer." The sales of *Eliminator* tower over the band's catalog—of the more than twenty-five million albums ZZ Top has sold in the United States, roughly half are copies of *Eliminator*.

Eliminator was not just a smash success in the United States; it became a worldwide phenomenon after hitting the Top 10 in several countries from Australia to Holland, including reaching number two in Canada and number three in the United Kingdom. The album has periodically reentered album charts all over the world. For example, in February 2023, just weeks before the album's fortieth anniversary, *Eliminator* reached number seventeen on the album chart in Hungary.

Regardless of who played what on the album, the trio needed to figure out exactly how they would perform these new songs live when the Eliminator Tour started on May 6, 1983, at the Hirsch Memorial Coliseum in Shreveport, just four months after the conclusion of the El Loco-Motion Tour. Manning even accompanied the band on tour to assist with the syncing of the live performances with the backing tracks. Regardless of how much he played on the actual record, it was up to Beard to keep the band on the beat during live performances.

Some of the backing tracks that the band used were recordings of Jamison's backing vocals, which the band continued to use long after the Eliminator Tour. In a 2012 interview with *Popdose*, Jamison remembered visiting the band backstage at a concert and having an awkward moment with Ham about the use of his vocals.

> *I remember walking into the Mid-South Coliseum one time, and they didn't know I was coming to the show. I walked in and here's Bill Ham, the manager, and Billy, and Bill goes, "Uh Jimi, you know we use your background*

vocals as backing tracks live. We just wanted to let you know that." He
thought I was going to sue them or something, and I said, "Hey, that's cool,
man—that's fine," and he breathed a sigh of relief because he didn't know
what was going to happen because he never told me that they were going to
do that, but I didn't mind them doing it at all.[4]

Naturally, the supporting tour for *Eliminator*, the album that redefined the group's sound and won them heaps of new fans, featured a heavy helping of new material. Every song on the album, except "Thug," "Dirty Dog," and "If I Could Only Flag Her Down," would make the set lists during the tour, but the band wisely included songs dating back to *Rio Grande Mud*, showcasing their back catalog. In addition to playing tour dates, ZZ Top also promoted the album with explosive live performances on television in Europe, including energetic renditions of "Got Me Under Pressure," "Gimme All Your Lovin'," "Sharp Dressed Man," and "Tube Snake Boogie," as well as a mini-set of pre-*Eliminator* classics on April 16, 1984, for a broadcast on Swedish national television.

While the band faced some criticism for adopting synthesizers in their music, it is hard to argue with that massive success. "They made a lot of money—and that's one thing, when people criticize them about using machines or sequencers," said Joe Hardy, an Ardent Studios engineer who worked with ZZ Top and Gibbons for decades. "They did a lot of great stuff before *Eliminator*, [but] *Eliminator* made them billionaires, so you can't argue with the money—because people vote with their dollars, about what they like. They won big on that record."[5]

In the face of the criticism, Gibbons has been unapologetic about his efforts to keep pushing ZZ Top into new territory throughout the band's career, citing examples of Muddy Waters and Bob Dylan shifting from acoustic to electric guitars and Jimi Hendrix's experimental sonic innovations. He has also frequently noted that the Grand Ole Opry originally did not allow drums but gradually accepted the instrument in country music starting in the 1940s (incidentally, Gibbons was the subject of a tribute night at the Grand Ole Opry in May 2021, featuring artists like Eric Church, Jimmie Vaughan, Lucinda Williams, and Larkin Poe, as well as his occasional collaborators Martin Guigui and Tim Montana). As popular music evolved, Gibbons was determined to have ZZ Top evolve with it. Manning points out,

When you talk about fans saying, "Oh gosh, they went from a three-piece blues band to Eliminator, *what happened?" Well, the Beatles went from "Please Please Me" to "I Am the Walrus" in a few years. It is crazy how the Beatles progressed. You take an artist like Madonna; she's certainly progressed in all sorts of ways over her career to do whatever it takes new to keep her career going. If they had stayed only a three-piece blues band, it would've been great and all the early fans would've loved it, but they never would've brought on millions of new fans. I don't for a minute regret progressing on that. We never thought about doing anything other than a core of the Texas blues sound or feel on the album. Maybe not every song would have it, but it would have to be something because you don't want to give away where you came from.*

Manning remains extremely proud of the success of *Eliminator*.

When you work on thousands and thousands of albums over your career, you start being able to tell things. Of course, you don't go to work unless you think you're doing something really good. Otherwise, why are you there? Why are you working on it if you don't love it and think that it is really going to do something? That's what we always did, but there are those very times when something just hits you and you kind of get a chill and you just know, wow, this is something super special and there's no doubt that this is going all the way. Certainly, on Eliminator, *and particularly on "Sharp Dressed Man," when we first recorded that, and that guitar sound and drumbeat came out, I just knew. There was that chill. Nothing could stop this, and it didn't.*

While Gibbons fully intended for ZZ Top to make a contemporary-sounding album with *Eliminator,* the band wasn't necessarily expecting to become music video stars. MTV was still in its infancy, and the promotional potential of the music video was still largely untapped. Jeff Ayeroff, senior vice president of Warner Bros. Records, had recently been put in charge of marketing for several artists, which included the creation of music videos. Ayeroff felt that ZZ Top, with their unique look, could make for an interesting video. However, Ham was skeptical because he had built their career on the idea of not overexposing them to avoid their becoming yet another rock band featured in magazines and tabloids and forgotten the following month.

Yet Ham still realized the selling power that MTV brought to the industry. Manning remembers,

I remember Bill Ham saying, "We got this new MTV thing, we've got to have videos and they've got to really knock people out." Whoever said, "Let's get Tim Newman," was brilliant because he had been doing commercials before then. I think Billy had seen a few of his commercials and was impressed. Bill and Billy wanted something visual. ZZ Top had always had a lot of humor in their songs. The song lyrics are often very humorous, and even musically with lots of stops and changes all out of nowhere. Billy is such a funny guy and is so intelligent and philosophical. He's such a brilliant guy and his humor—he's always being Reverend Willy G and having barbeque sauces or creating recordings of funny things. It's fun. Life is fun, and he's having it. They wanted to translate that into videos, and Tim Newman was just the perfect director to do that.

Newman, the son of famed Oscar-winning Hollywood composer Alfred Newman and part of the Newman entertainment family (Tim is cousins with another Oscar-winning composer and songwriter, Randy Newman), and the band conceived of a video that would feature ZZ Top as background characters in their own video for the first single, "Gimme All Your Lovin'," which helped relieve the idea of potentially overexposing the band.

Instead of the band, the music video stars three beautiful models driving the Eliminator coupe, which stops on a sweltering day at a remote gas station where a young man, played by actor and dancer Peter Tramm, is working as a pump jockey. He is mesmerized by the flirtatious women, and the three members of ZZ Top periodically appear in the video as something like spiritual guides, fading in and out and observing the proceedings. The trio toss the key to the Eliminator (with a ZZ Top–branded key chain, which would become one of the band's trademark pieces of merchandise) to the young man, who is taken for the ride of his life by the three women.

The "Gimme All Your Lovin'" video was shot at the Super Store 6, a gas station located north of Los Angeles in Palmdale, California, featured in numerous film and television shoots, including the blockbuster 1984 film *The Terminator*. ZZ Top wore coordinating outfits (leather jackets, white T-shirts, blue jeans, boots, and large sunglasses, with both Gibbons and Hill sporting fedoras); in addition to observing the proceedings and making a variety of coordinated hand gestures (a suggestion from Beard, who felt they were instructed to do too much standing around), they are shown performing the song at the gas station. For some visual distinction, Gibbons and Hill play unique guitars without headstocks. The music video, an obvious male fantasy, was a smash hit on MTV. The music video also revealed the true worth of Gibbons and Hill's long beards, trademark sunglasses, and coordinating fashion choices—the look hid the band's ages behind their rock-and-roll caricatures. In their mid-thirties by the release of *Eliminator*, the members of ZZ

Top were at least a decade older than most of the contemporary music video stars.

After the immediate popularity of "Gimme All Your Lovin'" on MTV, ZZ Top and Newman created a video for "Sharp Dressed Man," which is generally considered to be the first music video to be a direct sequel to a previous video. Shot at night, which immediately contrasts it with the previous video, the "Sharp Dressed Man" video again stars Tramm, who is now a well-dressed parking valet at what appears to be a Hollywood club. Once again, the three Eliminator girls show up, as well as ZZ Top, who slide the Eliminator key to the young man. He again drives off with the women. When they return, presumably after an extremely memorable night, the young man is now truly sharp dressed in a well-tailored white suit, and a fourth woman, whom he made eyes at earlier that evening as she emerged from her car, grabs him and starts dancing aggressively with him. ZZ Top is revealed to be the band performing at the club, and Gibbons and Hill demonstrate some impressive dance moves of their own as they play the song.

The "Sharp Dressed Man" video was voted the best music video of 1983, and ZZ Top was honored as the year's Video Vote Champion by *Friday Night Videos* viewers who called a 1-900 number to cast their votes (a year later, in November 1984, the group appeared on the series to promote that year's voting for the Video Vote Champion in a vignette that depicted Gibbons, Hill, and Beard as the crew of Apollo 11).

The third *Eliminator* music video was made for the more offbeat song "TV Dinners." Though originally titled "Troubles," "TV Dinners" received a new set of lyrics after Gibbons spotted a woman in a nightclub in Memphis wearing a white jumpsuit with the words "TV Dinners" on the back. The song, a peculiar ode to microwavable food, was different enough in content from "Gimme All Your Lovin'" and "Sharp Dressed Man" to warrant a unique approach to its music video.

The "TV Dinners" music video was directed by Marius Penczner, a musician turned filmmaker who had developed a working relationship with Ardent Studios as a keyboardist for bands like Target, Ruby Starr & Grey Ghost, and Black Oak Arkansas. Ardent founder and owner John Fry contacted Penczner in 1982 with the idea that Ardent could expand its operations with a fully equipped video production studio to service the rapidly expanding appetite for music videos. "In doing so, Ardent could offer clients, particularly those interested in getting exposure on MTV or eventually VH-1, a more cost-efficient option of one-stop audio/video shopping," recalls Penczner. "Given that I had just won an Emmy for a short film I directed as well as having a music artist background, Fry offered me a position in Ardent's new film and TV division since he thought I was a natural fit."

Since Ardent had a nearly decade-long working relationship with ZZ Top, Fry reached out to Bill Ham to pitch Ardent's new video production services for producing a music video for ZZ Top. Penczner recalls,

> Warner Bros. and ZZ Top had just wrapped a terrific intro video for "Gimme All Your Lovin'" directed by Tim Newman. And "Sharp Dressed Man" and "Legs" seemed like natural follow-ups for Newman given the beautiful women, hot rod, disappearing ZZ thematic he had established. But Ham told Fry the band might, just might, be interested in working with us if we could come up with something creative and quirky for a track called "TV Dinners." That was if, and it was a big if, at the time, we could develop a concept that management and the band liked.

A complication that Penczner faced was that the band had already embarked on the Eliminator Tour and would only be available for filming for a short period during the soundcheck of their May 13, 1983, concert at the Mid-South Coliseum in Memphis. Penczner remembers,

The challenge for me was coming up with a concept within that framework that we could pull off on a small budget as well as do most of the production and post in-house. To differentiate us visually, my preference was for a darker, more urban futuristic look along the lines of the films The Thing *and* Blade Runner, *both released the year before. The action would take place in a high-tech—for the eighties—remote outpost during a storm. Inside, along with the kind of grungy dining and recreation area you'd expect to find in a place like that, this single location would also contain a master computer console and, more importantly, a large bank of surveillance monitors and regular TVs which we could use to showcase the band.*

To link the "TV Dinners" music video to the previous *Eliminator* music videos, the production team created a custom *Eliminator* driving arcade game, and the video also included an appearance by ZZ Top's now famous key chain.

The music video's principal visual effect was the inclusion of a stop-motion monster that emerges from a microwaved TV dinner. "The last piece was finding a storyline hook that could generate some dramatic tension for the outpost guy to deal with while keeping the TV dinners theme," recalls Penczner.

To solve that, I worked in an exchange between our hero and a tiny gremlin hiding in the dinner tray. Fortunately, I was in the process of wrapping visual effects on an independent feature film I directed called I Was a Zombie for the FBI, *which would later appear on the USA Network. In that film we had a stop-motion monster, we called ZBeast, which was animated by a very talented friend of mine named Bob Friedstand who had been on the visual effects teams of movies like* Star Trek: The Motion Picture. *Since Bob still had the ZBeast armature, he agreed to animate the model for the "TV Dinners" special effects shots.*

The stop-motion beast was an immediate hit with ZZ Top. "Once the band, and especially Billy Gibbons, saw the test footage of the monster, the band and management signed off on the visual effects and greenlit the production," says Penczner.

The production team shot footage of ZZ Top performing the song during the soundcheck at the Mid-South Coliseum, for which the band chose to wear light-blue jumpsuits. The production crew also filmed ads for an upcoming Schlitz Rocks America TV commercial campaign promoting the Eliminator Tour, which is why the band is wearing the same clothing in both the "TV Dinners" music video and the ad campaign.

ZZ Top's promotional partnership with Schlitz caused an issue with MTV when the beer was included in the first cut of the "TV Dinners" music video. "Coincidentally, since late-night TV dinners with a beer on the side seemed to naturally go together, one of the props used on the Ouija board dinner tray that the art director gave the outpost guy was a can of Schlitz," reveals Penczner. "However, given how new the music video format was at the time, we weren't fully conscious about how serious concern over product logos might be until MTV's legal department flagged the beer shots. Fortunately, the editor was able to mask the logos with a green 'radioactive' glow enough to satisfy the lawyers and get approval." Similarly, Newman was angered when the band's management asked him to include a shot of Schlitz products in the "Sharp Dressed Man" music video that also had to be edited out when MTV would not allow the product placement to air (the network apparently did not have an issue with the prominent placement of the Coca-Cola vending machine in the "Gimme All Your Lovin'" music video, however).

The "TV Dinners" music video was another hit for ZZ Top and received substantial airplay on MTV. "One thing I've always admired about ZZ Top, and Billy Gibbons in particular, is that they have never been afraid to take creative chances," adds Penczner. "In this case, 'TV Dinners' opened the door to the more than sixty music videos I directed for various artists afterward, so I will always be grateful to Billy and the ZZ Top family for taking a chance on the video and me."

Though the "TV Dinners" music video was unique in its creativity and sense of surrealism, the final music video ZZ Top produced for *Eliminator* was "Legs," which reunited the band with Newman in early 1984, almost a year after the album was released. The band's bigger video hits were clearly "Gimme All Your Lovin'" and "Sharp Dressed Man" (it likely didn't help its cause that the "TV Dinners" single didn't chart on the *Billboard* 200). The "Legs" video features the Eliminator coupe and three models coming to the rescue of a timid, picked-on diner waitress, helping her get revenge on a cast of various people who torment her during her workday and giving her a stunning makeover that allows her to impressively strut her stuff and walk off with the only person who seems kind to her, the hamburger cook at the restaurant. Yet again, the band members themselves are background characters in the video, with a few shots of ZZ Top performing the song and additional shots of them reacting to the proceedings in the video, including plenty of new hand signals. The music video was shot at the Old Orchard Shopping Center in Valencia, California, and the set designers dressed up numerous local businesses with mock signage.

The "Legs" music video would ultimately become the most iconic of the four videos because of a new contraption that soon became another one of the band's most identifiable gimmicks: the spinning, fuzzy-fur custom Dean guitars that would become yet another visual trademark of the group. The guitars were created with sheepskin that Gibbons had purchased when the band was in Scotland in November 1983 on the Eliminator Tour. The spinning apparatus was based on a device designed by Gibbons's former Moving Sidewalks bandmate, Don Summers, who used it in the late 1960s with his bass as a stage effect, most notably at the infamous concerts that the Moving Sidewalks opened for the Doors.

The four creative music videos for *Eliminator* ensured that ZZ Top was a constant presence on MTV, which prolonged the number of weeks that the album and singles stayed on the charts. The channel recognized the band's unlikely yet tremendous popularity, and ZZ Top was one of only six live performances during the first-ever MTV Video Music Awards ceremony at New York City's Radio City Music Hall on September 14, 1984. The audience, including the band members' mothers, who came as their guests, all donned fake beards as the band performed "Sharp Dressed Man." ZZ Top also walked away with two awards, one for Best Group Video for "Legs" (ZZ Top was also nominated for "Sharp Dressed Man" in the same category) and another for Best Direction in a Video, which was presented to Tim Newman for "Sharp Dressed Man" ("Gimme All Your Lovin'" was also nominated in the same category).

What's most fascinating about the success of *Eliminator* is how much of a slow build it was. The band's enthusiastically received MTV Video Music Awards performance came eighteen months after the release of the album and seven months after the Eliminator Tour had ended in February 1984. In the summer of 1984, "Legs" even reached number thirteen on the *Billboard* Dance Club Songs chart, finally giving Gibbons the dance hit he craved when he was inspired to create *Eliminator*. This incredible run not only amounted to nearly two years of success for just one album but also set ZZ Top up to take time to determine their next move. Few artists have ever undergone such a significant change to their sound as ZZ Top did with *Eliminator*, and even fewer have had the explosive chart success of *Eliminator*.

10
BLASTING OFF

Billy Gibbons and Bill Ham decided the right move was to lean even more into the digital experimentation that had boosted the popularity of *Eliminator* with the follow-up album *Afterburner*. With the opening synthesized sonic blast of the album's first single and opening track, "Sleeping Bag," *Afterburner* signaled that ZZ Top was fully embracing the digital transformation the band had begun with *Eliminator*. The cover art highlighted this as well, with the Eliminator coupe now depicted as a shuttle circling the Earth with Billy Gibbons, Dusty Hill, and Frank Beard looking on, each as a nebula floating in space on the back of the album. The trio had rocketed quite far from the plains of Texas.

For the first time since *Tres Hombres*, however, Terry Manning was not along for the ride. He recalls,

> *I had several big projects I was producing, and I had moved to England with a whole year of things booked for me. Bill Ham came in and said, "We got to do this now!" and I said, "Bill, I just can't. I'm committed. If you can wait, I'll be happy and would love to do it because I love them." But Bill was so jumpy, and he went ahead and did things. Now we had some things pre-done that we recorded for* Eliminator *that we didn't use, part of "Can't Stop Rockin'" and maybe another song or two. I think they took some of that and went ahead and redid things or whatever for* Afterburner.

Stepping into the primary engineering role vacated by Manning was Joe Hardy, a longtime staff member of Ardent Studios. He would later recall working on much of the album without Ham's involvement or even notice, though, as was typical for ZZ Top's 1970s and 1980s albums, Ham is credited as the album's producer. "I wouldn't say that we defied Bill," Hardy said. "We just went behind his back and did stuff. When I did *Afterburner*, we had all of the rhythm tracks and all of the bass tracks done in Houston on a Fairlight. . . . He never said, 'Who did the drums, where did they come from? Where did you record them? Why wasn't I there?' It was just very strange."[1]

Hardy would continue as Gibbons's engineer of choice on all subsequent ZZ Top albums—except for 1990's *Recycler*, which featured the return of Terry Manning—as well as Gibbons's first two solo albums, up until Hardy died in 2019. Hardy also played piano on ZZ Top's *La Futura*, various instruments on Gibbons's *Perfectamundo*, and bass on Gibbons's *The Big Bad Blues* (he likely performed bass and other instruments on various ZZ Top recordings as well).

Once again, the album's credits gave no indication that synthesizers or keyboards were used in its production, though much of the bass and drum tracks were performed on a Fairlight CMI, according to Hardy.

While often thought of as a direct sequel to the *Eliminator* sound, *Afterburner* incorporates far more studio technology than its predecessor, including an even heavier reliance on keyboards and synthesizers, producing an overall more pop sound than *Eliminator*, with all the bells, beeps, and whistles that encapsulated pop hits in 1985. And yet, the album is so much more complex, with songs like "Delirious" utilizing so many studio sonic tricks in the groove that it's something of an art unto itself.

As part of that approach, *Afterburner* also fully embraced sampling, or the reusing of a sound recording in another recording, a common practice in hip-hop and rap but not in mainstream rock music of the 1980s. ZZ Top used samples on *Afterburner* to achieve the album's drum sound, though of course all drums were credited to Beard. One of the bands that Gibbons sampled was Ministry, a Chicago-based band founded by multi-instrumentalist Al Jourgensen in 1981. Though Ministry and Jourgensen would later be recognized as a pioneering force in industrial metal, the band's 1983 debut album *With Sympathy* had a synth-pop sound that had evolved into a harder industrial sound by the group's second album, 1986's *Twitch*, and an even more aggressive sound on the following album, 1988's *The Land of Rape and Honey*. Ministry performed at a Houston club named Numbers on January 24 and 25, 1990, and Jourgensen was paid a visit by Gibbons, who felt he had a score to settle with him. Jourgensen remembers,

> *That was amazing. First of all, I was already a superfan, obviously. The first ZZ Top record I heard was* Rio Grande Mud, *and I went back and bought the first one. By the time* Tres Hombres *came out, I was hooked for life, man. That was it! The best boogie band in the universe, as far as I'm concerned. The owner of this club in Houston, which was called Numbers, came up to me at soundcheck and says, "Billy Gibbons wants to take you out to dinner." I thought it was some kind of practical joke. But sure enough, soundcheck is over and he shows up in a white suit with a driver and what I believe was a 1934 Merc—just a sharp-dressed man, if you know what I mean!*

Naturally, Jourgensen accepted the offer even if he wasn't sure why it was being extended. "So he takes me and my guitar player, the late, great, Mike Scaccia, to this Italian place," he continues. "I didn't know what to say, so when we got there, I said, 'Billy, I don't mean to be rude, but why are we here?' He just matter-of-factly says, 'Well, I owe you one, man. You resurrected my career.' He said he had sampled all of my drum samples from Ministry and put them on ZZ Top records."

Far from upset with Gibbons, Jourgensen was amused by a tremendous irony that the ZZ Top guitarist was unaware of.

I said, "That's pretty funny man, because we sampled you to get the Min-istry sound—so you just sampled yourself back!" I'm sure he heard it and something sparked recognition in him and he said, "I'm taking that," even though it was his to start with! But the coolest part about it was instead of having to go through lawyers, he figured he just owed me dinner. We were having dinner, and I just couldn't fucking believe he was wearing a white suit with that big-ass beard and not a speck of spaghetti sauce was on there, while Mikey and I are chowing down and covered in food. I was like, this guy is dapper, man! Ever since then, we've been close buddies.

In light of all the new approaches to creating the sound of *Afterburner*, there also seems to have been a conscious effort to create lyrical spiritual sequels to some of the songs on *Eliminator*, with "Woke Up with Wood" and "Planet of Women" out to cover the "I Got the Six" sleaziness and a now obligatory song in praise of an inanimate object, "Velcro Fly." And yet there are also obviously more tender songs as well, including two of the singles, "Stages" and "Rough Boy," the latter becoming the group's most successful ballad and the closest thing they ever did to the then in vogue "power ballad." However, parts of the album did veer too closely to rehashing the *Eliminator* sound—for example, "Dipping Low (In the Lap of Luxury)" borrows liber-ally from "Gimme All Your Lovin'," which might explain why the song was buried in the back half of the album.

The album's space-age concept was inspired, in part, by Ty Reveen, an illusionist, hypnotist, and internationally renowned stage and special effects creator for live entertainment who was responsible for designing and creating the innovative stage effects for the Afterburner World Tour. Reveen is the son of groundbreaking Australian-born, Canada-based hypnotist and illu-sionist Peter Reveen, known as Reveen the Impossiblist, an award-winning and world-renowned performer who, in addition to his own tremendous popularity, helped establish Las Vegas as the premier locale for magicians and illusionists to perform; he managed the career of Lance Burton, a stage magician who became a Vegas institution and was so popular that he signed a thirteen-year contract with the Monte Carlo resort in 1994, the longest contract ever given to a Las Vegas performer up until that point. Ty Reveen and his brothers were introduced to the world of live entertainment at a very young age as part of Reveen the Impossiblist's stage show.

"At the time I met ZZ Top, my father was the number one theater performer coast to coast in Canada," says Reveen. "I grew up on the road of his traveling show with my brothers. All four of us traveled with the show for most of our lives, and I was always in the center of the magic community because my father was an illusionist and hypnotist."

Observing the increasing spectacles of rock concerts, the younger Reveen saw an opportunity to utilize his experience in illusions to enhance rock concerts. He explains,

> *After touring with my father professionally since the age of twelve, and at that time he had hypnotized so many tens of thousands of people and played to millions of people across Canada and the United States and about nine different countries that we toured, in 1984 I noticed that all these professional musicians like Earth, Wind & Fire, Alice Cooper, and Michael Jackson were starting to hire magicians to come up with ideas to make their rock shows more spectacular. I told my father I wanted to take some time off and dedicate some time to being involved with the development of rock shows.*

He initially approached Loverboy, a Canadian rock band with five Top 40 hits in the United States by 1984, at an afterparty following one of their shows. "I was telling the guys that I was retiring from my dad's show and was going to Vegas to start coming up with ideas for rock shows and that I think I could make their show a lot more exciting," recalls Reveen, then adding with a laugh, "They were feeling pretty good at the time," and the band asked him to pitch ideas for their show.

At the time, Loverboy was working on their fourth album, *Lovin' Every Minute of It*, which would be released in August 1985. The title track features lyrics about a rocket in space, which Reveen took inspiration from for his design. "I thought, 'Okay, rocket ship,'" recalls Reveen. "I went out and bought a dashboard of the space shuttle and I thought that would look pretty cool." Reveen designed a stage production for Loverboy that involved the dashboard of a rocket ship, but the band's production team never called him back. When he finally got in touch with representatives of the band, they said that they were working with a team out of Hollywood for Loverboy's next concert tour.

However, Reveen was undeterred.

> *I knew I was sitting on a really hot idea because it was a giant dashboard of a rocket ship that spanned forty feet wide, and the idea was to take the audience on a trip into outer space as they sat in the arena. Then I was making some stuff for Lance Burton, who ended up having a huge show in Las Vegas at the Monte Carlo, and he was having a party at his house. When I came over he said, "Hey, Billy Gibbons is here. Do you want to meet him?" I said, "ZZ Top Billy Gibbons? Are you kidding me, is he here?" So, I walk into this room in a pretty little house, and I said, "Billy, I am your biggest fan, I absolutely love your music, you're the first concert I ever saw when I moved here from Australia. I'm pleased to meet you, and I want you to know that I'm the greatest designer for magic and special effects for rock shows."*

Reveen adds, "It just came out of my mouth." Noting his connections to the live entertainment scene in Las Vegas, Reveen invited Gibbons to see shows throughout the city the next day to demonstrate possibilities for ZZ Top's next tour. "I met him at two o'clock the next day, knocked on the door, and the first thing he did was hand me one of those ZZ Top keychains."

After speaking with Gibbons about his family's background in magic and live entertainment and showing him around Las Vegas, Reveen intrigued Gibbons by sharing his keen understanding of the realities of transporting stage effects from city to city, night after night. "I explained to him that your show has to be put together fast, it's got to tear down fast, and it's got to require as few people as possible," recalls Reveen. "He really had an appreciation for my understanding of logistics."

At that point, Reveen wanted to pitch Gibbons a concept for ZZ Top's next tour. "I asked him, 'What is your album about, and what do you have in mind?' And he said, 'Well, we don't have a theme for the album. We're three guys, we write our music, and we try to make our show seem as spectacular as it can.'" However, Gibbons invited Reveen to come up with a concept for ZZ Top's next world tour, scheduled to launch in August 1985.

Reveen decided to adapt his concept for Loverboy into something suitable for ZZ Top. He developed an idea that the stage show would first resemble the dashboard of the Eliminator coupe (by a stroke of luck, he found a friend with a 1933 Ford that he could use as a design sample), which would turn into a spaceship deck during the concert. He created a scale model demonstrating the design and even incorporated miniature trucks to show how the stage could be transported from arena to arena. Lastly, Reveen developed an astounding effect that would serve as the standout surprise of the concert—a twenty-foot-tall skull of a longhorn bull with laser beam eyes that would be positioned above the drum riser and, seconds before the start of the concert, snort up a white sheet covering the drums as the band launched into the first song.

As ZZ Top was recording the follow-up album to *Eliminator* at Ardent Studios, Gibbons asked Reveen to come to Memphis to pitch his staging idea to himself, Ham, and J. W. Williams, the band's longtime tour manager. Reveen recalls that he was only allotted fifteen minutes for his initial presentation. Reveen brought his scale models with him and says he spent over three hours presenting his entire concept, from snorting longhorn skull to coupe dashboard to spaceship, to the group, including demonstrating how the entire stage could be transported by truck. After seemingly approving the idea, the group proposed coming back the next day to hear the pitch again with a larger group, including Gibbons and Beard. Reveen recalls,

> *Bill Ham walks in and he seemed kind of agitated and says, "You know, this all looks very colorful, and it looks good on the model. But we're the little ol' band from Texas. What does going into outer space have to do with our band?" And I said, "Are you kidding me? Your home base is Houston, the place of the world's biggest space station. You guys have more territorial rights to outer space than anybody! You could take it so far by putting all kinds of outer space stuff in your videos." They all kind of jumped up, and I could see they were trying not to high-five and hug each other. So that was another meeting that was supposed to be fifteen minutes that went into three hours. Billy told me later that in the fifteen years of ZZ Top, I presented the most impressive and detailed presentation they'd ever seen.*

Shortly afterward, the band and management approved the concept, and the stage was built by FM Productions, a San Francisco live concert production company founded by legendary promoter Bill Graham.

Ultimately, the snorting longhorn skull evolved into a snorting Tutankhamun head to tie into the Egyptian references in the lyrics of "Sleeping Bag" and the visual presented in that song's music video (though Reveen noted it might have been viewed as a rip-off of Iron Maiden's elaborate Egyptian-influenced production on their 1984 World Slavery Tour, and later KISS would utilize a similar Sphynx head as part of the production of their 1990 Hot in the Shade Tour). Otherwise much of Reveen's spectacular staging ideas remained intact. His space-themed concepts influenced the artwork of *Afterburner*, the space-age music videos, and even the lyrics of songs like "Planet of Women."

Because of all the audio and visual effects, the Afterburner World Tour was a heavily choreographed and programmed stage show. The tour won critical acclaim for its immersive production, and the snorting curtain in particular was widely praised. "*Rolling Stone* called it 'the greatest cocaine gag in the history of rock and roll,'" remembers Reveen. "Every time I turned on MTV and they were talking about ZZ Top, Mark Goodman said, 'Do not miss the opening of ZZ Top! It is the greatest opening of anybody in the history of rock and roll!'" Reveen was nominated as one of the top three stage designers of 1986 and 1987 by *Performance* magazine's Reader Poll Awards. Reveen also reflects on his close creative relationship with Gibbons during that period.

> We had so many talks over the months that went into this. He said, "When you first walked up to me and said that you wanted to put some magic in our shows and make them exciting because nothing is more exciting than great magic and rock and roll, I knew that we were on a path where we were going to work together. I didn't know you were going to be such a great asset." A year or so later he came to visit me in my shop, and he said, "I really thank my guardian angels that brought us together." But he was really passionate about making people enjoy his show.

Reveen, who is also the inventor of the world's first portable high-performance confetti and streamer cannons, which he created for the Afterburner World Tour, has gone on to design stage effects for musicians like Madonna, Paul McCartney, Dolly Parton, Garth Brooks, Gloria Estevan, and Miley Cyrus and for illusionists like David Copperfield and Criss Angel.

Performance magazine later cited the Afterburner World Tour as the highest-grossing world tour in both 1986 and 1987. The massive, prolonged success of *Eliminator* often obscures just how successfully *Afterburner* capitalized on the blockbuster sonic approach of its predecessor. *Afterburner* peaked at number four on the *Billboard* 200, five spots higher than *Eliminator*, and remains the highest-charting album in ZZ Top's career. It also stayed on the album chart for seventy weeks. While *Eliminator* eventually sold more than twice as many copies as *Afterburner* and "Gimme All Your Lovin'," "Sharp Dressed Man," and "Legs" remain the untouchable *Eliminator* triumvirate performed at nearly every ZZ Top concert over the past forty years, pound for pound *Afterburner* yielded more chart and radio hits. "Sleeping Bag" tied the *Billboard* Hot 100 chart peak (number eight) of "Legs," and "Stages," "Rough Boy," and "Velcro Fly" were all Top 40 singles ("Gimme All Your Lovin'" was the only other Top 40 single from *Eliminator*). "Velcro Fly" also has the distinction of being the band's final Top 40 single. Songs from *Afterburner*, including those only released as promo singles, also dominated the *Billboard* Top Rock Tracks chart: "Woke Up with Wood" (peaked at number eighteen), "Delirious" (peaked at number sixteen), "Velcro Fly" (peaked at number fifteen), "Can't Stop Rockin'" (peaked at number eight), "Rough Boy" (peaked at number five), and "Sleeping Bag" and "Stages" (both peaked at number one).

ZZ Top attempted to follow up their incredibly popular music videos from *Eliminator* with four music videos for songs from *Afterburner*. Unfortunately, Warner Bros. pulled the deal with Tim Newman to direct the "Sleeping Bag" music video, a personnel change that the band was reportedly unaware of until shortly before the video shoot. Nonetheless, the "Sleeping Bag" music video generally follows the narrative pattern established by Newman's *Eliminator* videos. It opens with a montage of a grandmother reading fairy tales to her granddaughter before bed as she gradually grows up to become a woman portrayed by actress Heather Langenkamp, best known for starring in the hit horror film *A Nightmare on Elm Street*, which had been released the previous year. She is awoken from her sleep, then subsequently robbed of a valise full of money by a pair of unscrupulous thieves. She escapes, aided by a passing bicyclist (portrayed by actor John Dye, later star of the TV series *Touched by an Angel*), and the two manage to escape when ZZ Top appear on the scene and use magic produced by their coordinated hand motions to aid the fleeing couple. However, the would-be robbers pursue the couple in the famed Bear Foot monster truck, but they are saved by three women in the Eliminator coupe. Though the Eliminator coupe is destroyed and given a proper burial by the couple, it is somehow resurrected as a space shuttle that launches from one of Egypt's pyramids and puts an end to the robbers before zooming out into space. The video is also intercut with clips of ZZ Top and the three women dancing robotically to the synthesized beats.

The "Rough Boy" music video continues where the "Sleeping Bag" video left off, with the Eliminator shuttle docking in a mothership that is more than a little reminiscent of the spaceships in *Star Wars*. The interior of the mothership reveals a host of visual effects, and the video used camera tricks to show floating disembodied body parts of the band members performing the song. The entire purpose of the docking is so the Eliminator shuttle can get washed, which is excuse enough to have numerous wet women (and a long pair of disembodied female legs) sensually clean the vehicle. The music video marked ZZ Top's sole MTV Music Video Award win in 1986 in the category of Best Art Direction in a Video. Both the "Sleeping Bag" and "Rough Boy" videos were directed by Steve Baron, an Irish-born filmmaker who had previously directed Michael Jackson's landmark "Billie Jean" music video as well as the music video for A-ha's "Take On Me," both often cited by critics as among the best music videos of the early MTV era.

The "Stages" music video is similar to the "TV Dinners" one in the sense that it is more of a performance video featuring ZZ Top on stage playing the song, which is depicted as being broadcast throughout space on satellites. Much more inventive is the music video for "Velcro Fly," which features a bevy of dancing women throughout history in various stages of undress on animated backgrounds utilizing green screen technology and stock black-and-white footage of women dancing. Then the three members of ZZ Top don't do so badly themselves as they cut a rug in a choreographed dance routine, including a unique effect in which the three band members leer at a beautiful woman by leaning over at an absurd angle without losing their footing, like cartoon characters, an effect suggested by Reveen that was achieved by bolting to the floor of the studio three sets of boots for the band members to stand in so that they would not topple over (Reveen proudly notes that the effect came several years before Michael Jackson received acclaim for a similar maneuver in his "Smooth Criminal" music video in 1988). At the end of the sequence, Gibbons, Hill, and Beard move their hands over their head in a motion reminiscent of Curly Howard of the Three Stooges—a tribute likely inspired by the fact the music video was filmed on a soundstage formerly used for filming by Curly, Larry, and Moe.

The "Velcro Fly" music video's director, Daniel Kleinman, had previously won acclaim for directing more than a dozen music videos, including the Simple Minds' "Don't You (Forget about Me)" video. He would go on to win further notice for his inventive title design sequences for various James Bond films, starting with 1995's *GoldenEye*. Another notable member of the crew for the "Velcro Fly" music video was the pre–*Forever Your Girl* Paula Abdul, who at the time was primarily known as a choreographer before launching her singing career. She was responsible for creating the hand jive "Velcro Fly" dance that the band does in the music video, as well as the more complex routines by the female dancers. Abdul later won the best choreographer award for "Velcro Fly" at the American Video Awards, a short-lived competitor of the MTV Video Music Awards, though it actually debuted a year before MTV's ceremony. When ZZ Top appeared on *American Idol* in 2008, Abdul, a judge on the show at the time, seemed particularly thrilled to see her former dance students. The song itself would get a second lease on life after it was cited as part of the "soundtrack" of popular author Stephen King's The Dark Tower book series and was even sampled in the audiobook version of *The Dark Tower III: The Waste Lands.*

Midway through the Afterburner World Tour, ZZ Top took a nineteen-day break to cross a new line by performing on network television in the United States. On May 16, 1986, ZZ Top appeared on *The Tonight Show*, the late-night television institution hosted by the iconic Johnny Carson since 1962. The show had featured the biggest names in entertainment, and even Ham, no matter how adverse he was to the band performing on American television, must have realized what it meant for the band to be invited to perform on the show.

After some praise from the legendary Carson and his surprised acknowledgment that they had never performed on a network television show before he introduced them, the band rocked into "Sharp Dressed Man." Also unique for ZZ Top, the group was accompanied by *The Tonight Show* band, the NBC Orchestra, led by jazz trumpeter Doc Severinsen, who wore a fake ZZ Top beard for the occasion. (Upon my inquiring via email if he remembered playing with ZZ Top on *The Tonight Show*, Severinsen responded, "I was glad to have that unique experience as a ZZ Top 'member.' My sex life improved immediately.") The extra instrumentation seemed to throw the group off, however. Gibbons had to re-sing the opening line after starting too early, and there appeared to be a moment of miscommunication between Gibbons and Hill after the "Sharp Dressed Man" guitar solo. However, ZZ Top and the NBC Orchestra then launched into a flawless rendition of "Tush" featuring a stellar slide solo by Gibbons (and demonstrating how good "Tush" could sound with a horn section). After the commercial break, Carson came back on wearing a fake ZZ Top beard and trucker hat himself. The message was clear: while it may have taken nearly two decades, ZZ Top fever had officially swept the nation.

Nonetheless, the nagging question about the appearance was why the band didn't perform a song from *Afterburner* or at least one of the two Top 40 singles from *Eliminator*. The likely answer is that ZZ Top would not be able to replicate its complex backing-track system for a live-to-tape television performance; this might also explain why the band had trouble getting through "Sharp Dressed Man"—and also why, in comparison, ZZ Top was able to breeze through "Tush," a song that they had performed countless times live as a trio without technological support. Regardless, the performance was proof that ZZ Top had ascended to the upper tier of American pop culture. Just six weeks later, ZZ Top, with Gibbons and Hill donning captain's hats, performed on MTV's barge in New York City's harbor during the July 4, 1986, events celebrating the one hundredth anniversary of the Statue of Liberty. Without their high-tech stage show to provide backup, the band stuck mostly to covers, but the crowd of celebrities didn't mind grooving to oldies at all.

In reality, ZZ Top mania was also growing beyond the borders of the United States. Perhaps no appearance highlights this better than ZZ Top's live appearance on a Japanese television show in March 1986, an utterly bizarre display shot just after dawn in the swamps of Henderson, Louisiana, just hours after performing in a Baton Rouge concert on the Afterburner World Tour. Probably because they never expected the footage to be shown in the United States, Gibbons and Hill inexplicably appear to be sporting thick wigs with braided ponytails and are dressed in tan slacks and blue sports coats, as if about to walk into a yacht club. The band's introductory interview focuses primarily on the same subject seemingly every ZZ Top interview starts with—their facial hair. After a few more awkward questions, the band clumsily mimes "Stages" from *Afterburner* while various locals in fishing boats look on, wondering what the heck they are watching. The performance culminates in the launch of fireworks that appear way too close for comfort (Hill in particular looks backward as if concerned that Beard and his drumkit will catch on fire). Minutes later, the drizzle that had been pelting the band all morning turns into a thunderstorm, and ZZ Top heads on their way to Biloxi for their next gig the following night. It's a peculiar sequence of events, but then again, ZZ Top is a peculiar band.

After grossing over $24 million while playing more than 170 concerts to over 2.5 million fans throughout the United States and Europe in 1986 from January through October on the Afterburner World Tour, ZZ Top scaled back their touring commitments in 1987, playing just a handful of concerts in Japan, Australia, New Zealand, and Hawaii in February and March. As per usual, the tour was not without incident. About two hundred audience members in the crowd of sixty thousand were arrested at the Auckland, New Zealand, concert at Western Springs Stadium on March 14. The group was banned from playing the stadium again by the Auckland City Council not only for the arrests but for exceeding the noise limit (ZZ Top would not return to Auckland until 2000).

The music industry finally accepted that ZZ Top was one of the industry's top bands, and *Billboard* devoted a fifty-six-page supplement to the band in its October 3, 1987, issue. Ads from every segment of the entertainment industry congratulated ZZ Top on the completion of the Afterburner World Tour and the band's incredible success over the previous five years (Ham would later claim it was the publication's highest-selling issue in its nearly one-hundred-year history). At that point, it was hard to think of ZZ Top as "that little ol' band from Texas" when their fame was now truly worldwide and the only thing small about them remained the number of group members. Unsurprisingly, following the worldwide tour, the group did not hit the road in 1988.

Naturally, ZZ Top's explosive popularity over the previous four years meant Warner Bros. had ample opportunity to profit off the band's back catalog, especially since the lengthy Afterburner World Tour kept ZZ Top out of the recording studio for an extended period. Ham saw this as a way to issue the earlier albums on compact discs, but in a package that he felt would appeal to recent fans whose knowledge of ZZ Top began with *Eliminator*.

Ham wasn't alone in his attempts to revitalize material originally recorded on analog tape for CD. As decades' worth of music originally released on vinyl recordings was being reissued on the increasingly popular CD, music journalists and audiophiles frequently criticized the "thin" sound of the music on the new format, with many labels not bothering to utilize the original master tapes and instead simply transferred second- or third-generation copies onto CDs that reproduced imperfections in analog recordings, like tape hiss and static. By the late 1980s, the music of some of the most significant artists in music history was instead remastered digitally by audio engineers before being issued on CD to ensure better quality sound.

However, Ham decided to take a different approach to ZZ Top's catalog. With the band preoccupied with the lengthy world tour for *Afterburner*, which stretched from December 1985 through October 1986, then from February 1987 through March 1987, Bill Ham understandably saw the extended gap between albums as an opportunity to push ZZ Top's back catalog sales. However, Ham believed the sound of the band's original recordings would not appeal to the fans who had discovered the band from *Eliminator* and *Afterburner*. Having negotiated ownership of the master tapes from London Recordings before ZZ Top signed with Warner Bros., Ham opted to rerelease ZZ Top's earlier albums on CD as a stopgap release between albums. With the recent success of the synthesizer-heavy *Afterburner* in mind, Ham believed that the massive success of *Eliminator* and *Afterburner* gave the general audience the impression that the ZZ Top "sound" was seeped in synthesized drums, bass, and guitars and thus the albums, as originally recorded in the 1970s, were not suitable for the audiences of the late 1980s. He decided that he would ask Terry Manning to remix the albums to sound more like ZZ Top's current music.

"Bill had called me and said, 'Quick, we have to remix all the albums for digital!'" Manning remembers. "I said, 'Bill, we don't need to mix anything. They can be transferred. You want to keep everything original—the things people know, love, [have] bought, and fallen for over time. You don't want to re-do anything we did.'" Ham also wanted the process completed in an incredibly short amount of time (though marketing materials claimed the process took "months," Manning says Ham wanted the remixing done over four days). A combination of that short amount of time, his busy production schedule with other artists, and a general disagreement about the whole point of the remixes led Manning to opt out of participating in their creation.

However, Ham was convinced that the albums needed to be remixed to sound more like *Eliminator*. Without Manning, Ham and *Afterburner* engineer Hardy worked together on the remixed albums for a box set of ZZ Top's first five albums (except for the live side of *Fandango!*, which was not remixed), adjusting much of the original instrumentation with synthesized parts utilizing a Wendel drum machine. Manning recommended Bob Ludwig, one of the most renowned master engineers in the industry who has worked on thousands of albums, including ZZ Top albums, to remaster the original recordings for CD. The new mixes were then handed off to Ludwig for remastering. "When Bob Ludwig got the remixes he called me up and said, 'What have you done?' and I said, 'Bob, I didn't do it,'" remembers Manning. "He said, 'This is horrible, but I have to master it. But they didn't make some of the edits you made.' I said, 'Well, I'm not surprised,' so I had to guide him through what the edits would be to try and recreate them. It was just a disaster."

The band's seventh album, *El Loco*, was also included in the compilation but not remixed. *Degüello*, which had already been reissued on CD in its original mix, was not included in the collection. The six albums were packaged on three CDs and issued as a box set named *The Six Pack* with space-age cover art that looked much more *Afterburner* than *Tres Hombres*.

A band releasing remixes of older music is not unheard of, but *The Six Pack* was unique in that the original versions of those recordings were not available on CD for years afterward, and classic songs like "La Grange" were swapped out for the remixed versions for radio airplay on many station playlists. Fortunately for fans of the original classics, the 2003 box set *Chrome, Smoke & BBQ* used the original versions in a new remaster, but that was only a handful of tracks. Not until ZZ Top's music was widely available for download did the original recordings of the first five albums again become available.

While the band took a break from the road, they began taking another approach to monetizing their music. In late 1987, L'eggs pantyhose offered ZZ Top a multi-million-dollar deal to use "Legs" in its commercials. Instead of the original track, the commercials used two versions rerecorded by other artists, an upbeat version for its Sheer Energy line and a slower version for its Sheer Elegance line. The trio also began branching out into other media projects. They appeared in the Disney Channel television special *Mother Goose Rock 'n' Rhyme* as the Three Men in a Tub (the tub being souped up like the Eliminator coupe) alongside other rock luminaries, like Little Richard, Paul Simon, Cyndi Lauper, and Stray Cats. The special aired in May 1990.

Most notably, ZZ Top made their first film appearance in *Back to the Future Part III*, the third film in the box office hit comedy movie series about a teenager, Marty McFly (portrayed by Michael J. Fox), who encounters his family at various points in history via time travel. In *Back to the Future Part III*, McFly travels back to 1885, and much of the movie features Western set pieces reflecting the aesthetic of classic Western movies. ZZ Top recorded a new song for the film, "Doubleback," and appeared in the film in cameo roles as a Western band playing an 1885 version of "Doubleback," even executing their now trademark guitar spins (with Beard, playing a marching drum, executing his own instrument spin for once). In the film, the trio is dressed in period clothing, and in the behind-the-scenes footage, Hill jokes that it was the only movie that they could appear in that would let the band wear their own clothes.

Jokes aside, the hit film was a perfect fit for the group, and they were approached because the director wanted them for the film. "Director Bob Zemeckis was a big ZZ Top fan, so he asked our music supervisor to inquire," remembers the movie's cowriter and producer, Bob Gale (Zemeckis's appreciation for ZZ Top likely explains how a Chiquita travel guitar, codesigned by Gibbons, ended up in the opening scene of 1985's *Back to the Future*).

We all had a blast working with Billy, Frank, and Dusty on Back to the Future Part III. *They were three of the nicest guys any of us had ever met. They were very happy to be there, loved that they were performing in a Western, and developed a wonderful rapport with the local musicians we'd hired to be the rest of the band. One of my fondest memories of the entire production was filming the town festival scenes with them. In between takes, the guys stayed on the set and jammed with the other musicians, and it was totally joyful. In fact, director Bob Zemeckis actually held up shooting after one of the takes because he was enjoying hearing everyone play together!*

Both the film and the single were released in May 1990, with "Doubleback" hitting number fifty on the *Billboard* Hot 100 chart. The movie was yet another hit in the franchise, grossing $245.1 million worldwide and setting ZZ Top up for success with their long-awaited tenth studio album to be released later in 1990.

11
ZZ LITE

For some fans, *Afterburner* and its spectacle-full tour was a bridge too far from what they had loved about ZZ Top's classic sound. ZZ Top may have sensed those concerns, and their next album, *Recycler*, became the band's first of many records to be promoted as a "return to roots." In one significant aspect, it was a return: *Recycler* marked the return of Terry Manning as engineer and would be his final album working with ZZ Top. "When some things with *Afterburner* didn't go the way Bill Ham wanted, he begged me to come back for the next album," explains Manning.

The proposed "return-to-roots" approach to *Recycler* was inspired, in part, by the band's involvement with Mississippi's Delta Blues Museum after the release of *Afterburner*. In September 1987, ZZ Top took a break from recording at Ardent Studios to visit Clarksdale, Mississippi, the home of the Delta blues. The band visited an exhibit on the history of the Delta blues, at the time housed in the local library, the Clarksdale Carnegie Public Library. The following year, Billy Gibbons helped raise $1 million to support the construction of a museum in tribute to the legendary music that had inspired ZZ Top in Clarksdale, which included Gibbons financing the creation a guitar out of a piece of wood recovered from the sharecropper shack that blues icon Muddy Waters purportedly grew up in. The guitar, created by the Pyramid Guitar Company in Memphis and dubbed "Muddywood," embarked on a tour nationwide to Hard Rock Cafe chains to help raise funds and awareness for the museum; "ZZ Top's Muddywood World Tour"–branded merchandise even contributed to the fund-raising. On April 21, 1988, the band appeared at the museum to donate the Muddywood guitar and were, in turn, made honorary citizens of Clarksdale. The museum later moved to a stand-alone building in 1999 in a restored freight train depot in downtown Clarksdale. In the decades since, Gibbons has continued to support and fund-raise for the museum.

This renewed blues influence is most evident on the album's most enduring track, "My Head's in Mississippi," a powerful slice of guitar-driven electric boogie blues; its surreal lyrics, seemingly about the mental confusion of a hangover, live up to Gibbons's oft-cited direction of the band as the Salvador Dalí of the Delta. The song became a fan favorite, and the band has regularly performed it live, albeit typically in an abbreviated form. Other standout tracks on the album that showcased the blues include "2000 Blues," the type of slower blues tune that had not been heard on a ZZ Top album in years.

Though the band felt a renewed connection to the blues because of this activity, they did not completely abandon the synthesizer-based sound of the previous two albums. Songs like "Lovething" feature keyboards; yet others, like "Concrete and Steel" and "Give It Up," hang more in the straightforward rock zone with "Doubleback" (which was included on the album), all indicating ZZ Top had taken a step back from the pop-rock of "Stages." Curiously, Dusty Hill had no lead vocal songs on *Recycler*, the first ZZ Top album not to feature a lead or colead vocal from him.

While *Recycler* peaked at number six on the *Billboard* 200, it dropped off the chart after thirty-seven weeks, spending a far shorter time on the chart than its two predecessors. The singles also struggled. None of them entered the Top 40, though "Doubleback," "Concrete and Steel," and "My Head's in Mississippi" all topped the Album Rock Tracks chart, and "Give It Up" hit number two. Like for *Eliminator* and *Afterburner*, ZZ Top produced four music videos for *Recycler*—"Doubleback" (largely using footage from *Back to the Future Part III*), "Give It Up," "My Head's in Mississippi," and "Burger Man."

Though the music videos for *Recycler* still retain some of the trademark humor, they are more high concept and performance driven. The "My Head's in Mississippi" music video depicts a story about a convict in a chain gang who is rescued by a beautiful woman on horseback, with ZZ Top appearing as performers in a club where the escapees run to hide. Gibbons appears to be playing the Muddywood (or a copy), with Hill playing a similarly styled bass. "Give It Up" features the trio performing on film accidentally projected in a junkyard by a stray dog. Of course, both videos feature plenty of beautiful dancing women, and "Give It Up" even features a stop-motion dancing robot that emerges from the junkyard and vaguely resembles one of the android skeletons from the Terminator film series.

However, the standout music video from *Recycler* is the unlikely "Burger Man," a black-and-white video that draws inspiration from 1950s monster movies. The music video opens at a burger stand that is visited by a rough-looking customer driving a truck full of toxic waste barrels. He harasses the young woman behind the counter before leaving, but while he is dumping the toxic waste in a lake, he falls in while still clutching his burger. As one might expect, he becomes a mutated burger monster, a bizarre cross between the Creature from the Black Lagoon and McDonald's Mayor McCheese, and returns to the burger stand to kidnap the counter girl. Watching these proceedings from space in a UFO, ZZ Top arrive on the scene after being beamed to Earth with a trio of scantily clad alien women. They then use their righteous music and a giant ZZ Top–branded spatula to flip the burger monster into space. It's all as ridiculous as it sounds, and perhaps the last pure example of ZZ Top's absurdist humor in a music video (which had to be expected for a song titled "Burger Man").

After seven dates across Canada in early October 1990 and a one-off appearance at the Hard Rock Cafe in Orlando as another fund-raiser for the Delta Blues Museum, ZZ Top returned to the Cotton Bowl in Dallas on

October 20 for the first time since opening for the Rolling Stones in 1981 with a concert that raised money for the Texas Special Olympics. The stadium show kicked off a short US tour that lasted through mid-December before the band returned to the road in January to kick off a nine-month world tour that would also visit Europe and mark the band's first-ever concert in Mexico.

The elaborate stage design of the Recycler World Tour included a car junkyard in keeping with the "recycler" theme of the album, with Frank Beard's drum set on the back of a flatbed truck and a moving crane that would "pick up" Gibbons and Hill during the show as they performed the end of "Got Me Under Pressure." Afterward the bearded pair and Hill were "recycled" in a car crusher (naturally, two mannequins stood in for Gibbons and Beard for the effect). They then humorously emerged in their evening finest from two rolling blocks of crushed automotive parts to perform "Sharp Dressed Man." Also included on the stage were a pair of conveyor belts (or moving sidewalks, if you will) that allowed Gibbons and Hill to engage in some clever choreography, including moonwalking. The effect was originally proposed by Ty Reveen for the Afterburner World Tour, but the band held off on including it until the next major tour.

Popular beer brand Miller Lite signed as the promotional sponsor of ZZ Top's Recycler World Tour. Unlike the Schlitz sponsorship of the Eliminator Tour, Miller Lite's sponsorship was a true branding partnership, complete with television commercials featuring "La Grange," posters, and a unique limited-release "ZZ Lite" neon bar sign. That "ZZ Lite" logo became ubiquitous during the tour promotion, branded nearly anywhere it could be mentioned.

The heavy promotional push caused a difficult situation between ZZ Top and the opening act, the Black Crowes, during the second leg of the Recycler World Tour, which began January 4, 1991, at the University of New Orleans Lakefront Arena. The Black Crowes, a southern rock–influenced hard rock band, were touring behind their critically acclaimed debut album, 1990's *Shake Your Money Maker*, winning over the rock press with their distinct throwback raucous style. The album was released by future ZZ Top producer Rick Rubin on his Def American label, likely helping endear it to the rock press. For instance, the Black Crowes were voted Best New American Band by *Rolling Stone* in 1990. On the surface, pairing a beloved veteran rock act with a fiery up-and-coming group of rock-and-roll upstarts appeared the perfect bill, even if the Black Crowes, with their back-to-the-1970s look, contrasted substantially with ZZ Top in all their superstar special effects glory.

However, less than three months into the five-month tour, Miller and ZZ Top's management cut the Black Crowes off the tour after lead singer Chris Robinson repeatedly made anti–corporate sponsorship remarks during the band's opening sets. The timing of the removal was particularly poor on the part of Miller and ZZ Top's management because it came after the March 25, 1991, show, the second of three concerts at the Omni Coliseum in Atlanta, the hometown of the Black Crowes. That alone ensured the abrupt end of the Black Crowes' participation in the tour would become a hot local story.

Of course, it did not remain a local news story. The resulting publicity, much of which cast ZZ Top as aging hacks against the more honest newcomer Black Crowes, was a substantial boost to the younger band. Less than two weeks after they were removed from the tour, *Shake Your Money Maker* peaked at number four on the *Billboard* 200, two spots higher than the peak of *Recycler* on the same chart, which it had hit one month after its 1990 release (at that point, *Shake Your Money Maker* had been in release for over a year). That same week *Recycler* dropped from number forty-two to number fifty on the *Billboard* 200. The Black Crowes' then current single, "She Talks to Angels," peaked at number thirty on the *Billboard* Hot 100 a few weeks later, and the band was featured on the cover of the May 30, 1991, issue of

Rolling Stone (under the cover line "What's So Bad about the Black Crowes?")
in a story that highlighted the controversy.

Ultimately, the Miller Lite situation helped the Black Crowes a lot more
than it hurt ZZ Top. The move to throw the Black Crowes off the tour was
largely portrayed as a management decision, and how involved the members
of ZZ Top were in the decision is not clear, though both Gibbons and Bill
Ham spoke publicly in support of Miller's sponsorship. Regardless, by the
end of the tour, ZZ Top was the third-highest-grossing music concert tour of
the year, grossing $25.977 million, playing to 1.275 million fans, and selling
out 94 of 105 concerts, demonstrating that even if audiences were not buying
Recycler in the numbers they had the band's previous two albums, ZZ Top was
still a significant concert draw.

Sadly, tragedy struck the ZZ Top family while the band was in Europe
on the Recycler World Tour. Bill Ham's wife, Cecile, and her Cadillac disappeared on July 2, 1991. Two days later, Ham reported her missing; foul play
was immediately suspected and later confirmed when Cecile's credit cards
were discovered being used across Texas (there had been sixty charges over
the first eight days since Cecile's disappearance). More than a month later,
on August 7, the Cadillac was found in the possession of a twenty-two-year-
old man named Spencer Corey Goodman after a merchant in Eagle County,
Colorado, refused to accept one of Cecile's credit cards and alerted police.
After his arrest, Goodman revealed that he had horrifically abducted Cecile,
stole her car, murdered her, and disposed of her body in a field. Upon his
return to Texas the next day, he led police to her remains. Goodman had been
released on parole just one day before he killed Cecile. He was eventually con-
victed of her murder and executed by lethal injection in January 2000. By the
time Cecile's body was found, the Recycler World Tour had returned to the
United States. A notoriously private individual, Ham did not speak publicly
about his wife's murder aside from offering a reward for information about

her disappearance and remarking that he was attending the murder trial to see justice served.

As the final obligation to Warner Bros. for the contract the band signed in 1978, ZZ Top released a new compilation album, *Greatest Hits*, in April 1992. It contained only two pre–Warner Bros. tracks, "La Grange" and "Tush," and both were included in their remixed forms from *The Six Pack*. Though most of the band's major *Billboard* Hot 100 hits from their five Warner Bros. albums were included, the compilation also included older songs that weren't hits or even released as singles, like "I'm Bad, I'm Nationwide" and "Pearl Necklace," though they were nonetheless popular with audiences, and left off songs that were more recent hits on the Album Rock Tracks chart, like "Stages," "Velcro Fly," and "Concrete and Steel." Naturally, it was also wise for Warner Bros. not to overload *Greatest Hits* with songs from ZZ Top's most recent albums, *Afterburner* and *Recycler*, even if they were bigger hits than the included earlier album tracks, especially since the label likely wanted to continue to reap the benefits of ZZ Top catalog sales.

Greatest Hits also included two new songs, a cover of the Elvis Presley hit "Viva Las Vegas," which was released as a single, and "Gun Love," a blues-rock song that would have been right at home on *Recycler*. Two years later, Warner Bros. released a second compilation album, *One Foot in the Blues*, which consisted of selections not featured on *Greatest Hits* that mostly reflected the band's bluesier work (though the older material included on the release was the remixed *Six Pack* versions).

The barrage of electronic accompaniments in "Viva Las Vegas" appropriately matches the neon gaudiness of the Las Vegas Strip and also serves as a sonic grand finale to the band's 1980s sound. The band appeared to have sensed that too, wearing some of their most ostentatious outfits yet—long leopard-print suit jackets, with Gibbons and Hill wearing oversized cowboy hats—on the cover of *Greatest Hits* and in the "Viva Las Vegas" video (which also features multiple costume changes for the band). It seemed impossible for the band to get any flashier in the video. The song ended up being the band's last major international chart hit, though it did not chart on the *Billboard* Hot 100 (it peaked at number sixteen on the Album Rock Tracks chart). The *Greatest Hits* album was a top seller, reaching number nine on the *Billboard* 200 and becoming a Top 10 album in Australia, New Zealand, and several European countries. Within weeks it was certified as a platinum album by the Recording Industry Association of America (RIAA) and eventually achieved triple platinum status, ZZ Top's highest certification outside *Eliminator* and *Afterburner*.

Six weeks after the release of *Greatest Hits*, RCA Records announced that it had signed ZZ Top to a monster five-album deal reportedly worth more than $30 million, with the band earning a guaranteed $5 million advance per album, more than double the $2 million advance per album the band had received from Warner Bros., plus an estimated $5 million signing bonus. The deal was at least $1 million more per album than what Warner Bros. had offered ZZ Top to sign a new contract.

From a pop culture standpoint, RCA executives at the time likely felt like they had struck gold. In what might have been taken as a good sign, the number one song on the *Billboard* Hot 100 the week after the deal was announced was rapper Sir Mix-A-Lot's "Baby Got Back," a spiritual successor to "Tush" in songs about fine derrieres. However, over on the Album Rock Tracks chart, which ZZ Top had been dominating just a few years earlier when it was known as the Top Rock Tracks chart, their recent tour rivals the Black Crowes were in the midst of an eleven-week run at the top of the chart with "Remedy" from their second studio album, *The Southern Harmony and Musical Companion*, which they would in turn dethrone themselves with their next single, "Sting Me." Other modern bands in the mix on the chart were the Red Hot Chili Peppers ("Under the Bridge"), Pearl Jam ("Even Flow"), and

Nirvana ("Come As You Are"), though a few legacy artists with big hits in the early MTV era, like ZZ Top, were still holding strong in top positions, like Ozzy Osbourne ("Road to Nowhere"), Def Leppard ("Make Love like a Man"), and Bruce Springsteen ("57 Channels and Nothin' On").

Another warning sign that ZZ Top was no longer on the cusp of pop culture's cutting edge was that the band's music videos for *Recycler* did not receive any nominations at the 1991 MTV Video Music Awards (the music video for "Doubleback," released several months before the album, was nominated for Best Video from a Film at the 1990 MTV Video Music Awards but lost to Billy Idol's "Cradle of Love" video). The awards frequently reflected popularity and airplay on the channel, and while RCA doubtlessly did not expect ZZ Top to maintain their mid-1980s popularity, the label must have believed that ZZ Top would retain enough fans from their heyday to make the long-term, five-album deal beneficial for both parties.

Even from that perspective, the deal was a major gamble for RCA. Despite ZZ Top's massive success in the 1980s, the record deal is extraordinary in hindsight and again demonstrates Ham's prowess at selecting the right legal team and terms for negotiations (it also likely helped that Ham's other major client, country musician Clint Black, was signed to RCA Nashville). ZZ Top, while still one of the top rock acts in the United States, was already on a trajectory of commercial decline. While as of 1992 *Eliminator* had been certified platinum seven times by the RIAA, *Afterburner* had been certified platinum three times by that point (still a big success, of course), and *Recycler* had been certified platinum. ZZ Top also hadn't had a Top 40 hit since "Velcro Fly," released six years before. RCA, at the time owned by German company Bertelsmann Music Group, was likely counting on the band's international appeal, considering the recent ZZ Top singles had stronger chart success in Canada, Germany, the United Kingdom, and other territories than in the United States (for example, "Viva Las Vegas" was a Top 10 hit in Ireland,

Sweden, and the United Kingdom). The band, of course, was thrilled to have such a lucrative deal, and Hill told *Guitar World* around the release of their first RCA album, *Antenna*, that the deal was especially exciting to him since RCA had been Elvis Presley's record label.

Noted music attorney John Branca, who handled the negotiations of record contracts worth tens of millions of dollars for Michael Jackson, the Rolling Stones, and Bob Dylan, among others, was the key player in the ZZ Top negotiations. Branca keenly understood the investment that RCA was making in the group, telling the *San Diego Union-Tribune*, "If down the road some of these artists fail to perform, labels will think harder about these big-money deals."[1]

Unfortunately for ZZ Top, Branca was right on target when it came to the band's deal with RCA. Because of changing tastes in popular music and pop culture, as well as the decline in album sales in the following decade, ZZ Top's $30 million record deal quickly became something of an albatross for RCA.

12
RETURN TO THE ROOTS, AGAIN

Because of ZZ Top's declining album sales, plenty of commentators were skeptical of the band's new deal with RCA. Billy Gibbons himself addressed those concerns with a joke backstage during the 1993 Rock and Roll Hall of Fame ceremony (during which ZZ Top inducted Cream). Asked when the band would release their first RCA album, Gibbons quipped, "We won't do one. That's the best part of the deal."

Obviously, the response was just a quip because the band was already working on music for their eleventh studio album. Like *Recycler*, the album was promoted as a "back-to-roots" release. Even the album title, *Antenna*, was intended to harken back to the band's earlier days, a direct reference to their *Fandango!* track "Heard It on the X" and the border-blasting radio stations that influenced their sound. The album's artwork was also a throwback because the cartoon rendition of the band was recycled from a 1980s piece for ZZ Top International, the band's official fan club.

The RCA record deal also signaled a new way that ZZ Top was doing business internally. For the first time since his "Asleep in the Desert" songwriting credit on *Tejas*, Gibbons received sole credit for writing songs on a ZZ Top album, as five of the eleven songs are solely credited to him. The tradition of splitting the songwriting credits three ways that began with *Degüello* ended, though it was briefly revived for the band's 1999 album *XXX*. Perhaps because Bill Ham was increasingly involved in his other musical ventures and had health issues (he had a major scare in 1994 when his aorta ruptured), *Antenna* also marked the first time that Gibbons was credited as an album's producer alongside Ham. While the band did return to Ardent Studios, ZZ

Top was again recording without Terry Manning, who had since moved to Nassau, Bahamas, to work at the famed Compass Point Studios, though Joe Hardy was back to engineer the album.

Despite these changes behind the scenes, *Antenna*, released in January 1994, is still largely in the vein of *Recycler* in its combination of synthesized sounds and heavily fuzzed guitar in songs, though the album generally lacks the layers of synthesized sounds on the band's 1980s albums. The songs are generally longer. At fifty-one minutes, ten minutes more than *Recycler*, *Antenna* became the band's longest album to date.

In contemporary reviews much was made about the song "Cover Your Rig," an ode to safe sex from a band previously known for lascivious lyrics. The song was noted as another tacit acknowledgment on the band's part that the goofiness of the *Eliminator* era was over. Of course, the song immediately following on the album, "Lizard Life," thrust right back into standard sleazy territory, showing that the boys didn't want to demonstrate too much personal growth.

The first two singles from *Antenna* demonstrated that ZZ Top was, like with the two singles from *El Loco*, trying to cast a wide net to see what the market would respond to more. The lead single and opening track of the album, "Pincushion," is an effect-laden mid-tempo rocker with a slight industrial tinge to its barrage of grinding guitars. On the other hand, the second single (and incidentally, the second song on the album), "Breakaway," is one of the smoothest grooves that the band ever released, an almost tropical-sounding tune incorporating a conga-like rhythm. But neither song reached the *Billboard* Hot 100, though "Pincushion" was number one for four weeks on the Album Rock Tracks chart, while "Breakaway" peaked at number seven on the same chart, indicating that RCA was able to push the songs out for significant airplay on rock radio.

MTV airplay was another story. Music videos like the ones for "TV Dinners" and "Velcro Fly" were out of step with the aesthetic of 1990s music
videos, which were far more expensive and, in most cases, less humorous
than their 1980s counterparts. In 1984, Duran Duran's "The Wild Boys"
video was the first music video to cost more than $1 million to produce. By
the release of *Antenna* in 1994, many videos had far exceeded that budget,
like Madonna's "Express Yourself" and Guns N' Roses' "Estranged" (both $5
million) and Michael Jackson's "Black or White" ($4 million), while videos
exceeding $1 million were increasingly commonplace. Moreover, music vid-
eos at the time became a training ground for future feature filmmakers like
Zack Snyder, who directed ZZ Top's "World of Swirl" music video (though
that video liberally uses clips from the 1994 comedy movie *In the Army Now*,
starring comedian Pauly Shore, which features the song on its soundtrack).

The cost of a ZZ Top video never reached seven figures, but the *Antenna*
music videos marked a departure from the group's previous award-winning
videos. There is a country mile of difference in tone between the music videos for "Burger Man" and "Viva Las Vegas" and those for the songs from
Antenna. The "Pincushion" video was directed by Julien Temple, who at the
time had been one of the most sought-after music video directors in the business for over a decade, particularly after directing videos for Duran Duran,
the Rolling Stones, David Bowie, and Tom Petty, among many other artists.
Though the video starred a beautiful woman like previous videos (in this
case, actress Joyce Hyser), it was more high concept than the group's 1980s
videos, featuring the group performing in a spike-filled room. The tone is
considerably less humorous than that of their previous videos, although there
are over-the-top sequences interpreting the song's title with a voodoo doll
sequence. None of the album's videos got significant airplay on MTV, as the
channel had already initiated its move away from broadcasting videos in favor

of other programming and was generally devoting its music video playlists to emerging alternative rock and rap artists.

Another visual change for the band went beyond coordinating outfits or video aesthetics. When ZZ Top resurfaced to promote the album, fans noticed that Gibbons appeared to have lost a considerable amount of weight. His generally slender figure was now rail thin, a physique he has maintained ever since. This led to rumors about his health, though the band's management either outright ignored questions about his condition or answered by saying it was a personal choice.

Despite some highlights and some positive critical reviews (including in the *Los Angeles Times*), *Antenna* was an underwhelming start to ZZ Top's contract with RCA. The album sold just fifty-four thousand copies in its first week, debuting at number fourteen and dropping down the charts after that until disappearing altogether after twenty-three weeks (the shortest time one of ZZ Top's albums had spent on the *Billboard* 200 since *El Loco*). Unfortunately, that disappointing debut for the label ended up being the commercial high point for the band at RCA. In interviews, Gibbons downplayed his concern for the lackluster sales of their RCA debut, first blaming it on tough competition. "There's a lot of product out there," he said at the time. "I guess what's really getting crazy is that there's a lot of formats to play it on. It's not like you go to a record store; you now go to record, CD, tape, and laser disc stores. But it's doing well in foreign markets, even in places we haven't been yet." He told the *Austin American-Statesman*, "We just make them. The record company has to sell them. If I had wanted to be in the business of selling records I would have got a job in a record store instead of starting a band." In reality, Gibbons must have been in a similar mind-set as after the initially underwhelming response to *El Loco*. He knew ZZ Top needed a hit record to justify RCA's substantial investment in the band.[1]

The Antenna Tour featured a stage setup patterned after an old-fashioned tube radio that doubled as an elevated stage, but aside from some spectacular lighting effects (including at one point the radio exploding into pieces after the band performed "Antenna Head") and dancing girls, the tour otherwise marked a scaling back on the stage gimmicks and visual effects that proliferated in the tours for *Afterburner* and *Recycler*. Nearly all the *Afterburner* songs, some of which featured complex stage gimmicks during the previous two tours, were henceforth dropped from the set lists. The Antenna Tour marked the next phase of ZZ Top live performances as the band jettisoned many of their 1980s hits in favor of new songs. Of all the *Afterburner* songs, only "Rough Boy" has continued to regularly appear in the band's set lists. Other popular songs from the album, including "Sleeping Bag," "Velcro Fly," "Planet of Women," "Stages," and "Can't Stop Rockin'," largely or completely disappeared from live performances, with "Pincushion," "Breakaway," "World of Swirl," "Fuzzbox Voodoo," "Antenna Head," and "PCH" from the new album all making appearances on set lists during the tour.

Though the Antenna Tour carried on through the end of December 1994 with a monthlong stint in Europe, a five-year gap between albums would not follow, as between *Afterburner* and *Recycler*. The origins of the band's twelfth album, *Rhythmeen*, began when Texas-born filmmaker Robert Rodriguez, who had recently had a box office hit with the action film *Desperado* (1995), approached ZZ Top about writing a song for his next film, *From Dusk Till Dawn*, an action-horror vampire film set in a Mexican strip club called the Titty Twister. The band offered Rodriguez a new cut, "She's Just Killing Me," a grinding, boogie-down tune that would have been right at home playing for the girls at the Titty Twister. Gibbons initially considered the song unpolished, remarking, "I thought, 'This is crazy! It's rough and raw and needs redoing.' But it was to their liking, and it got us thinking, 'Do we really need to do so much smoothing and polishing these days?'" The film and its soundtrack album—which also featured "Mexican Blackbird" from *Fandango!*—were both released in January 1996, eight months before *Rhythmeen*. The "She's Just Killing Me" music video—featuring ZZ Top performing as the house band at the Titty Twister (shot at Houston's now defunct Urban Art Bar) and two of the stars of the movie, George Clooney and Salma Hayek—was also directed by Rodriguez and would be ZZ Top's last music video for nearly two decades.

According to Gibbons, the raw sound of "She's Just Killing Me" inspired the tone for the rest of the new album. Of course, Gibbons also again incorporated some additional musical influences, this time African drumbeats (inspired in part by the book *Savannah Syncopators: African Retentions in the Blues* by Paul Oliver). To signal that, around this time Gibbons became interested in collecting African art and adopted his trademark Bamileke nudu hat, which he later claimed he had acquired in Cameroon in a trade for one of his cowboy hats with a tribal chief. ZZ Top played several dates in South Africa in July and August 1996 at the end of the first leg of the international tour, which the band had dubbed the Continental Safari Tour, and some fans have speculated that Gibbons ventured north to Cameroon after these shows for the hat trade. However, footage from earlier in the Continental Safari Tour shows that Gibbons was already wearing the hat on stage before the South African tour. Thus the timeline for when Gibbons acquired his first nudu hat is not known, but it originated as part of the aesthetic of both *Rhythmeen* and the Continental Safari Tour.

And yet some of the album's tracks are influenced by other sources. The album's most successful single, "What's Up with That," which spent twelve weeks on *Billboard*'s Mainstream Rock Tracks (the new name for the Top Rock Tracks chart) and peaked at number five, integrates the melody of the Staple Singers' 1971 hit "Respect Yourself." "Respect Yourself" songwriters Luther Ingram and Mack Rice receive cowriting credit, and curiously, though Terry Manning engineered the original Staple Singers tracks, he was not involved in this re-envisioning of the song. "What's Up with That" also marks the band's first collaboration with blues harmonica player James Harman, who would play with Gibbons on several occasions until he passed away in 2021. Similarly, "My Mind Is Gone" incorporates the melody of Stevie Wonder's "Pastime Paradise," which had recently returned to prominence after being sampled by rapper Coolio for his huge 1995 hit "Gangsta's Paradise" (the opening verse of "Gangsta's Paradise" ends with the line "Even my mama thinks that my mind is gone"). With those two tracks alone, the album demonstrates Gibbons's attempts to write music that would appeal to the band's aging original fan base ("What's Up with That") and also hopefully attract notice from younger audiences ("My Mind Is Gone"). If nothing else, *Rhythmeen* offered the most variety of sonic influences on a ZZ Top album since perhaps *Degüello*. Gibbons was again credited as producer alongside Ham and was solely credited for writing three of the twelve tracks. Hardy, who again engineered and mixed the album, is credited with cowriting four of the album's songs with Gibbons, while the traditional Gibbons-Hill-Beard credit appears on five songs, including a distorted blues tune the band aptly titled "Vincent Price Blues" after the horror movie icon.

Rhythmeen was ZZ Top's third album in a row purported to be a "back-to-roots" effort. (*Billboard* said it "harkens back to the venerable Texas power trio's early, stripped-down, blues-based rock rather than the more produced and synthetic sound of its later work." Gibbons remarked, "We've made no secret that we've left the synthesizers behind and have returned to early ZZ style.") It was also the first in decades to not be wholly recorded at Ardent Studios, with parts of the album being recorded in Hollywood and Houston.[2]

The album's credits have also led to repeated rumors and speculation that Frank Beard does not perform on the album. In the "Extra Super Solid Thanx" section of the liner notes, Greg Morrow is listed for "Gangzz Clangzz &

Percussion Thangzz." Morrow is a renowned Tennessee-based session drummer who has recorded with countless top-name rock and country artists, including Don Henley, Bob Seger, Lynyrd Skynyrd, Luke Bryan, Bad Company, Allison Moorer, and Trace Adkins, among many others. In other words, Morrow, whom Gibbons would later refer to as "one of the great drummers in the business today," isn't the type of musician one would bring into the studio just to play shakers. In more recent interviews, Morrow has noted that he performed on some ZZ Top songs during this period and continued to work with Gibbons professionally by playing drums on Gibbons's first two solo albums, *Perfectamundo* and *The Big Bad Blues*, while also engineering the former. In a 2018 interview with *Shindig! Magazine*, Gibbons also ambiguously referred to Morrow as "our dear friend and drummer from days gone by." In 2019, Morrow was interviewed on the *Surviving the Music Industry* podcast, and when asked if he drummed on ZZ Top's albums, he mentioned that he had begun working with them, without providing specifics, in 1996 (the year that *Rhythmeen* was released).[3]

Some fans have even speculated that Gibbons or future band member Elwood Francis, who is also mentioned in the "Extra Super Solid Thanx" section, may have played bass on the album instead of Dusty Hill, who only has one lead vocal ("Loaded") on the album. However, Francis is credited with "guitar," and in an interview with *Guitar World* shortly after the album's release, Gibbons credited Francis for assisting with the various guitar tunings during the album sessions. Curiously, in a retrospective interview on each ZZ Top studio album, Gibbons referred to *Rhythmeen* "as the truest test of ZZ Top as a trio. If you listen to that record, there are no overdubs. That was pure band going in and saying: 'Okay, we think we know these songs, we're gonna try and lay 'em down.'" With the knowledge that Morrow played on the album in place of Beard for at least some of the songs (if not all), that remark seems as disingenuous as descriptions of the *Eliminator* sessions as the band playing as a trio in the studio. Beard and Hill received cowriting credits for five of the twelve tracks on *Rhythmeen*, so it's entirely possible that Gibbons was referring to songwriting sessions that produced these songs; as with all ZZ Top recordings since *Eliminator*, however, there remains speculation about who exactly played what.[4]

The release of *Rhythmeen* was preceded by the globe-spanning Continental Safari Tour, which began June 14 at the Brixton Academy in London and ran through most of Europe, including cities in countries where ZZ Top had never performed before, like Poland, Estonia, and Latvia, and a landmark performance in Moscow (where they drew twenty thousand to the famed Gorky Park). ZZ Top also appeared at several European summer music festivals, including making their first-ever appearance at the Montreux Jazz Festival (the band would later play the festival again in 2003, 2013, 2016, and 2019). The first leg of the tour wrapped up in August after eight performances in South Africa, just two years after South Africa's first nonracial elections marking the end of apartheid. The tour's production design was based on an African aesthetic and saw the return of some earlier classics like "Brown Sugar," "Nasty Dogs and Funky Kings," and "Party on the Patio" to the set lists.

Rhythmeen was released on September 17, 1996, and debuted at number twenty-nine on the *Billboard* 200. Unfortunately, that was also its peak, and it fell off the chart before the end of 1996. On October 2, the band performed "What's Up with That" live on the *Late Show with David Letterman*, accompanied by both Harman and Letterman's band, led by renowned bandleader Paul Shaffer. Two days later, Gibbons made a then rare solo appearance on the show to perform with the house band again. The appearances were followed by the US leg of the Continental Safari Tour, concluding with a November 23 performance in Shreveport, Louisiana. During the tour, ZZ Top made a brief appearance in the opening credits of an episode of the sitcom *Ellen*, which aired on November 20 (though it was likely filmed earlier that month when ZZ Top was in Los Angeles for a November 11 performance at the Universal Amphitheater). The band ended the year with another television appearance playing another one of the album's singles, "Bang Bang," at the Billboard Music Awards on December 4.

All that was pretext, however, for the biggest television performance the band would ever give in their career. On January 26, 1997, ZZ Top was part of the halftime show for Super Bowl XXXI at the Superdome in New Orleans. The performance was promoted under the banner "The Blues Brothers Bash" and featured actors Dan Aykroyd, John Goodman, and Jim Belushi performing as their Blues Brothers characters, developed in a popular *Saturday Night Live* skit featuring Aykroyd and Belushi's late brother, John Belushi, which had become a hit feature film in 1980. Aykroyd and Goodman were preparing to film a sequel to the film, *Blues Brothers 2000*, which was released the following year. The halftime show also served as a promotional vehicle for Aykroyd's House of Blues restaurant and music hall chain, which had opened its first location outside Boston five years previously. Later that year, ZZ Top would perform at the Myrtle Beach, South Carolina, location, and the band would go on to perform at the West Hollywood (2007, 2009, and 2012), Orlando (2009), Atlantic City (2009), Las Vegas (2012), and Anaheim (2018) locations. The performance also included iconic soul singer James Brown, with ZZ Top arriving at the end of the performance to mime "Tush" and "Legs" and then participate in the closing song, a lively cover of "Gimme Some Lovin'" by the Spencer Davis Group. Super Bowl XXXI, broadcast by Fox in the United States, had 87.87 million viewers, the highest-rated program in the history of the network at that point. Later that evening, at an afterparty at the House of Blues location in New Orleans, Gibbons and Hill joined the Allman Brothers Band to perform "Rock Me Baby" and "One Way Out."

Just days after the Super Bowl performance, ZZ Top returned to Europe for a month of shows and then took a two-month break before embarking on the Mean Rhythm Global Tour, which launched on May 2 at the Music Midtown Festival in Atlanta and included several summer festivals and state fairs. The tour included a concert at the University of Texas Frank Erwin Center in Austin on May 15, which was declared "ZZ Top Day" by then governor of Texas George W. Bush. ZZ Top concluded the tour with a concert in Honolulu on October 11, the group's first concert in Hawaii in a decade.

ZZ Top's continued success on the road was obvious, but album sales were another story. Only four years after signing the biggest record deal of their career, the sales of ZZ Top's first two RCA albums led to speculation that RCA was suffering from buyer's remorse. "If the band didn't deliver the sales necessary to justify the deal, there was a danger that RCA might eat the contract and cut its losses," wrote Joe Nick Patoski in a revealing profile of Gibbons in *Texas Monthly* in December 1996, only three months after the release of *Rhythmeen*. "When the first release of the RCA deal, 1994's *Antenna*, sold just over a million copies, that danger seemed more real. To keep the machine going, the next release would have to do better. That release is *Rhythmeen*, and while the jury is still out on its success, the signs are fairly ominous." In short, it was a diplomatic way for Patoski to say that *Rhythmeen* had stalled out of the gate.[5]

Just seven months after that *Texas Monthly* article, and after all the singles off *Rhythmeen* failed to break into the *Billboard* Hot 100, the band was playing defense in an article titled "ZZ Top Doesn't Worry about Drop," which focused on the decline in the band's album and concert ticket sales since signing the RCA deal. "It's like if Michael Jordan only scored 22 points a game, what a drag, because he did score 50," Hill argued. "He had the flu and he scored 38. I don't know how to respond to that. Selling a million records used to be a big deal. I guess it's not anymore."

Hill's analogy was way off the mark. The sales figures for *Rhythmeen* were more like a case of Jordan's game completely collapsing to single digits. *Antenna* may have gone platinum, which was still considered a disappointment, but *Rhythmeen* failed to even go gold and was ZZ Top's lowest-charting album since *Rio Grande Mud*. As of February 2002, SoundScan reported the album had sold 310,000 units in the United States. The album's stronger European sales on the back of the high number of concerts they played on the continent couldn't save it, as even those numbers were lower than the European sales figures for *Antenna*.

Those who had worked with the band previously also sensed something was awry with ZZ Top's RCA years. "I thought *Eliminator* was great, but then they started straying away from the farm," shares Robin Hood Brians about the group he had formerly worked with at his studio. "Boy, the stuff they did on RCA, golly, I just listened to that, and I said, 'They're lost. They're just lost.' Once you have established who you are, the only group who have ever gotten away from that were the Beatles. But the new stuff that they did was so far out, so exciting, and so original that they got away with it. But most singers, most groups, find their farm and they stay on that farm. And ZZ Top didn't."

On the other hand, virtually no artists have been able to sustain a level of success on par with *Eliminator* and *Afterburner*, even if fans still appreciate the music they are putting out. "Nobody can stay that hot, sell that many records, for very long, and the mass audience brought by MTV didn't prove to be all that loyal," points out Matthew Wilkening, founding editor in chief of *Ultimate Classic Rock*. "But there was a bit of a creative drop-off too. It's probably the one time in their career they held on to something for too long. *Afterburner* was about straight down the middle, half genius and half retread, and the ratio dipped even further for *Recycler*. But they found a nice groove after that; there are always two or three songs worthy of placement on the all-time ZZ Top mix tape on every album after that."

Yet "two or three songs" strong songs per RCA album was not going to keep the band on the charts. With *Antenna* and *Rhythmeen*, ZZ Top was obviously trying to follow the lead of their earlier albums in incorporating contemporary sounds into their trademark groove. But *Eliminator* and *Afterburner* were able to capture the zeitgeist at the right moment because of a variety of factors. It would be much harder for any band, even one with a creative talent like Gibbons at the helm, to accomplish that incredible feat again.

13
THE END OF THE WOLFPACK

In an overview of ZZ Top's fifteen studio albums, the band's 1999 album, *XXX*, is the most puzzling. If 1976's *Tejas* is generally thought of by fans as an overlooked gem, *XXX* is viewed as a forgotten misfire that was released to coincide with the thirtieth anniversary of the band's founding.

XXX, the first ZZ Top album on which Billy Gibbons is solely credited as producer, is a Frankenstein in ZZ Top's discography, not only because of its monstrous sound but because of the way it was put together as a purported part-studio, part-live album. The biggest question about *XXX* (pronounced "three X," according to Gibbons in contemporary interviews, and intended as a reference to the band's thirtieth anniversary, Dos Equis beer, poison, and pornography) is what it was supposed to be. Despite the title, it was not a thirtieth-anniversary retrospective, and the album's packaging makes no other effort to recognize the milestone (in fact, the packaging is bereft of detail, not even noting where the studio or "live" tracks were recorded). If the part-studio, part-live presentation was intended to be a twenty-fifth-anniversary celebration of *Fandango!*, that was not noted anywhere.

The album was released in April 1999 after ZZ Top took the entirety of 1998 off from touring. Eight of the album tracks are studio recordings, while the four tracks that end the album are purported to be "live recordings collected world wide [*sic*]," according to the liner notes. In interviews promoting the release, the band members said the live songs were recorded in surprise club shows, though there is no record of ZZ Top performing live between the October 11, 1997, concert in Hawaii that ended the Mean Rhythm Tour and the first concert on the XXX Tour at the Cheyenne Frontier Days Festival on

July 23, 1999. At that point *XXX* had already been released and recorded, so there does not appear to have been a logical occasion when the songs would have been recorded live, and surprise ZZ Top club shows would still have made headlines in the cities where they occurred. In addition, the crowd noise on the songs sounds like that from an arena rather than a smaller venue. Of the four songs, the only one for which there is evidence that ZZ Top actually performed it live is the Dusty Hill–sung Elvis Presley cover "(Let Me Be Your) Teddy Bear," but that was long after the album had been released.

Beyond that, there are several other indications that these tracks are studio recordings with overdubbed crowd noise. The first of the four tracks, "Sinpusher," is simply "Pincushion" with different lyrics (though the two versions are registered as separate compositions with BMI). Gibbons bizarrely explained to the *Washington Post* that the band changed the lyrics just for this release because he couldn't remember the original lyrics, which makes little sense considering that ZZ Top had been performing the song live for several years (with backing-track accompaniment) by the time *XXX* was recorded and would continue to perform it regularly in concert over the next eighteen years with its original lyrics. Even if this was a onetime live performance of a version with new lyrics, that does not explain the presence of accompanying "backup shouters" during the chorus who are obviously rehearsed and do not sound like Hill or Beard.

Other factors also point to the four tracks originating as studio recordings. "Hey Mr. Millionaire" features vocals by guitar icon Jeff Beck, and Gibbons was open about the fact that Beck dubbed his vocals onto the track. Gibbons attended Beck's March 19, 1999, concert at the Roseland Ballroom in New York City. While backstage he asked if Beck would be willing to sing—not play guitar—on a ZZ Top song. Beck loved the quirky idea of doing something so off the wall, particularly because he was not known to be a vocalist. "I went up to Jeff's hotel room with a Sony MiniDisc recorder and one of those little stereo microphones that go with it," Gibbons would later recall. "And we recorded the vocal right there in the hotel room. The engineer for our album had told me, 'Just get something on tape and we can insert it using Pro Tools. We can pitch-correct it and time-stretch it if we need to.' So I just had to get him to sing his vocal part in the hotel room. 'You know how much trust this entails?' Jeff said to me. 'Because I can't actually sing, you know.'" The backing vocal (which is not particularly distinctive on the song) must have been a late addition to the album because *XXX* was released the following month.[1]

Curiously, while Beck joined ZZ Top on stage on several occasions before he died in 2023, including regularly during the aptly named joint Beards 'N Beck Tour in 2014 and 2015, they never performed "Hey Mr. Millionaire" together. Indeed, it seems ZZ Top has never performed the song live. Instead, Beck and ZZ Top typically played the *Afterburner* ballad "Rough Boy" together while on stage, a song that Gibbons has noted is a personal favorite of Beck's (a live recording of ZZ Top performing the song with Beck is included on the 2016 ZZ Top compilation *Tonite at Midnight: Live Greatest Hits from around the World*). Gibbons also performed "Rough Boy" with Beck's band at Beck's guest-filled "50 Years of Jeff Beck" concert at the Hollywood Bowl on August 10, 2016, and Gibbons performed "Rough Boy" with Beck's band on both nights of the May 2023 "A Tribute to Jeff Beck" concerts organized by Eric Clapton at the London's Royal Albert Hall. Oddly enough, during his 2019 tour, Beck occasionally played "Hey Mr. Millionaire," though the song was by then two decades old before making its live debut.

Finally, the most damning evidence that the four songs weren't recorded during a live concert is that there exists a bootlegged alternate extended version of the song "Dreadmonboogaloo" from the album sessions that features overdubbed crowd noise as if this song were originally intended to be part of the "live" portion of the album but was instead cut down and the crowd noise removed. It's possible that at one point the entire album was meant to be presented as a "live" recording before it got the *Fandango!* treatment instead, which would explain why there is no information on where the songs were recorded anywhere on the packaging.

Though they lack crowd noise, the eight studio tracks on *XXX* sound similar in tone to the four "live tracks," with Gibbons experimenting with some rap phrasing and playing with heavily distorted guitar riffs on songs like "Crucifixx-A-Flatt" and the band playing some unique tricks with tempo on the down-tuned and grungy dirge "Made into a Movie." The song most reminiscent of standard ZZ Top is the album's first single, "Fearless Boogie," one of the few songs from the album that the group performed live on the XXX Tour.

XXX was yet another sales disappointment. It debuted and peaked at number one hundred on the *Billboard* 200 and spent only four weeks on the chart, the group's lowest-charting album since *Rio Grande Mud* (though that album managed to spend ten weeks on the chart). The two singles, "Fearless Boogie" and "36-22-36," both reached the Top 40 on the Mainstream Rock Airplay chart, but neither made much of an impression elsewhere. As of February 2002, SoundScan reported the album had sold 140,000 units in the United States. That month, RCA executive Joe Galante, who had made the deal with ZZ Top in 1992, told *Billboard* in an article recounting massive record deal busts that ZZ Top's reported $30 million record deal with RCA was "falsely inflated," which was likely an attempt to save face. That month, Mosaic Media Group, managed by former Dick Clark Productions CEO Allen Shapiro, acquired Bill Ham's publishing company, Hamstein Music, acquiring ZZ Top's entire catalog in the process, demonstrating the continued value of ZZ Top's classic music even if audiences weren't buying the new releases in large numbers.[2]

And yet, despite the album flatlining, the XXX Tour kept the trio busy on the road. It's probably not much of a surprise that they did not play many songs from *XXX* on tour—in addition to a few performances of "(Let Me Be Your) Teddy Bear," the group played "Poke Chop Sandwich," "Fearless Boogie," and "36-22-36," and they also played "Fearless Boogie" during an appearance on *The Late Show with David Letterman*.

After completing the XXX Tour in New Zealand in May 2000, ZZ Top was forced to cancel the European leg, titled the Fearless Boogie Tour, when Hill was diagnosed with hepatitis C. It marked the first of a few tour cancellations over the next two decades because of Hill's health. Otherwise, ZZ Top played just two dates in 2001: a special performance on January 18 at the Marriott Wardman Park Hotel in Washington, DC, called "The Best Little Ball in D.C.," to mark the presidential inauguration of Texan George W. Bush and a live performance at the unveiling of the uniforms of the new Houston Texans football team in September.

ZZ Top did return to touring in 2002, first for a one-off appearance at the Houston Livestock Show in February (which they would play again in 2003, 2007, 2009, and 2012), then for an appearance on Country Music Television's newly launched program *CMT Crossroads*, which paired country musicians with musicians from other genres. ZZ Top was paired with superstar country duo Brooks & Dunn. Ten years later, Gibbons would appear on another episode of the series with a variety of musicians to perform with Joe Walsh. After a brief five-show tour in May 2002 of various casinos, naturally dubbed the Casino Tour, ZZ Top went into the studio to work on the follow-up album to *XXX*. The band finally returned to Europe over two years later for twenty-two dates in October 2002, including three concerts, two in Germany and one in Belgium, where the band's drum tech John Douglas, who also designed Beard's elaborate drum sets, sat in for Beard after Beard had to have emergency appendectomy surgery in Paris, the only time that one of the members of ZZ Top missed concerts until Hill left the road shortly before his death in 2021. Douglas would later become the fill-in drummer for Aerosmith starting in 2019 after the band's drummer Joey Kramer faced health issues.

ZZ Top's fourth RCA album, 2003's *Mescalero*, was originally scheduled for release on April 15, 2003, but RCA pulled it just days before the on-sale date (reviews of the album were already circulating in newspapers) and delayed it indefinitely. Famed music mogul Clive Davis, now president and CEO of RCA, considered scrapping the album entirely or reworking it in the vein of Santana's 1999 RCA album *Supernatural*, which featured the classic rock group collaborating with contemporary musicians on about half the tracks. *Supernatural* was a huge commercial success on par with *Eliminator*, with the bonuses of two number one hit songs, nine Grammy Awards, and enough critical praise to completely reverse Santana's ailing fortunes (before *Supernatural*, Santana hadn't had a Top 40 hit or a platinum album in nearly twenty years). *Supernatural* was released just three months before ZZ Top's *XXX*, and the contrasting successes of the two legacy artists couldn't have been more obvious to either RCA or ZZ Top.

The previous year, and perhaps inspired by the band's *CMT Crossroads* appearance, RCA tested the waters for such a collaborative release with a tribute album featuring other artists performing ZZ Top's music. *Sharp Dressed Men: A Tribute to ZZ Top* features several country artists, including Willie Nelson, Hank Williams Jr., Dwight Yoakam, Brooks & Dunn, and Kenny Chesney, covering most of ZZ Top's greatest hits. Curiously, while the album was released by RCA, only one song from the band's three RCA albums up to that point was included on the collection, Hank Williams III's version of "Fearless Boogie," which was originally from *XXX*. The only support appearance by ZZ Top to promote the release was a surprise performance of "Tush" at the CMT Flameworthy Video Music Awards on June 12 alongside Brooks & Dunn (though the country duo performed "Rough Boy" on the tribute album). *Sharp Dressed Men: A Tribute to ZZ Top* was a Top 10 album on the

Billboard Top Country Album chart and also peaked at number eighty-one on the *Billboard* 200, a higher chart position than *XXX* reached three years earlier. While that was still a win, it likely caused frustration for the band and RCA, in the face of their then ten-year-old mega-deal, that other artists could sell ZZ Top songs better than ZZ Top could (of course, those other artists were country superstars performing mostly well-seasoned hits).

Nine years later, which was several years after ZZ Top's contract with RCA ended, RCA released *ZZ Top: A Tribute from Friends*, a covers album featuring a wide-ranging group of artists like Steven Tyler, Mick Fleetwood (who by that time shared ZZ Top's manager), Grace Potter and the Nocturnals, Wyclef Jean, and Wolfmother. Gibbons, Hill, and Beard were credited as executive producers on the latter album, and Gibbons performed on two of the tracks, "Just Got Paid" with heavy metal band Mastodon and "La Grange" with country music singer-songwriter Jamey Johnson. Unlike with the earlier tribute album, none of the songs covered on the album were from ZZ Top's RCA years.

Perhaps because of the success of *Sharp Dressed Men: A Tribute to ZZ Top*, Gibbons was, for his part, receptive to the collaborative album concept. However, he implied that it would be the result of an edict from RCA rather than a personal preference, likely because it would have shattered the "same three guys, same three chords" image that the band continued to promote. "I met with [Davis] in New York, and I was kind of leaning toward at least entertaining the possibility of perhaps igniting one of these collaborative excursions," Gibbons said at the time. "I'm content to let it percolate a little bit, but I guess we'll get our marching orders from the record company, probably sooner rather than later." Those plans never came to pass for *Mescalero*, and RCA announced in July that the album would be released on September 9. Unfortunately, by that time the album had leaked online, which potentially impacted its sales.[3]

The album stood in obvious contrast to *XXX* in several respects. Running over an hour, it is the longest studio album ZZ Top has ever released. While the songwriting of *XXX* returned to the Gibbons-Hill-Beard credit, only one song on *Mescalero*, "What It Is Kid," is credited to the trio (the Japanese-only bonus track, "Sanctify," also credits Gibbons-Hill-Beard as songwriters). Twelve of the album's seventeen songs are credited solely to Gibbons. The album's colorful artwork, featuring sombrero-wearing skeletons, is also far different from the darker, simple artwork of *XXX*. The most notable difference is the instrumentation. While *XXX* went for a contemporary sound, *Mescalero* makes a sincere attempt to include a variety of instrumentation, almost like a throwback to the creativity of *Degüello*.

Gibbons invited a father and son duo who had played marimba for him at a Mexican restaurant to perform on the title track to give it a unique groove, while the country-influenced ballad "Goin' So Good" features a pedal steel guitar. Yet some of the album's strongest tracks are the ones that stick to the standard ZZ Top structure, like the Hill-sung "Piece" and the raucous rocker "Buck Nekkid."

Drummer Greg Morrow was again acknowledged in the "Special Thanks" section of the liner notes alongside two other session players on the album, pedal steel guitarist Dan Dugmore and James Harman, once again providing harmonica.

The release of *Mescalero* came about a month before Warner Bros. released *Chrome, Smoke & BBQ*, a four-disc box set spanning Gibbons's Moving Sidewalks through the two new songs on ZZ Top's *Greatest Hits*. Notably for fans, it included the original studio mixes for the songs from the band's first five albums, which had never been available on CD and had not been available commercially since before the 1987 release of *The Six Pack*. While the box set was a welcome release for ZZ Top fans, it obviously overshadowed the release of *Mescalero*. It also highlighted the lack of success of ZZ Top's RCA period because Warner Bros. chose not to license any RCA recordings for the box set; nor did the band's old label license any RCA tracks for the following year's two-disc compilation *Rancho Texicano: The Very Best of ZZ Top*, which also used the original album mixes. It wasn't until 2014's *The Baddest of ZZ Top* (one disc) and *The Very Baddest of ZZ Top* (two discs), released by Warner's Rhino Records imprint, that compilations containing tracks from ZZ Top's London, Warner Bros., and RCA albums were finally released.

It also likely didn't help the band's relationship with RCA when *Rancho Texicano* outperformed *Mescalero* on the *Billboard* 200, peaking at number thirty compared to *Mescalero*'s chart debut at number fifty-seven, which was also its peak. According to SoundScan, *Mescalero* sold just 17,600 copies in the United States in its first week, a veritable sales implosion signaling that the album would struggle to reach six figures in unit sales. Five years after its release, *Mescalero* was reported to have only sold 103,000 copies in the United States.

Warner Bros. had impeccable timing with the release of *Chrome, Smoke & BBQ*. The compilation came out just a month before the Rock and Roll Hall of Fame announced that ZZ Top would be inducted the following year. ZZ Top joined one of the most storied Hall of Fame "classes," alongside George Harrison, Bob Seger, Traffic, Jackson Browne, the Dells, and, most notably, Prince, whose astounding guitar solo during the tribute performance of Harrison's "While My Guitar Gently Weeps" is considered one of the greatest moments in the history of the institution's induction ceremonies. ZZ Top was inducted by Keith Richards during the March 15, 2004, ceremony at the Waldorf Astoria in New York City, after which the band played "La Grange" and "Tush." Though it seemed like a prime opportunity to push *Mescalero* again to tie into the publicity of the ceremony, RCA appeared to have no interest in doing so.

For a short period, RCA continued to consider the ZZ Top collaborative album concept following *Mescalero* as perhaps a last-ditch opportunity to salvage the final album on its contract with the band. Gibbons even began working on a song with the rock band Wilco for the potential album. Interestingly, after not appearing on any non–ZZ Top albums for three decades, Gibbons was already in the process of demonstrating that he could play nice with others. He performed "Put It Right Back" on bluesman John Mayall's 2001 album *Along for the Ride*, "Walkin' with Sorrow" on Hank Williams III's 2002 album *Lovesick, Broke & Driftin'*, and "Hillbilly Stomp" on Kid Rock's 2003 self-titled album. But the floodgates of Gibbons collaborations seemed to open after *Mescalero* quickly fell off the charts. Gibbons appeared on B. B. King's 2005 guest-laden album, *B. B. King & Friends: 80*, performing on a new recording of one of King's standards, "Tired of Your Jive."

That year Gibbons also got married, marking another behind-the-scenes development that would have previously been kept quiet. As the members of ZZ Top were nontraditional rock stars, their individual love lives were not frequently the subject of speculation or gossip by the media. Since they frequently attended media functions as a trio, there was no need for any of them to be accompanied by a significant other (as if Bill Ham would ever have allowed it, anyway). Beard at least had been married to his wife, Debbie, since 1982, and Hill married his longtime girlfriend, Charleen McCrory, in 2002 in a ceremony in Houston with Beard as his best man (Gibbons was also in attendance). It was Gibbons's turn to walk down the aisle on December 14, 2005, to marry Madison, Arkansas, native Gilligan Stillwater in the affluent Houston neighborhood of River Oaks. The wedding went largely unreported at the time, and the couple maintains a significant degree of privacy, but Stillwater has occasionally attended various media events with Gibbons since their marriage.

Over the next five years, Gibbons appeared on recordings by a wide variety of artists, including Les Paul, Nickelback, Queens of the Stone Age, Al Jourgensen, Vivian Campbell, Billy Sheehan, Sam Moore, Brooks & Dunn,

Gov't Mule, and Ronnie Wood, among others in quick succession. Gibbons's appearance on Brooks & Dunn's 2009 single "Honky Tonk Stomp" gave him his first—and as of 2023, only—Top 20 hit on the *Billboard* Hot Country Songs chart. He also popped up for some television collaborations, including the 2006 Academy of Country Music Awards as part of the musical tribute to country star Buck Owens, who died earlier that year. "Doing these collaborations has opened a few extra avenues to stretch out and find fresh footing in strange lands," Gibbons later remarked.[4]

Strange lands indeed—Jourgensen, who had already had an eventful dinner with Gibbons back in January 1990 where they discussed sampling, had the opportunity to work with Gibbons in the studio on the songs "Prune Tang" and "Dead End Streets" on the 2006 album *Cocked and Loaded* by one of Jourgensen's bands, Revolting Cocks. Jourgensen recalls,

That session was awesome. That's imprinted in my memory for life. He shows up at the studio in El Paso—he just took a train there from California, but he stopped in New Mexico and got a bunch of hatch chili peppers, fresh ones. Tony Rancich, the owner of the studio, is a wine aficionado, and I think he broke open an $80,000 bottle of Château Lafite Rothschild, or something. He set up these crystal glasses for us on top of the grand piano in the studio, all very proper. All of a sudden, Billy says, "Hey, man, I know—let's have a chili eating contest!" So we took a bite of a raw chili and then swigged some wine down with it, right? We didn't even use the glasses—Billy just took a big bite of a chili and then took the bottle and started chugging it. Then I had to take a bite and did the same thing. We kept doing it until Billy ended up puking all over his beard.

Whether Gibbons was just enjoying some downtime with colleagues or attempting to create a blueprint for an RCA collaborations album, the latter was no longer in the cards. In September 2006, ZZ Top announced that the band was no longer under contract to RCA. Without outright stating as much in the media release, RCA had clearly decided to cut its losses with ZZ Top. While other artists have fulfilled a contractual obligation for a final album with a compilation or live album release, RCA did not release a fifth ZZ Top album in any form (unless the two tribute albums released in 2002 and 2011 were counted toward the contract), likely determining that a "best of" or "live" album of songs that didn't sell anywhere close to expectations the first time around wouldn't sell any better the second time around if packaged differently.

Ironically, in December 2021, just five months after Hill's death, ZZ Top announced it had sold the rights to their publishing catalog, recorded music royalties, and performance royalties for a reported value of $50 million to BMG Rights Management and KKR & Co. Inc. BMG Rights Management was previously part of Sony BMG, which in 2006 was the parent company of RCA, the label that severed its relationship with ZZ Top at that time.

The bigger bombshell of that 2006 announcement was that, after nearly forty years, ZZ Top was splitting with manager Bill Ham's Lone Wolf Management. "Lone Wolf will always be grateful for the overwhelming loyalty and support from fans around the world, the labels, the promoters, the agencies, the vendors, the media, and so many others who helped make this possible," the company said in a statement. "We wish the band all the best for continued success."

"I love Bill, but it just seemed like we were stalled," Hill explained several years later. "So we could stay there or see if we could move on in a new direction. And the only way we could do that was to get a new feel for things and that included new management. If you think about it, we were together a lot longer than most people have managers."[5]

The split was initially reported to be contentious, and Gibbons served up one of his typically cryptic answers when he spoke about the split in an interview shortly after Ham died in 2016, remarking, "There was a peculiar mandate that appeared that was tethered with a previously undisclosed non-compete clause, and the actual details of that were never quite clear," though Gibbons suggested he still consulted with Ham in an unofficial advisory capacity after the formal dissolution of the partnership.[6]

Ham, of course, was in no dire straits after the split from ZZ Top. His Hamstein Music publishing company had dominated the country music charts, and he had hit singles with dozens of artists across music genres before selling the company's assets to Mosaic Media Group in January 2002 in a multi-million-dollar deal. One of Ham's final projects before his death in June 2016 was producing a musical about another Texas musical icon, *A Night with Janis Joplin*, which ran on Broadway from October 2013 to February 2014. Yet all that success had started with ZZ Top.

Carl Stubner, who became ZZ Top's manager a few months after their split with Ham, understood that ZZ Top needed to broaden their appeal beyond greatest hits concert tours, though by expanding the band's brand awareness, those concert tours would likewise benefit. As the manager of the legendary drummer Mick Fleetwood, Stubner played an essential role in reuniting the *Rumors*-era lineup of Fleetwood Mac a decade after they last recorded an album together for the blockbuster 1997 live album *The Dance* and its accompanying MTV special. It was the biggest reunion of a legacy rock band of the decade next to the 1994 *Hell Freezes Over* reunion of the Eagles and the 1996 reunion of the original members of KISS in their trademark makeup, as the industry realized that nostalgic reunions of beloved 1970s bands could generate enough money to temporarily quiet any inner-band turmoil.

But a large-scale reunion was the one trick that ZZ Top couldn't pull off. Unlike countless other classic rock bands, ZZ Top had two unique factors that made them an attractive client: the band's instant recognizability by anyone who had even a passing familiarity with ZZ Top, and—to Gibbons's point of constantly highlighting "same three guys, same three chords"—the authenticity of having the most consistent lineup in rock and roll. Whereas bands like Foreigner and Lynyrd Skynyrd featured an endless parade of replacements as original members of the groups quit, retired, or passed away, fans going to a ZZ Top concert knew they would be seeing the group's classic lineup, whether or not they had actually heard that lineup on any of the band's albums in decades.

The approach required the acceptance that regularly issuing new albums that struggled to sell in the six figures despite excessive promotion was not a wise or even sustainable means to continuing the ZZ Top brand. Like most of the demographic attending classic rock concerts, the primary audience going to see ZZ Top live wanted to hear a sampling of the band's 1970s and 1980s hits and buy a shirt or other branded merchandise. It was a formula that many classic rock bands had been following since at least the early 1990s—and even more so a decade later after the collapse of physical music sales—but one that ZZ Top had been slow to adopt, most likely because the contract with RCA to deliver new music was their priority. The band also began pushing out live releases to capitalize on their catalog—first 2008's *Live from Texas*, followed by 2011's *Live in Germany 1980*, and 2016's *Tonite at Midnight: Live Greatest Hits from around the World*, as well as live DVDs like *Live from Texas* (2008) and *Live at Montreux 2013* (2014).

Merchandising was not a new phenomenon for rock bands: Beatlemania launched dozens of products bearing the faces of the Fab Four, and in the following decade KISS tapped into their kid-friendly image to take merchandising to new heights with items like a comic book, action figures, a pinball machine, a board game, trading cards, Halloween costumes, makeup kits, and lunch boxes. ZZ Top had previously dabbled with merchandising to the degree that most rock bands did, offering the requisite badges, posters, stickers, and T-shirts. The group got more adventurous after the success of *Eliminator*, selling model kits of the Eliminator coupe and key chains like the one featured in the "Gimme All Your Lovin'" music video. Though more knock-off key chains were probably sold than officially licensed ones, a source told *Billboard* in 1987 that ZZ Top sold $500,000 worth of key chains in just one year. Nonetheless, the band's focus at the time remained on music sales and touring (for example, ZZ Top–branded TV dinners in the mid-1980s seem like a major missed merchandising opportunity).

Rock band merchandising exploded in the early 1990s after the Rolling Stones pioneered offering concert merchandise at retailers during the band's 1989–1990 Steel Wheels Tour and a wave of KISS nostalgia followed the band's 1996 reunion tour (including far-fetched items like the infamous KISS Kasket, for those who wished to rock on with KISS into eternity). However, ZZ Top's merchandising program did not shift into full gear until they began with their new management. Items like sunglasses (both cheap and otherwise), coasters, automobile shop rags, barbecue tool sets, Zippo lighters, and glassware became available, as well as some more unique branded products. For example, in 2021 ZZ Top and Waco, Texas–based distiller Balcones Distilling released a ZZ Top–branded bourbon, dubbed Tres Hombres. Beard—whose drink of choice since getting sober was Tab diet cola—became, like Angus and Malcolm Young of AC/DC, Nicko McBrain of Iron Maiden, Gene Simmons of KISS, and James Hetfield and Kirk Hammett of Metallica, one of many musicians who are sober or nondrinkers whose bands have released branded alcohol.

Independent of ZZ Top, Gibbons has also released his own line of merchandise, including cowboy boots, guitar straps, socks, pillowcases, and many other items. In 2012, Gibbons released his own line of condiments named BFG Sauces, and he later teamed with singer-songwriter Tim Montana—with whom Gibbons would occasionally record music as the Whisker Brothers—for a new line of hot sauces, barbecue sauces, and salsas under the name brand Whisker Bomb.

The new management team also made sure to maximize the potential of ZZ Top's popular back catalog of hits. While ZZ Top created songs for 1990's *Back to the Future Part III* and 1996's *From Dusk Till Dawn* and occasionally licensed songs for films like *Teachers* (1984), *One Crazy Summer* (1986), *The Santa Clause* (1994), *In the Army Now (*1994), and *Private Parts* (1997) and television shows like *Miami Vice* and *Knight Rider*, the band's media licensing would kick into another gear under their new management, with ZZ Top music appearing in over a hundred film and television productions as well as video games, commercials, and internet media. While the band's previous management wasn't opposed to licensing in most cases (the L'eggs panty-hose ad featuring "Legs" was enough evidence of that), the new team fully embraced the public's appetite for ZZ Top tunes in other media.

To support these new approaches, the band needed continued visibility. By the mid-2000s, ZZ Top could no longer count on airplay on radio stations outside the classic rock format, and MTV was no longer featuring music videos by even current artists in its programming amid a never-ending barrage of reality shows. The answer to those issues was for the band to increase their television appearances. While ZZ Top continued to occasionally make media appearances as a trio, including providing their voices in a 2007 episode of the animated series *King of the Hill* and a short cameo in a 2010 episode of the popular sitcom *Two and a Half Men*, Gibbons became the far more visible face of the band, appearing on television shows like *Criss Angel Mindfreak*, *Whisker Wars*, *Hell's Kitchen*, *CSI: Miami*, *Pawn Stars* (where Gibbons is reunited with one of his 1970s Nudie suits, which he had misplaced), *Jay Leno's Garage*, and dozens of others. Most of these TV programs had an older viewing demographic, meaning they were all opportunities to remind middle-aged and older adults about the band they probably remembered seeing on MTV decades earlier and who might even have one of those ZZ Top key chains stashed somewhere in the attic.

Most notably, Gibbons had a recurring role on the crime procedural television series *Bones*, portraying the father of forensic artist Angela Montenegro (played by Michaela Conlin). Though Gibbons's character is never named on the show, the show's creator, Hart Hanson, intended the character to be a fictional version of Gibbons himself because he wanted an instantly recognizable rock star to play Montenegro's father. Conlin shares,

> *Before we started filming the episode where we learn who Angela's father is, our showrunner Hart Hanson told me they had cast Billy in the role. I remember being a bit nervous to meet him. My dad used to blast ZZ Top in the car when he picked me up from school as a kid. He's been a rockstar and in the public eye for so long, I wasn't sure what to expect. We were introduced on his first day of the episode and I remember being struck by how open and gracious he was. He was incredibly kind and generous to every member of our cast and crew. He was always thoughtful, prepared, and open to trying new things. It was a joy having him on set.*
>
> *During the run of our show, ZZ Top played my hometown. I reached out to the band's tour manager to ask if it was possible for my father to see him live. Billy not only invited him but dedicated a song to him during the performance and invited him backstage after the show. It made my dad's year. I feel lucky to have had the opportunity to work with him. He's as professional, soulful, and genuine as they come.*

Whereas Beard and Hill typically retreated from the spotlight when not on the road with ZZ Top, Gibbons appeared to fill nearly every waking hour with media appearances or playing with other musicians either live or in the studio. For the first time, Gibbons was widely acknowledged as the band's front man, and he fully emerged as the public face of the band. These one-off appearances and collaborations also helped reestablish Gibbons's reputation as a guitarist, demonstrating his blues-rock chops, which may have gone unnoticed by the general public in the decades following the flashy fuzzy spinning guitars, leggy models, and hot rods in the music videos or the special effects–laden concerts of the 1980s.

The new management did not solve all the band's problems, however. ZZ Top still focused on grinding it out on tour, and that sometimes went awry. ZZ Top headlined the 2010 High Voltage Festival in London and suffered embarrassing headlines when the event was poorly attended, attracting only about half of its thirty-thousand capacity on each of its two days.

All these initiatives were in part in service of ZZ Top's main financial prerogative, which was the touring production. The band's tours, which strategically included more and more major cities and smaller markets in the United States as well as internationally, were trimmed to a much more manageable production with fewer stage effects and fewer personnel. For some tours and venues, the visual effects were limited to several video screens. "The last show I saw from them in 2013, I said, 'Billy, you used to be a little more into it,'" shares Ty Reveen, who designed the elaborate Afterburner World Tour stage. "They had the exhaust pipe microphones and these two rectangle projection screens. I said, teasing him about it, 'I mean, who cares, they're just going to remember seeing you, but it kind of looks like you just went down to Costco and bought a couple of big televisions.' He said, 'Well, what we got here is a lean, mean, money-making machine.'" Gibbons was right because the band no longer needed elaborate stage productions to compete with other stadium and arena bands. ZZ Top could continue touring as long as they were physically able based on their reputation and fans' love of their big hits alone.

But the band's new management was aiming for one piece of the legacy puzzle: a hit comeback record that would solidify the band's reputation as one of the great American rock bands and, as Stubner told the *Houston Chronicle* in November 2007, perhaps even win a Grammy Award.

14
BACK TO *LA FUTURA*

When ZZ Top signed with their new management, they were without a record deal. Based on the way the RCA deal went for the band and the label, they could count out signing with a major label. Plus, the landscape had changed for legacy rock bands. ZZ Top weren't alone as an aging rock band whose fans had diminishing interest in hearing new music from them.

It would take a superstar producer who owned a record label to get ZZ Top to create an album that would erase the disappointments of the last decade and a half of underwhelming and underperforming albums. Luckily, Billy Gibbons had already been acquainted for years with someone who fit that description: Rick Rubin.

Rubin, whose chest-length beard rivals that of Gibbons and Hill, developed his reputation as a producer working mainly with rap, punk, and metal musicians, helping turn artists like LL Cool J, the Beastie Boys, and Run-DMC into superstars while also producing bands with strong fan followings like Slayer and Danzig. By the early 1990s, his work with established artists like Red Hot Chili Peppers, Mick Jagger, and Tom Petty had brought him renown throughout the industry. His reputation and clout led him to approach country legend Johnny Cash—at that point in his sixties and without a record contract—to record an album of songs featuring him performing alone with his guitar. The resulting album, *American Recordings*, was released in 1994 and became a critical hit for its stark, haunting sound and song selection, which included some of Cash's own songs, traditional American music, and surprising covers of songs by contemporary artists like Nick Lowe and Glenn Danzig. Cash would continue to work with Rubin until he died in 2003, resulting in five additional albums, a box set of outtakes from all the sessions, and, most significantly, a legacy of late-career excellence that bolstered Cash's critical and commercial fortunes in his final years and solidified his place in history as one of the premier voices in American country music.

Unsurprisingly, numerous other veteran artists have worked with Rubin with similar hopes of late-career revival success, including Donovan (1996's *Sutras*) and Neil Diamond (2005's *12 Songs* and 2008's *Home Before Dark*), though Rubin continued to primarily work with contemporary artists.

In July 2008, ZZ Top announced that it had signed a record contract with Rubin's American Recordings. This came after months of speculation that ZZ Top and Rubin were working on an album together. Ironically, at that time American Recordings was an imprint of Columbia Records, whose parent company is Sony Music Entertainment, which is also the parent company of RCA Records, the label that ZZ Top had recently parted ways with—though ultimately a shift in ownership of American Recordings landed the label under Universal Music Group by the time the ZZ Top album was released.

Gibbons and Rubin had become acquaintances in the early 1990s. In April 1993 Gibbons attended a show by noted underground punk band Fugazi at the Hollywood Palladium with Rubin—which led to Gibbons writing a song for Cash's sessions with Rubin. The song, titled "I Witnessed a Crime," also features Gibbons on electric guitar. The tune, which fits firmly among Cash's outlaw country material, has remained officially unreleased despite being widely bootlegged (in a Q&A on his website, Gibbons even encouraged fans to look for it on YouTube).

As expected of a superstar producer who started with a wunderkind reputation to amass a career that has now spanned decades, Rubin also has had his detractors, particularly among artists from veteran bands who disagreed with his approach to production—or questioned that he even *had* an approach. Malcolm Young of AC/DC spoke negatively of his experience working with

Rubin on the band's 1995 album *Ballbreaker*, and both Tony Iommi and Geezer Butler of Black Sabbath have admitted to being perplexed by Rubin's suggestions and decisions while recording their 2013 album *13*. However, Rubin's continued success and ongoing professional relationships with artists like Red Hot Chili Peppers and his perpetual status as a go-to producer of revival and comeback records for legacy artists somewhat counter those alternate impressions.

As for ZZ Top, the band's experience with Rubin appears to have fallen somewhere between those views. For starters, the recording of the album was drawn out over a four-year period; recording started in Rubin's Shangri La Studios in Malibu with producer Dave Sardy, followed by the primary sessions at Foam Box Studios in Houston overseen by Joe Hardy. Rubin reportedly disliked several of the band's early demos. Gibbons later said,

> *I believe that it would be safe to say one of the most admirable traits that has endeared our band with Rick is his remarkable sense of patience. Rick is in no way going to get set into motion where it may be hasty or hurried. He really is sincere when he works with any artist, of which there have been many. And he said, "Let's keep working on it until it's right." It's funny, you may find yourself returning to a particular track, it may be months tucked away in the can, and you say, "Oh yeah, I remember that. Let's come back to that." So I really think Rick is one of the rare individuals that is willing to let the material develop and reach a logical zenith.*[1]

Both Sardy and Hardy are credited for mixing and "additional production" as well as for playing the piano and Hammond B3 organ on the album, while Sardy received credit for cowriting the song "Flyin' High," and Hardy received credit for cowriting "I Gotsta Get Paid" and "Big Shiny Nine." Though credited with Gibbons as the album's producer, Rubin's work with the band was at times minimal, and it was more than four years after ZZ Top announced in July 2008 that they had signed to American Recordings before *La Futura* was finally released. Naturally, neither Rubin nor ZZ Top spent much downtime during production, with ZZ Top playing more than two hundred concerts across the United States and Canada and making multiple tours of Europe during that period and Rubin working with dozens of other artists.

The album was purported to be yet another return to form for the band—unsurprisingly, in interviews Gibbons compared it to *Tres Hombres* and *Eliminator*—and, perhaps to signify that unity, it marked the first time since *El Loco* that a photo of the trio was featured on the cover of a ZZ Top studio album. In addition, all tracks are listed as "Performed by Billy F. Gibbons, Dusty Hill, Frank Beard" to indicate that there were supposedly no outside musicians performing Hill's or Beard's parts. Yet Chad Smith of the Red Hot Chili Peppers—who, in addition to working with Rubin in his main group, has also worked with Rubin on other projects—revealed on Twitter that he was the drummer on two of the songs on *La Futura*. Furthermore, Hill and Beard are only credited with cowriting "Chartreuse," and Hill's lone lead vocal for the project, "Drive by Lover," is not on the main album but is featured on the deluxe edition release.

That's not to say the album doesn't have moments where it shines. At more than twenty minutes shorter than *Mescalero*, *La Futura* is a leaner, more focused record that truly harkens back to classic ZZ Top at points in a way that the RCA albums did not. "Chartreuse," a song about the greenish-yellow French liqueur, is an obvious offspring of "Tush," and songs like "Heartache in Blue" are reminiscent of the band's love for the blues and are examples of songs that would've been buried under layers of studio overdubbing on an album like *XXX*. But the album's true gem is its opening track, "I Gotsta Get Paid," perhaps ZZ Top's most successful attempt at matching their Texas blues with hip-hop. The song incorporates the melody of a rap song by

Texas rapper DJ DMD titled "25 Lighters." One of ZZ Top's engineers, G. L. Moon, had worked on the original song, and the band incorporated it into a gritty blues song that features vocals by both Gibbons and Hill. It became the first ZZ Top song since "She's Just Killing Me" to have a music video, a throwback video featuring fast cars in the desert driven by beautiful models.

La Futura was an upgrade in terms of sales—it tied the *Billboard* 200 chart high of *Recycler* at number six and hit the Top 10 on the charts in several countries across Europe. According to SoundScan, its first week sales were thirty-one thousand copies, nearly double what the band's previous album, *Mescalero*, sold in its first week. *La Futura* reached number one on *Billboard*'s Top Hard Rock Albums chart and number five on the Top Rock & Alternative Albums chart, and it was a Top 10 album in Canada and eight European countries. While "I Gotsta Get Paid" did not have chart success, it received critical praise (*Texas Monthly* called it "ZZ Top's best new song in decades") and became the first new staple of ZZ Top's live show since "Pincushion." "Chartreuse" also was added to set lists from 2012 to 2017, and "Flyin' High" was played regularly from 2013 to 2016. The marketing support for the album brought renewed attention to ZZ Top, including high-profile interviews on programs like *The Howard Stern Show*. Based on that the band also promoted the album heavily, playing nearly two hundred concerts on the La Futura Tour from October 2012 through August 2014, the band's heaviest concert schedule since the 1990s.[2]

La Futura was certainly a more successful record than its predecessor and perhaps ZZ Top's best-selling album since *Antenna*, but not overwhelmingly so (like *Rhythmeen*, *XXX*, and *Mescalero* before it, *La Futura* also did not ship enough units to receive a gold album certification from the Recording Industry Association of America)—and that came after a years-long process of recording with Rubin. It also secured no significant award nominations and no Grammy recognition, as Carl Stubner had once hoped. While ZZ Top had enough leftover songs from the *La Futura* sessions to get the band started on a follow-up, Gibbons was inspired to do something different that would not take mobilizing the entire ZZ Top operation.

Over forty years after the breakup of the Moving Sidewalks, specialty archival music label RockBeat Records released *The Moving Sidewalks: The Complete Collection*, a two-disc CD set that compiled the band's singles, album, and demos, in September 2012. Though three songs from the Moving Sidewalks' lone LP, *Flash*, appeared on the 2003 ZZ Top box set *Chrome, Smoke & BBQ*, and various other tracks had appeared on compilations of Gibbons, Hill, and Beard's pre–ZZ Top music and in other collections of garage rock, this was the first time that all the band's material was available in a single package for fans of Gibbons.

Four months after the release of the compilation, Gibbons announced that he would be reuniting with Dan Mitchell, Tom Moore, and Don Summers as the Moving Sidewalks for a performance at B. B. King's Blues Club & Grill in New York City. Though the timing suggested it was the result of new interest in the group because of the release of *The Moving Sidewalks: The Complete Collection*, the reunion had been in the works for quite some time. For many years the Moving Sidewalks had a standing invitation to play at New York City's Cavestomp!, an annual music festival devoted to garage rock that on occasion reunited early rock-and-roll groups. However, the timing never worked out for a Moving Sidewalks reunion because of Gibbons's schedule with ZZ Top. For the 2013 edition of the festival, Gibbons was between a ZZ Top tour of Australia and a spring US and European tour and was able to make the March 30, 2013, show in New York. The former bandmates started rehearsing for the performance just after the holidays in Houston.

The B. B. King show featured the Moving Sidewalks performing all four of their original singles, "99th Floor," "Need Me," "I Want to Hold Your Hand," and "Flashback," with most of the cuts from the *Flash* album like "You Make Me

Shake," "You Don't Know the Life," and "Pluto—Sept. 31st." The group also performed a few covers, including Jimi Hendrix's "Foxy Lady," "Red House," and "If 6 Was 9" and the Troggs' "Wild Thing," but no ZZ Top songs. The performance was sold out (opportunities to see Gibbons play in a club that small were few and far between) and received positive reviews. One month later, the Moving Sidewalks played a second gig as part of the 6th Annual Austin Psych Fest, a music festival that also featured on the bill Roky Erickson of the 13th Floor Elevators, whose band inspired the name of the Moving Sidewalks. On September 28, 2013, the band made their last public appearance together at the Deacons of Deadwood Motorcycle Club Charity Ball at the Bayou Music Center, which featured Jimi Hendrix's sister, Janie Hendrix, in attendance, creating a full circle moment for the Moving Sidewalks.

Though in interviews promoting B. B. King's Blues Club & Grill, Gibbons hinted at the band possibly recording together again, and new recordings were teased on the band's Facebook page, new music from the Moving Sidewalks never materialized. However, the experience of performing live and recording with a group that wasn't ZZ Top may have partially inspired Gibbons to finally make the leap into recording new music without the ZZ Top banner.

In July 2015, Concord Records, the nonjazz imprint of the esteemed Concord Jazz record label, announced that it would release Gibbons's first solo album, titled *Perfectamundo*, in November of that year. On the album, Gibbons was backed by a new group dubbed "The BFG's," featuring Mike Flanigin on Hammond B3, Alx Garza on bass, Martin Guigui on Hammond B3 and piano, G. L. Moon on guitar, ZZ Top studio favorite Greg Morrow on drums, and the always-present Joe Hardy on various instruments (Hardy and Gibbons also coproduced the album).

Gibbons would later say that the album was inspired when ZZ Top was invited to perform at the 2014 Havana International Jazz Festival in Cuba, a world-renowned event established in 1978 by Argentina-born composer Guigui, whom Gibbons invited to play on *Perfectamundo*. While the band was unable to perform at the festival that year, the invitation inspired Gibbons to explore the Afro-Cuban rhythms that influenced him on previous ZZ Top albums as well as his experience under the tutelage of Tito Puente for his own project. Press for the album heavily leaned on the Puente and Cuban connections, but the album also featured covers of well-trodden classics like Roy Head's "Treat Her Right" and Big Joe Williams's "Baby Please Don't Go," which may have worked on a ZZ Top album, and others like the sonic montages of "Hombre Sin Nombre" and "Quiero Mas Dinero."

Gibbons also had more flexibility as a solo artist, and parts of *Perfectamundo* were recorded in Pontevedra, Spain, as well as Los Angeles, Austin, and, of course, Houston. In a lot of ways, *Perfectamundo* marked the culmination of Gibbons's decade-long solo endeavors and collaborations. "As a guitarist, he's a gosh-dang genius," remarks Matthew Wilkening of *Ultimate Classic Rock*. "So tasteful, so lyrical, and such a master of mood. Watching him break out of ZZ Top's previously closed-off habitat with solo albums and countless guest appearances has been one of the more exciting developments in recent rock history."

Perfectamundo debuted on the *Billboard* 200 at number forty-eight and dropped off the chart immediately afterward, but without the pressure or expectations of a ZZ Top release, that seemed like a respectable showing for Gibbons's first-ever solo album. Though not strictly a blues album, *Perfectamundo* also topped the *Billboard* Blues Albums charts, holding that position for five weeks.

Gibbons hit the road with The BFG's for his first proper solo tour with Guigui serving as the band's musical director. With The BFG's in tow, Gibbons performed at the 2015 Havana International Jazz Festival (Guigui directed a short documentary, *Billy Gibbons & The BFG's Go to Cuba*, which documented the trip). On the road, The BFG's played most of the *Perfect-amundo* album, though they also played a few ZZ Top songs, including the requisite "La Grange" as well as "Ten Foot Pole," the standout *El Loco* track that Gibbons's main band had not performed live since the Recycler World Tour. One of the tour stops was at the Cullen Performance Hall at the University of Houston, a homecoming show that included Beard in attendance, where Gibbons was warmly received.

While it may not have been his original intention, with his solo album and band, Gibbons was in a sense preparing for life after ZZ Top. Hill's health issues had already resulted in canceled tour dates in 2000, 2007, and 2014, and again in 2016 just six months after the release of *Perfectamundo*, followed by one final set of cancellations in 2017. It was entirely possible that at some point Hill's various aliments would not allow him to tour with ZZ Top any longer. While in many ways Gibbons is the essential component of ZZ Top, the group would be treading in uncharted territory should Hill be forced to leave the band, because no rock group of that level of success had ever maintained a stable lineup as long as ZZ Top had. Certainly, other legacy bands like the Rolling Stones and the Beach Boys had continued to tour long after many of the original members had left the band or passed away, but ZZ Top's longevity was credited in part to the group's stability, making the trio a very different beast.

Similarly, the Canadian rock trio Rush was facing a similar dilemma at roughly the same time. While Rush may have formed initially in 1968, the band's stable three-man lineup of Getty Lee, Alex Lifeson, and Neil Peart did not come together until 1974, four years after Hill joined ZZ Top. Rush became inactive after playing its final concert in 2015 and formally disbanded in 2020 after Peart's death. It wasn't yet clear if fans would even accept a ZZ Top in any other configuration.

While Gibbons couldn't control Hill's health issues, he could continue to promote himself separately from ZZ Top to ensure he would have a career and be recognizable outside the group. While the goofy videos, spinning, fuzzy guitars, and chest-long beards may have made ZZ Top millionaires and world famous, they did obscure just how good a guitar player and musician Gibbons really is—and his solo albums and tours gave him another opportunity to prove that in a form devoid of ZZ Top's associations (except, of course, Gibbons's signature physical look, which was not going to change).

To that end, it's not surprising that Gibbons's next solo album was something more traditional, a blues album titled *The Big Bad Blues* released in September 2018. The album features six original songs, four covers, and a song penned by Gibbons's wife, Gilligan Stillwater, titled "Missin' Yo' Kissin'." Gibbons admitted in interviews that after going off the beaten path with *Perfectamundo*, he decided to go back to his wheelhouse for a more traditional sound on his second solo album, and it's no surprise to see two Muddy Waters songs ("Standing Around Crying" and "Rollin' and Tumblin'") and a Bo Diddley song ("Crackin' Up") on this release alongside some bluesy originals penned by Gibbons, like the grinding "Hollywood 151." The album again features Morrow on drums, but this time he shares drumming duties with former Guns N' Roses drummer Matt Sorum. Other musicians include future ZZ Top bassist Elwood Francis on guitar and harmonica, James Harman on harmonica (his last appearance on a ZZ Top–related project before he died in 2021), and Hardy on bass. In support, Gibbons launched the Big Bad Blues Tour with a one-off show at the 2018 San Diego Blues Festival, followed by two dozen dates across the United States.

The Big Bad Blues also proved to be a relative sales and critical success—though it debuted and peaked at number seventy-three on the *Billboard* 200, it spent thirty-nine weeks on the *Billboard* Blues Album chart (peaking at number two, held out of the top spot by Joe Bonamassa's 2018 album *Redemption*) and won the Best Blues Rock Album award at the Blues Foundation's 2019 Blues Music Awards. The award, presented on May 9,

2019, at the ceremony in Memphis, was accepted on Gibbons's behalf by Stillwater. The album was also named one of the Top 50 Blues Albums of 2018 by *Living Blues* magazine, the oldest periodical devoted to the blues. While *Perfectamundo* was a departure from Gibbons's work with ZZ Top (though, truthfully, ZZ Top did tend to experiment with new sounds), *The Big Bad Blues* could have been the late-career revival that ZZ Top had been angling for under different circumstances. Many ZZ Top fans wouldn't have faulted the aging band for doing a straight blues record, though it would certainly have marked an acceptance of commercial limitations that the band seemed to resist throughout the RCA years.

If *The Big Bad Blues* represented a template that ZZ Top could have followed to deliver a respectable blues album, his third solo album, 2021's *Hardware*, represented Gibbons's solo version of the classic ZZ Top sound. For one, the album was recorded as a trio with Gibbons on guitar and vocals, Alabama-born left-handed guitarist Austin Hanks (who cowrote "Flyin' High" on *La Futura*), and Sorum on drums, with all three also playing bass. The only other musicians on the album are members of the Americana rock band Larkin Poe, who provided additional vocals for the song "Stackin' Bones." While the album has a generally harder rock sound than classic ZZ Top, of Gibbons's three solo albums it is perhaps the most similar to the classic ZZ Top arrangement. The album's title is a reference to Gibbons's longtime collaborator Joe Hardy, who died in 2019.

Gibbons released four music videos for songs from *Hardware* that were all shot in the Pioneertown, California, area—where the album was recorded—and directed by Texas filmmaker Harry Reese, who had previously worked with Gibbons as the cinematographer of the "Missin' Yo' Kissin'" music video. The four *Hardware* videos included one for "She's on Fire," which was essentially a modern take on ZZ Top's classic *Eliminator* videos. The clip features the *Hardware* trio performing in the desert with a dancing, short-shorts-wearing redhead model, who arrives on the scene in one of Gibbons's many prized cars, his 1984 Chevy El Camino—the conclusion of the video even features Gibbons, Hanks, and Sorum leaning over and striking a pointing pose reminiscent of ZZ Top's classic hand signals. The video for "My Lucky Card" features Gibbons arriving, performing, and gambling at Pappy & Harriet's Pioneertown Palace, a local institution near Joshua Tree National Park that began its life as a Western-style movie set and later converted into a popular honky-tonk music hall and restaurant.

While Gibbons's solo work obviously took precedence over recording with ZZ Top, his solo tours amounted to a limited number of dates in smaller venues, and Gibbons's primary focus remained touring with ZZ Top. While ZZ Top was no longer recording new music, the band had one last major project to undertake before the end of the beloved Texas trio.

15
NOT JUST OLD MEN TALKING

As part of Carl Stubner's new strategy for marketing ZZ Top came the idea to produce a documentary about the band's history. The concept came off the back of a trend of successful, well-received in-depth music documentaries about legacy bands and artists who had a range of professional successes, including 2005's *No Direction Home* (Bob Dylan), 2007's *Runnin' Down a Dream* (Tom Petty and the Heartbreakers), 2008's *Anvil! The Story of Anvil*, 2009's *When You're Strange: A Film about the Doors*, 2010's *Rush: Beyond the Lighted Stage*, 2012's *Searching for Sugar Man* (Sixto Rodriguez), and 2013's *20 Feet from Stardom* (about backup signers). *Searching for Sugar Man* and *20 Feet from Stardom* even won the Academy Award for Best Documentary Feature Film, and the other films similarly won other accolades and acclaim.

In addition to celebrating the history of these artists, these documentaries marked yet another entry point for new fans to discover the artist or lapsed fans to relive the phenomenon of artists they had enjoyed in their youth. The documentaries also had the dual purpose of serving as definite visual documents of these artists and influencing how they would be perceived for decades to come. While artists' music would ultimately serve as what defined their legacies, documentaries could support that perception by highlighting and celebrating key accomplishments of their careers while also downplaying any unsavory aspects of their histories. History is written by the victors—and for rock-and-roll artists and bands with long histories and intricate relationships, releasing an official documentary to crystalize the record for posterity went a long way in constructing a legacy narrative. As ZZ Top approached the band's fiftieth anniversary, it would be an ideal opportunity to release a film chronicling the band's history—particularly because the band spent so much of its career promoting mystery and mystique.

Ahead of this trend, Canadian production company Banger Films, established by directors and producers Scot McFadyen and Sam Dunn, created a series of critically acclaimed and award-winning documentaries, including *Metal: A Headbanger's Journey* (2005), *Iron Maiden: Flight 666* (2009), *Rush: Beyond the Lighted Stage* (2010), and *Super Duper Alice Cooper* (2014). *Rush: Beyond the Lighted Stage* in particular was extremely well received, earning a Grammy nomination for Best Long Form Music Video (the category is now called Best Music Film) as well as winning the Audience Award at the Tribeca Film Festival, the Manhattan-based film festival where it premiered. The documentary delved deeply into the history of the three-man Canadian progressive rock band, including interviews with family and friends of the band members, offering an insider's view of a band that many critics had dismissed over their decades-long career for not fitting into the rock-and-roll archetype.

Though Rush and ZZ Top have little in common musically beyond the three-man lineup, they share fan loyalty and, until their later years, a general disregard by the critical establishment. Based on those past successes, Banger Films seemed to offer the right team—one with a deep reverence for the cultural power of music—and professional touch to create a documentary about ZZ Top. The film was to be distributed by Eagle Rock Entertainment, a UK-based film production and distribution company that specialized in music documentaries and live performance films. At the time the ZZ Top documentary was produced, Eagle Rock was a subsidiary of Universal Music Group (in 2020, the company was consolidated into Mercury Studios, which would continue to focus on music-based films). The resulting film, *ZZ Top: That Little Ol' Band from Texas*, was released in August 2019, the outcome of more than four years of production in which the content and direction of the project changed substantially for a variety of reasons that were both within and outside the control of the filmmakers.

Representatives of Banger Films were invited to meet with ZZ Top to discuss the potential project in Ontario when the band had a concert at Casino Rama, located north of Toronto on March 19, 2015. Included in the meetings was Ralph Chapman, the film's eventual cowriter with director Sam Dunn. Chapman had worked with Banger Films on *Metal Evolution* and *Rush: Beyond the Lighted Stage* as well as a twelve-part television series, *Metal Evolution*, which documented the history of heavy metal. As both a filmmaker and a fan with an encyclopedic knowledge of rock music, Chapman was looking forward to attending the Casino Rama concert and meeting ZZ Top. Unfortunately, during the meeting, it did not appear that ZZ Top's camp—particularly Gibbons—were all on the same page about the project.

"The meeting went poorly," Chapman recalls. "Billy was not in the state of mind where he wanted to discuss the film. He seemed wary of us, including me, Sam, and the other producers involved with Banger who came and were part of the team. I was excited to go because I had been a fan for decades and somehow I had never seen them, but from my impression—and it was a learning experience, that's for sure—what I got was a wary guy who didn't really seem to know what we were doing, almost." Recalling that initial meeting and Gibbons's skepticism, Chapman adds, "His big quote was, 'I don't want this film to be just a bunch of old men talking.'"

That put the Banger Films team in a challenging situation—as of March 2015, when that initial meeting took place, the three members of ZZ Top were all officially senior citizens, and many of the people associated with the band whom it would make sense to feature in the documentary were the same age or older. Making a documentary about an aging rock band without including "old men talking" would be difficult from a narrative standpoint. However, conversations about the project continued, with Gibbons even indicating that he wanted to be involved in scripting the documentary in addition to being one of its main subjects.

After a period of conversations with the band members and management about the project in preproduction, the decision was made to have Dunn and Chapman accompany Gibbons on his tour bus during ZZ Top's 2016 Hell Raisers Tour to hash out ideas for the film. "At that point he wanted the film to be nontraditional, to say the least," recalls Chapman. He also remembers Gibbons still being wary of their participation, questioning if Banger Films was the right production company for the project. "Sam mentioned *Rush: Beyond the Lighted Stage*, which had a huge impact on the perception of that band. From Sam's point of view, the pairing made sense. Billy reacted the opposite, saying, 'We're not Rush.' That kind of poisoned the well at that point."

Bizarrely, the project was aided during the tour by an unfortunate circumstance when Hill went down with an injury before ZZ Top's April 14, 2016, concert in Lubbock, Texas, at the Lone Star Events Center. Hill dislocated his shoulder backstage, necessitating the cancellation of the concert and the postponement of fifteen concerts in the South over the next five weeks. While the tour resumed on June 23, 2016, at the Birmingham Academy in the United Kingdom, Hill's injury left the documentary in a state of uncertainty.

The challenge of making *ZZ Top: That Little Ol' Band from Texas* wasn't just related to Hill's health issues; it would also require revealing much about a band that had traditionally been reluctant to share information about its inner workings. "Because the story is so built on myth, people are reluctant to go on camera and challenge the myth, even if they are part of the myth," points out Chapman.

One such obstacle in telling the band's history involved getting vintage footage to use in the documentary. At the time, ZZ Top was not on overly positive terms with their former management, Bill Ham's Lone Wolf

Productions, which prevented access to the company's archive material. Ham had long been a proponent of supporting the mystique of ZZ Top and did not authorize the release of footage of the band performing, and it is entirely possible that such footage did not even exist in the first place. Lone Wolf was said to have recorded some of ZZ Top's past concerts, including the penultimate concert of the Worldwide Texas Tour on New Year's Eve on December 31, 1977, in Fort Worth, but the condition of these possible recordings was not known. Banger Films was in negotiations with Ham's company to gain access to that archive to see if anything was usable, but the legal issues were still pending upon Ham's death in June 2016. At that point, Banger Films and ZZ Top had already announced the project, and the January 2016 media release urged fans with archival photos and recordings of ZZ Top concerts to reach out to Banger Films. However, the finished film would eventually use animated sequences to cover for missing archival material.

With the lack of vintage performance footage available, Chapman, as one of the film's writers, had to come up with a concept that would anchor the documentary. Chapman proposed an idea of filming the trio performing together in a no-frills, stripped-down setting to serve as the connecting thread throughout the documentary and to recreate, to the best degree possible, the original jam session that had brought the three musicians together in 1970. "The jam came from me out of the necessity of having to come up with something," recalls Chapman. "We talked with Billy about it on his tour bus in Colorado Springs, and he nominally approved the idea, and we went from there. There was no myth in that. It was, 'We got nothing, so let's film them and try to recreate that vibe between those three musicians.' There is so much artifice attached to ZZ Top, but at the end of the day they were, for my money, such a great band who made great records."

The so-called jam session was filmed at Gruene Hall in Gruene, Texas, a venue built in 1878 that is recognized as the oldest continually run dance hall in Texas. The vintage venue, awash in classic advertising signage, is an iconic country music venue on the Recorded Texas Historic Landmark list. Gruene Hall was a choice location for the shoot to visually demonstrate the band's long history and connection with Texas, and it allowed the filmmakers the opportunity to film an opening sequence of ZZ Top arriving in a Ford hot rod (driven by Gibbons, naturally).

In the media release about ZZ Top's 2022 *Raw* album, stated to be the soundtrack to *ZZ Top: That Little Ol' Band from Texas*, the Gruene Hall session was presented as completely inadvertent, the implication being that a photo session of the band with their instruments for the documentary had turned into an "unplanned jam session." In reality, the performance was planned ahead of time and even rehearsed—with ZZ Top reviewing a proposed set list presented by the filmmakers before finalizing a set list of their own—making the album yet another part of the ZZ Top mystique. Chapman remarks, "The purpose of the jam was to create a spine that we could come to throughout the film that we could use in place of where no footage existed. The thing I am most proud of is the jam because that was my idea and I got to see it come to fruition."

The session is the highlight of the film, and it allowed the band to play songs that the group had not performed live in some time, including "Certified Blues," "Blue Jean Blues," and "Thunderbird," along with their usual repertoire, including "La Grange," "Tush," and "Gimme All Your Lovin'." Only a handful of the songs made it into the film, including the band performing a shuffle in C, the first music the trio ever jammed on together, though that was not included on the soundtrack album. The performances are not completely stripped—for example, Beard uses his monstrous on-stage drum set as opposed to the smaller kits he used back in the 1970s—but still serve as an enjoyable insight into how the band performs when not on an arena stage surrounded by spotlights and visual effects.

ZZ Top: That Little Ol' Band from Texas premiered at the Arclight Hollywood, a theater attached to Hollywood's landmark Cinerama Dome, on August 13, 2019, with both Gibbons and Hill in attendance with the film's director, Dunn, for a very short Q&A session (Beard was unable to attend as he was recovering from pneumonia at the time, and ZZ Top was launching a tour in Washington State three days later). As a chronicle of the band's early career, it does an admirable job, and Beard is forthright about his struggles with addiction in the 1970s in a way that had not been reported previously (in particular, his remarks about Eric Clapton not cost-effectively using heroin are sadly hilarious). The project, which Gibbons claimed to have wanted to be unconventional, evolved into a film that, while craftily made, is standard enough in its narrative approach to be an episode of the classic VH-1 music channel series *Behind the Music*. "From my point of view, the scope and ambition are muted," shares Chapman. "A lot of the lofty ideas fell away, and it becomes more conventional in my view, often out of necessity. There was definitely a process and a tone and scope shift in the film as it evolved. I'm delighted people like it, but it was way more traditional than what we set out to do." Past band insiders also have shared that while they enjoyed the film, the final product plays fast and loose with the group's history ("I wanted to say, 'C'mon, guys, that's not how it happened,'" shares one longtime member of the band's organization).

In 2020, the film became widely available on Netflix and received extremely positive reviews. However, even fans and critics who enjoy the documentary have questioned why it ends so abruptly after documenting *Eliminator*, leaving nearly thirty-five years of the band's history largely unexplored. In 2021, *ZZ Top: That Little Ol' Band from Texas* was nominated for a Grammy Award for Best Music Film, though it lost to another career-spanning documentary, *Linda Ronstadt: The Sound of My Voice*.

ZZ Top: That Little Ol' Band from Texas was the final band project to be released in Hill's lifetime, though the soundtrack, *Raw*, was not released until July 2022. The album, which features the band playing a selection of songs at Gruene Hall, was purported to be a raw recording of the "unplanned" session (hence the title), though it was subject to studio editing before release. For example, the versions of "Brown Sugar" and "La Grange" featured in the documentary differ from the versions on the album, and "Gimme All Your Lovin'" and "Legs" seem to have similar electronic accompaniment as the songs usually have when ZZ Top plays them live in a typical concert setting. Nonetheless, the soundtrack album does serve as an appropriate tribute to Hill, to whom the album was dedicated by Gibbons and Beard.

For many reasons, it seems entirely appropriate that ZZ Top—a remarkable band that fully embraced the idea of building a career on image and mythology as a vehicle for outstanding music—would end their incomparable run with a project that will continue to promote that mystique for decades to come following ZZ Top's own version of history. It seems that even Bill Ham couldn't have plotted that move any better.

EPILOGUE

THE DUST HAS LEFT THE BUILDING

In April 2018, ZZ Top engaged in the band's first-ever residency, booking five shows at the Venetian in Las Vegas (the band squeezed in gigs between in El Paso and Anaheim during the run). The run was a success, and ZZ Top kicked off their 50th Anniversary Tour with eight more shows at the Venetian in January 2019 (after Dusty Hill's death, ZZ Top returned for a third time to the Venetian for five shows in October 2021 and again another five shows in December 2022). ZZ Top was far from the only legacy band to take up the lucrative opportunity to participate in short residencies in Vegas, and it allowed the band to play "Viva Las Vegas" to enthusiastic crowds (after Hill's death, Billy Gibbons took over the lead vocal on the song).

The residency was initially meant to be the first step in something of a small ZZ Top Las Vegas takeover as the band's management continued to explore ways to market ZZ Top's music. In May 2019, the group announced that a jukebox musical featuring ZZ Top's greatest hits titled *Sharp Dressed Man* would be coming to a Caesars Entertainment venue in Las Vegas with Gibbons, Hill, and Frank Beard serving as executive producers and ZZ Top's manager, Carl Stubner, as one of the producers. The musical was set to launch in 2020 but was likely derailed by the impact of the Covid-19 pandemic on the entertainment industry.

The global pandemic resulted in ZZ Top's playing just a single concert in 2020, a one-off performance at the San Antonio Stock Show & Rodeo on February 14. ZZ Top had already announced a full calendar of tour dates in

2020, including another Las Vegas residency at the Venetian, a spring and early-summer tour with dates in the United States and Canada, and a fall US tour with fellow 1980s MTV rock stars Def Leppard, until ZZ Top, like all other major music acts, was forced to cancel all their shows for the foreseeable future.

After a seventeen-month break, ZZ Top resumed their 50th Anniversary Tour on July 16, 2021, at the Delaware County Fair in Iowa. However, the lengthy break had clearly taken a toll on Hill's health. At the July 16 concert he performed for the first time while sitting down on an amp on stage, which made the audience aware that his health issues may have been catching up with him. After two more dates, July 17 in Mount Pleasant, Michigan, and July 18 in Louisville, Kentucky, Hill stepped aside to return to Texas to see his doctor about his ailments, which led the band to cancel its July 21 concert in Evansville, Indiana. The tour resumed on July 23 in New Lenox, Illinois, with the band's longtime guitar and bass tech Elwood Francis filling in on bass. On July 28, ten days after his final show with ZZ Top, Hill passed away at his home in Houston at age seventy-two. ZZ Top canceled that night's gig in Simpsonville, South Carolina.

For a band that was endlessly promoted as "same three guys, same three chords" for over fifty years, to many it seemed inconceivable that ZZ Top could continue after the death of Hill. But the band largely became a "greatest hits" touring entity after the disappointing sales of *Mescalero* and following the end of their contract with RCA. While ZZ Top remained popular live performers and a reliable draw in nearly every market they toured, Beard and Hill's role in writing and recording had been minimized over the years, and Gibbons's three solo albums indicated he had little interest in recording another ZZ Top album. Particularly his third solo album, *Hardware*, released just one month before Hill's death, could have easily been released as a ZZ Top album with its car cover art, trio lineup, and three-minute boogie tunes, and most fans would be none the wiser that it featured a different bassist and drummer.

Yet ZZ Top was still a lucrative touring entity, and the band had very little issue, technically or musically, continuing in the wake of Hill's death. Much of that can be credited to how deeply involved Francis had been with the band. Francis was able to step into Hill's role so quickly not just because he decided to grow a lengthy beard during the time he was off the road but because he is a longtime associate of ZZ Top, having worked as a guitar technician with the group since 1995 (he received an "Extra Super Solid Thanx" credit on 1996's *Rhythmeen*). Francis's career as a technician began when he was in his early twenties and started touring with Joe Perry of Aerosmith on one of Perry's solo tours and later worked with other artists like guitar virtuoso Steve Vai, Guns N' Roses, Skid Row, and others, before beginning to work with ZZ Top in the mid-1990s. He first worked exclusively with Gibbons but later took over tech duties for Hill as well. In addition, since 1986 Francis has been a member of the punk rock band The Mighty Skullhead. He performed guitar and harmonica on Gibbons's second solo album, *The Big Bad Blues* (2018), and became one of the few musicians to share the stage with ZZ Top, occasionally joining the band on stage over the years to play steel guitar on songs like Johnny Russell's "Act Naturally," so Francis was obviously a longtime member of the ZZ Top family. With a substantial part of ZZ Top's set list filled with songs that featured preprogrammed instrumentation like "Legs" and "Sharp Dressed Man," the role also required someone already familiar with how those performances worked behind the curtain who could step into the role, though ZZ Top's Hill-sung songs have been dropped from set lists with a few exceptions (Gibbons sings lead on "Viva Las Vegas" when the band performs it during their Las Vegas residencies, for example).

Perhaps most powerfully, Gibbons indicated in many interviews that Hill told him to keep the band going (even that Hill himself suggested that Francis take his place). Whatever differences Gibbons, Beard, and Hill had behind the scenes and across fifty years of performing and recording together—and there undoubtedly were several disagreements—Hill may have recognized and appreciated that the trio had built one of the most famous and beloved brands in rock-and-roll history. By keeping ZZ Top going for at least a few more years, the band will continue to celebrate his life and legacy. And celebrate is what they have been doing because 2022 was ZZ Top's busiest touring year since the La Futura Tour.

Since the release of *La Futura*, Gibbons has occasionally mentioned other ZZ Top recording sessions and the potential of a new album that would again be produced by Rick Rubin (though that might be referring to leftover songs from the *La Futura* sessions). While Gibbons has said that Hill recorded vocals for ZZ Top songs before his death, with each passing year it seems less likely that there will be another ZZ Top album except for reissues of old material or, in the case of 2022's *Raw*, new recordings of the band's hits.

Yet most fans going to classic rock concerts in the twenty-first century are there to hear the hits, something that Gibbons and ZZ Top were forced to come to terms with after the disappointing sales of *Mescalero*.

And yet it appears that Gibbons is having more fun being the Reverend Willy G than ever before. On March 26, 2023, Billy Gibbons did what he typically does and showed up in an unexpected place—at one of Billy Joel's concerts at Madison Square Garden in New York City, a venue that ZZ Top had not performed in since 1994. Joel, who has been playing a monthly residency at the Garden since 2014, has regularly had special guests from across the rock-and-roll spectrum join him on stage during his Garden shows, but Joel seemed particularly excited about performing with Gibbons. Together the two performed "La Grange" and "Tush" with Joel's band (the latter sung by Joel's rhythm guitar player Mike DelGuidice). "Well, that was a fantasy come true," Joel remarked as Gibbons exited the stage.

The remark demonstrates how Gibbons continues to be held in high esteem by his peers and even musicians like Joel, whose music is substantially different from ZZ Top's and whose catalog has outsold ZZ Top's three-to-one worldwide. While Billy Joel may be able to sell out Madison Square Garden every month, to him Gibbons is still a rock star to look up to—and he's just one of countless artists to feel this way. Gibbons has also continued with his many offbeat collaborations, including joining Prince protégé Morris Day for the hip-hop-influenced song "Too Much Girl 4 Me" in 2022.

Fans who invest decades of time, attention, and money into their favorite musicians often feel a sense of ownership over particular musicians and their music libraries—the accusations of "selling out" are habitually thrown about when those musicians no longer adhere to the fans' idealized visions. ZZ Top is no different. For example, to this day ZZ Top fans still complain about *The Six Pack* remixes and the band's diminished output of new music or archival live releases. But in the twenty years since the doomed release of *Mescalero*, ZZ Top, like many of their contemporaries, have largely become a "greatest hits live" band, and Gibbons has at times seemingly put ZZ Top on the back burner to pursue other projects and bask in the glow of being a world-famous rock-and-roll icon.

"Billy is one of the singular unique artists of music history, in my opinion," remarks Terry Manning. "He is just so special, and it comes from his mind. He has an incredible brain and sees through so much. He's several steps ahead—musically and historically. He's one of those people who sees the future just before it happens. I just love him so much, and I think he's so brilliant." Many of Gibbons's collaborators feel the same way about his ability as a performer, even if he has only issued a few recordings in the past two decades (many individuals who have spent time with Gibbons have noted he has hours of recorded music across many genres that he has yet to release).

From many different perspectives, it's hard to fault Gibbons for embracing that adoration. Throughout his nearly six decades in the music business, he has mostly proven to have a keen understanding of what will appeal to mass audiences while still retaining a semblance of the original music that inspired him. After ZZ Top struggled to release successful music in the 1990s and early 2000s, Gibbons learned to think smaller, like solo albums with far fewer expectations, quick appearances to play a well-appreciated guitar solo, and tours in smaller markets to boost the success and legacy of ZZ Top in new and more practically successful ways. Even after Hill's death, the band remains instantly recognizable and among the most successful American rock bands in history.

And if Gibbons wants to simply rest on his rock-and-roll laurels and enjoy new ways to rock in his later years, he's earned the right to take as many spins as he wants in the Eliminator coupe until he's ready to pull off the road.

ACKNOWLEDGMENTS

I must first acknowledge Lee Sobel, who continually suggests great ideas for books.

Thank you to all the publicists, representatives, managers, and everyone who helped facilitate the many interviews that went into the creation of this manuscript.

I am indebted to my many interview subjects (most named in this book but some who chose to remain anonymous) for being so generous with their time and memories.

My deepest appreciation to the amazing team at Rowman & Littlefield Publishing Group, including John Cerullo, Barbara Claire, Melissa McClellan, and Emily Burr, who prepared this book for publication.

Lastly, cheers to Erin for all her support, always.

NOTES

Prologue

1. Andy Greene, "The Last Word: Billy Gibbons on Cars, Marriage, Touring with Jimi Hendrix," *Rolling Stone*, November 6, 2017, https://web.archive.org/web/20220402111913/https://www.rollingstone.com/music/music-features/the-last-word-billy-gibbons-on-cars-marriage-touring-with-jimi-hendrix-119888.

2. Alan di Perna, "ZZ Top: Use Your Illusion," *Guitar World*, February 15, 2008, https://www.guitarworld.com/features/zz-top-use-your-illusion.

3. Matt Wardlaw, "'He Will Lie about Anything': Producer Joe Hardy's Wild Ride with ZZ Top's Billy Gibbons," *Ultimate Classic Rock*, November 11, 2018, https://ultimateclassicrock.com/he-will-lie-about-anything-producer-joe-hardys-wild-ride-with-zz-tops-billy-gibbons.

Chapter 1

1. "ZZ Top to Rock Texas Inaugural Party," *Barstow Desert Dispatch*, January 19, 2001, 4.

2. Kyle Eustice, "Billy Gibbons Interview," *Thrasher Magazine*, https://www.thrashermagazine.com/articles/music-interviews/billy-gibbons-interview.

3. Jay N. Miller, "A Different Side to ZZ Top's Billy Gibbons," *Providence Journal*, January 23, 2016, https://www.providencejournal.com/story/entertainment/music/2016/01/24/different-side-to-zz-tops-billy-gibbons/32709665007.

4. Bruce Westbrook, "Mom Digs ZZ Top's Success," *Kerrville Daily Times*, October 19, 1986, 28.

Chapter 2

1. Chris Gill, "ZZ Top: The Hoard Tour," *Guitar World*, February 15, 2008, https://www.guitarworld.com/features/zz-top-hoard-tour.

2. David Fricke, "Billy Gibbons: My Life in 15 Songs," *Rolling Stone*, November 10, 2015, https://www.rollingstone.com/culture/culture-lists/billy-gibbons-my-life-in-15-songs-151784.

Chapter 3
1. Peter Blackstock, "Longtime ZZ Top Manager Bill Ham Dies at 79," *Austin American-Statesman*, September 3, 2016, https://www.statesman.com/story/news/2016/09/03/longtime-zz-top-manager-bill-ham-dies-at-79/10054824007.

Chapter 4
1. "Choice Programming," *Cashbox*, January 3, 1970, 13.
2. "Cowboy Band Living Up to Texas Myth," *Port Arthur News*, January 30, 1977, 3B.

Chapter 5
1. Richard Cromelin, "Doobie Brothers, Mike Bloomfield, ZZ Top: Palladium, Los Angeles, CA," *Los Angeles Times*, July 10, 1973.
2. Steve Simels, "The Simels Report," *Stereo Review*, November 1973, 111.
3. "Z.Z. Top Break, Bloodstone Repeat," *Radio & Records*, October 12, 1973, 20.
4. "ZZ Top and Friends Due at Sunday Fest," *Austin Daily Texan*, August 28, 1974, 24.
5. Robert Duncan, "ZZ Top in Bulgaria," *Creem*, October 1976.

Chapter 6
1. "Z.Z. Top Big Flop in Fairground Concert," *Des Moines Register*, June 8, 1974, 7S.
2. Richard Cromelin, "ZZ Top, Elvin Bishop: Long Beach Arena, Long Beach CA," *Los Angeles Times*, August 27, 1974.
3. Pete Markowski, "ZZ Top: *Fandango* (London FHU 8482)," *Sounds*, May 24, 1975.
4. Toby Goldstein, "ZZ Top, Brian Auger's Oblivion Express: Felt Forum, New York," *Billboard*, June 7, 1975.
5. Chris Charlesworth, "ZZ Top: Top Three," *Melody Maker*, June 7, 1975.
6. "Indoor Concerts Set by ZZ Top," *Arlington Daily News*, October 26, 1975, 5.

Chapter 7

1. Robert Duncan, "ZZ Top in Bulgaria," *Creem*, October 1976.
2. Scott Mervis, "ZZ Top–Aerosmith Concert at Three Rivers Stadium Was One Crazy Day," *Pittsburgh Post-Gazette*, June 21, 2009.
3. Jon Tiven, "ZZ Top A Go Go," *Blast*, August 1976.
4. David Eden, "Houston Band Brings Texas Flavor Along," *Albuquerque Journal*, August 1, 1976, D1.
5. Duncan, "ZZ Top in Bulgaria."
6. Duncan, "ZZ Top in Bulgaria."
7. Jeff Davenport, "Gimme a Break," *Houston Daily Cougar*, November 11, 1976, 8.
8. Tiven, "ZZ Top A Go Go."
9. John Rockwell, "The Pop Life," *New York Times*, January 14, 1977, 52.
10. "Sellout Concert Causes Damages," *Burlington Times-News*, October 18, 1976, 5B.

Chapter 8

1. Dianne Bennett, "Soundtrack," *Hollywood Reporter*, August 30, 1978, 10.
2. "Concert Reviews," *Variety*, February 6, 1980, 116.
3. Robert Palmer, "Pop: Z. Z. Top, Rock Trio," *New York Times*, May 4, 1980, 74.
4. "*Deguello*: Z. Z. Top." *Audio*, April 1980, 84.
5. John Rockwell, "The Pop Life," *New York Times*, May 2, 1980, C13.
6. Tony Scherman, "Front Man: Billy Gibbons," *Musician*, November 1990.
7. Paul Elliot, "ZZ Top: Heaven, Hell . . . or Vegas!," *Kerrang!*, April 25, 1992.
8. David Fricke, "Billy Gibbons: My Life in 15 Songs," *Rolling Stone*, November 10, 2015, https://www.rollingstone.com/culture/culture-lists/billy-gibbons-my-life-in-15-songs-151784.

Chapter 9

1. Josh Rotter, "Star Apps: ZZ Top," *Download*, July 4, 2014, https://finance.yahoo.com/news/s/star-apps-zz-top-010736239.html.

2. Paul Rees, "Sex, Cars and Videotape: How ZZ Top's *Eliminator* Conquered the World," *Louder Sound*, August 22, 2021, https://www.loudersound.com/features/the-story-of-eliminator-by-zz-top.

3. Billy Gibbons, Frank Beard, and Dusty Hill, "ZZ Top—*Eliminator* 40th—Billy Gibbons, Frank Beard, the Late Dusty Hill," interview by Redbeard, *In the Studio with Redbeard*, March 5, 2023, audio, 8:55, https://www.inthestudio.net/online-on-demand/zz-top-eliminator.

4. "The Popdose Interview: Jimi Jamison of Survivor," *Popdose*, December 18, 2012, https://popdose.com/the-popdose-interview-jimi-jamison-of-survivor.

5. Matt Wardlaw, "Why ZZ Top Went behind Their Producer's Back to Finish 'Afterburner,'" *Ultimate Classic Rock*, October 29, 2019, https://ultimateclassicrock.com/zz-top-afterburner-sessions.

Chapter 10

1. Matt Wardlaw, "Why ZZ Top Went behind Their Producer's Back to Finish 'Afterburner,'" *Ultimate Classic Rock*, October 29, 2019, https://ultimateclassicrock.com/zz-top-afterburner-sessions.

Chapter 11

1. Fred Goodman, "Christmas Is Early for Rock's Megastars," *San Diego Union-Tribune*, December 9, 1992, C8.

Chapter 12

1. Michael Point, "3 Men, 3 Chords: ZZ Simply Stays on TOP," *Austin American-Statesman*, November 1, 1994, E5.

2. Jim Bessman, "ZZ Strips Down," *Dallas Morning News*, August 22, 1996, 5C.

3. Martin Popoff, "ZZ Top's Mud Metal Master Billy Gibbons Goes to Cuba—'They Just Want You, the Billy Boy,'" *Brave Words & Bloody Knuckles*, December 9, 2015, https://bravewords.com/features/zz-tops-mud-metal-master-billy-gibbons-goes-to-cuba-they-just-want-you-the-billy-boy; "In Conversation with the Reverend Billy G—from the Coachmen and Moving Sidewalks to ZZ Top," *Shindig! Magazine*, January 2018, https://www.shindig-magazine.com/?p=2349.

4. David Sinclair, "Billy Gibbons' Personal Guide to Every ZZ Top Studio Album," *Louder Sound*, January 3, 2023, https://www.loudersound.com/features/billy-gibbons-personal-guide-to-every-zz-top-studio-album.

5. Joe Nick Patoski, "Still ZZ after All These Years," *Texas Monthly*, December 1996, https://www.texasmonthly.com/arts-entertainment/still-zz-after-all-these-years.

Chapter 13

1. Alan di Perna, "ZZ Top: A Texan in New York," *Guitar World*, February 19, 2008, https://www.guitarworld.com/features/zz-top-texan-new-york.

2. Melinda Newman, "Industry Analyzes Mariah Carey Deal," *Billboard*, February 9, 2002, 3.

3. Gary Graft, "Expect the Unexpected from Little Ol' Band from Texas," *Plain Dealer*, May 16, 2003, 10.

4. Pete Markowski, "ZZ Top: An Interview," *Rock's Backpages*, October 2012, https://www.rocksbackpages.com/Library/Article/zz-top-an-interview.

5. Markowski, "ZZ Top: An Interview."

6. Peter Blackstock, "Longtime ZZ Top Manager Bill Ham Dies at 79," *Austin American-Statesman*, September 3, 2016, https://www.statesman.com/story/news/2016/09/03/longtime-zz-top-manager-bill-ham-dies-at-79/10054824007.

Chapter 14

1. Alan Scully, "The Art of Patience: A Conversation with ZZ Top," *Leo Weekly*, September 30, 2015, https://www.leoweekly.com/2015/09/the-art-of-patience-a-conversation-with-zz-top.

2. Alan Scully, "How Billy Gibbons Got His Groove Back," *Texas Monthly*, August 2012, https://www.texasmonthly.com/articles/how-billy-gibbons-got-his-groove-back.

INDEX

Photo insert images are indicated by *p1, p2, p3,* etc.

Cotton Bowl, in Dallas, 181–82
Country Music Television, 207
Country Tavern, in Kilgore, 61
"Cover Your Rig," 190
Covid-19 pandemic, 241–42
Cow Palace, in San Francisco, 105
Cream, 2, 33
Creem (magazine), 103–4, 136
Cromelin, Richard, 81, 89
crowd noise, on *XXX*, 205–6
"Crucifix-A-Flat," 206
"Cruel Little Number," 6
Cullen Performance Hall, at University of
  Houston, 229

Daily Court Review, of Houston, 47
Daily Record Distributors, 60
Dallas (television show), 52
Dallas, Texas: Cotton Bowl in, 181–82;
  Memorial Auditorium in, 33
Dallas/Fort Worth International Airport, 112
Dallas Memorial Auditorium, 69–70
The Dance (album), 215
danceable rhythms, on *Eliminator*, 134–35
The Dark Tower (King), 170–71
Davenport, Jeff, 105
Davis, Clive, 208
Davis, Doug, 53
Day, Morris, 245
Deacons of Deadwood Motorcycle Club
  Charity Ball, 227
"Dead End Streets," 213
Decca Records, 57
Deep Purple, 81
Def American label, 183
Degüello (album), 16, 114–16; on *Billboard*
  charts, 117; reissue of, 175; reviews of,
  119; *Rhythmeen* compared to, 195
Delaware County Fair, 242
"Delirious," 160
Delta Blues Museum, 179, 181
Delta Promotions, 52–53
Denver, Colorado, 70

Denver Coliseum, 70
Des Moines Register (newspaper), 87
Desperado (movie), 193
Detroit, 27
Devo, 126–27
Diablo Stadium, Summer Festival of Rock
  at, 95
Diamond, Neil, 222
Diddley, Bo, 230
"Dipping Low (In the Lap of Luxury)," 162
"Dis a Ittly Bit!," 60
Disney Channel, 176
Dixon, Willie, 141
DJ DMD, 224–25
documentaries, 233
Donovan, 222
Doobie Brothers, 81
the Doors, 32–34, 80
Dot Records, 3
"Doubleback," 176–77, 180, *p5*
Douglas, John, 207–8
Doyle Jones's Recording and Gold Star
  Sound Services, 48
"Dreadmonboogaloo," 205
"Dream On," 142
"Drive by Lover," 224
Duffy, Lorraine, 14
Dugmore, Dan, 210
Duncan, Robert, 100, 104
Dunn, Sam, 234, 235, 239
Duran Duran, 191
"Dust My Broom," 116
Dylan, Bob, 148

Eagle Rock Entertainment, 234
the Eagles, 215
"Eclipse," 40
Edgar Winer Group, 82
The Ed Sullivan Show (television show),
  16, 50
Electric Ladyland (album), 36
Eliminator (album), 1, 2, 147, 157, 187;
  Afterburner compared to, 160, 168;

"Gimme Some Lovin," 198
"Give It Up," 180, 181
Gloversville, New York, 13
"Goin' Down to Mexico," 63
"Goin' So Good," 210
GoldenEye (movie), 170
Gold Star Studios, 23
Gone with the Wind (movie), 14
Goodman, John, 198
Goodman, Mark, 167
Goodman, Spencer Corey, 184
"Got Me Under Pressure," 182
Graham, Bill, 88, 166
Grand Ole Opry, 149
Grand Prize Beer, 14
Grand Rapids, Michigan, Civic Auditorium
    in, 90
Greatest Hits (compilation), 185–86
Greig, Lanier, 9, 45, 48–49
"Groovy Little Hippie Pad," 125, 126–27
Gruene, Texas, 237–38
Gruene Hall, 237–38
Grugahalle in Essen, West Germany, 121,
    122
Guigui, Martin, 227–28
guitars: Automatic, 10, 124; Chiquita
    travel, 125, 177; Gibson Flying V,
    36; Gibson Les Paul Standard (1959),
    39–40; Gibson Melody Maker,
    20; "Muddywood," 179–80; pink
    Stratocaster, 34; spinning, 156
Guitar World (magazine), 8, 188, 196
Gulf Brewing Company, 14
"Gun Love," on *Greatest Hits*, 185
Guns N' Roses, 191

Hall, Tommy, 24
Ham, Bill, 3–4, 47, 64, 184–85, 214–15;
    Afterburner relation to, 159–60;
    The Best of ZZ Top relation to, 108;
    collaborations relation to, 68; Daily
    Record Distributors relation to, 60;
    Fandango! relation to, 91; on Felt

Forum show, 94; Gibbons, B., relation
    to, 37; on Hendrix, 34; Jamison
    relation to, 147–48; Lange compared
    to, 61; London Recordings relation
    to, 82, 111; MTV relation to, 150;
    RCA Records relation to, 187; *Recycler*
    relation to, 179; remixes and, 174–75;
    Reveen relation to, 166; *Rhythmeen*
    relation to, 195; Scat Records of, 48;
    songwriting credits of, 142; strategy of,
    58–59; Stubner compared to, 11; on
    The Summit show, 96–97; *Texas Shuffle*
    produced by, 53; Worldwide Texas
    Tour and, 100; "ZZ Top and Friends'
    First Annual Texas Size Rompin'
    Stompin' Barn Dance and Bar-B-Q"
    and, 88; *ZZ Top's First Album* relation
    to, 62
Ham, Cecile, 184
Hammersmith Odeon, in London, 121
Hamstein Music, 5, 206, 215
Hanks, Austin, 231
Hanson, Hart, 219
Happy Days (television show), 48
Hardin, Tim, 53
Hard Rock Cafe, 179, 181
Hardware (album), 231–32, 242–43
Hardy, Joe, 8, 148, 223, 230, 231;
    Afterburner relation to, 159–60;
    remixes and, 175; *Rhythmeen* relation
    to, 195
Harman, James, 195, 210, 230
Havana International Jazz Festival, 227–28
Having a Rave Up with the Yardbirds
    (album), 91–92
Hawaii, Honolulu International Center in,
    70–71
Hawkins, Dale, 46–47
Hayek, Salma, 194
"Heard It on the X," 19, 93
"Heartache in Blue," 224
Hell Freezes Over (album), 215
"Hello, I Love You," 33

"ZZ Top and Friends' First Annual Texas
Size Rompin' Stompin' Barn Dance
and Bar-B-Q," 88–90
ZZ Top International, 189

ZZ Top's First Album (album), 5, 61, 62–65;
Rio Grande Mud compared to, 66
ZZ Top's Muddywood World Tour, 179–80